# PASSING THE THREE GATES

## INTERVIEWS WITH CHARLES JOHNSON

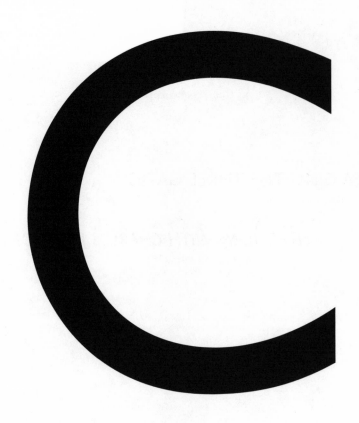

A

*V Ethel Willis White*

*Book*

*University of Washington Press*

*Seattle & London*

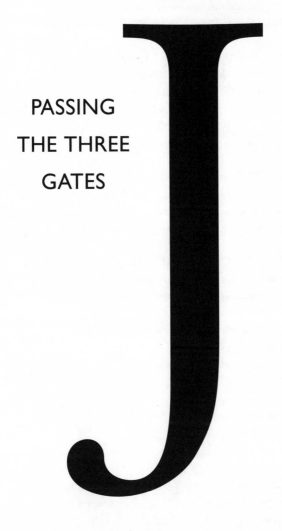

PASSING
THE THREE
GATES

INTERVIEWS WITH CHARLES JOHNSON

EDITED BY JIM McWILLIAMS

This book is published with the assistance of a grant from the
V ETHEL WILLIS WHITE ENDOWED FUND
established through the generosity of
Deehan Wyman, Virginia Wyman, and the Wyman Youth Trust.

Foreword © 2004 by Charles Johnson
© 2004 by the University of Washington Press
Printed in the United States of America
Designed by Audrey Seretha Meyer
FIRST EDITION
12 11 10 09 08 07 06 05 04 5 4 3 2 1

UNIVERSITY OF WASHINGTON PRESS
PO Box 50096, Seattle, WA 98145
www.washington.edu/uwpress

Library of Congress Cataloging-in-Publication Data
Johnson, Charles Richard, 1948–
    Passing the three gates : interviews with Charles Johnson / edited
by Jim McWilliams.—1st ed.
        p.   cm.
    "A V Ethel Willis White book."
    Includes bibliographical references and index.
    ISBN 0-295-98438-4 (acid-free paper)—ISBN 0-295-98439-2
(pbk. : acid-free paper)
    1. Johnson, Charles Richard, 1948—Interviews.   2. Authors,
American—20th century—Interviews.   3. African American authors—
Interviews.   4. African Americans in literature.   I. Title.
PS3560.O3735Z468   2004
813'.54—dc22                                            2004054987

The paper used in this publication is acid-free and recycled from
20 percent post-consumer and at least 50 percent pre-consumer waste.
It meets the minimum requirements of American National Standard
for Information Sciences—Permanence of Paper for Printed
Library Materials, ANSI Z39.48–1984.

# CONTENTS

# FOREWORD

## CHARLES JOHNSON

# T

*HE GREAT FIGHT*
*in life and in literature always is to prevent*
*some form of idea or situation from enslaving you.*
*It's to keep your mind open and your eyes open*
*and your life open, to find ways of not being limited.*

From my interview in *At the Field's End*

FIRST, AND BEFORE I write another word, I want to thank Jim McWilliams for his astonishing work in carefully selecting the interviews that appear in this volume and, of course, I wish to thank as well the distinguished University of Washington Press for making them available to the reading public. By my count, which is a conservative estimate, I've given more than 250 interviews for radio, television, newspapers, and magazines in America, Europe, and Asia since 1978. Seldom, if ever, do I revisit an interview after doing it, though I fondly remember the finest interviewers I've been privileged to meet, the ones who came prepared, having actually read my work thoughtfully, and guided me into conversations that were not only intellectually stimulating as they unfolded but also characterized by spontaneity, informality, and surprise—exactly what a reader would expect if he or she were privileged to enjoy a long dinner conversation with an author.

In these selections, McWilliams offers twenty of the best of these magazine, newspaper, and journal interviews, and yet he has achieved something far more startling and revelatory, at least for me. Jean-Paul Sartre said in his classic aesthetic work *What is Literature?* that it takes twenty years for a writer to be able objectively to read his own work as his audience does, not to see everywhere his own decisions and subjectivity and the countless things he considered saying as he worked from one sentence to the next, but instead—like his readers—finally to experience his creation as a finished object, a thing that stands separate from him, so mysterious and whole even *he* cannot remember where certain ideas, statements, and images came from. In other words, he has the delightful experience of encountering himself as a stranger. Thanks to Jim McWilliams, that has been, to a degree, my experience as I re-read these interviews, some of which I have not looked at in decades, and one or two of which I had completely forgotten I had done.

He begins this book with "Reflections on Film, Philosophy, and Fiction," an interview that is now twenty-five years old, conducted when I was thirty. At that time, I had only been teaching at the University of Washington for two years, my son was three years old, my daughter three years away from being born, my friend and mentor John Gardner was still alive and had just published his controversial literary manifesto *On Moral Fiction*, and I was in that delicate, even fragile place every first novelist knows only too well. As Gardner once said, 80 percent of novelists do not publish a second novel (sadly, a writer I much

admire, Ralph Ellison, is among them). When I did this interview with my friend, poet Ken McCullough, I had behind me
*Faith and the Good Thing* (1974) and ahead of me the challenge of the *second* novel, the one that says the first book wasn't
a fluke or a mistake, that says I—as a literary artist—was here
to stay. Furthermore, each novel (and especially the second) must
be an *advance* in technique and vision beyond previous works.
As I read this interview with McCullough, I can hear myself
working out methodically the aesthetic decisions and strategies
I would deploy in that second philosophical novel, *Oxherding
Tale* (1982), which I whimsically called my "platform novel"
because it became the foundation for the ten books I published
after it, none of which I would have cared to do if I hadn't completed *Ox*.

In all the interviews that follow, you will find—and I was
surprised to discover—the same issues of craft and culture raised
again and again: the artistic importance of formal virtuosity;
literary art as language performance; the need in fiction for specificity, imaginative storytelling, invention, and a cross-cultural,
interdisciplinary approach; the roles of consciousness, perception, and interpretation in the creation and reception of the
literary experience; the interplay between phenomenological
and Buddhist ways of seeing the world; and the need to both
*expand* and *deepen* in literature, film, and life our cultural images
in such a way that they capture the complexity and the poly-
semous character of the lives of people of color.

That aesthetic position is presented systematically in *Being
and Race: Black Writing Since 1970* (1988), which was my philosophy dissertation at the State University of New York at Stony
Brook and is the subject of the second interview McWilliams
selects for this volume. When this piece is placed together with
the interviews by my former student Nicholas O'Connell and
reporter Mary Lynn Lyke (who apparently spoke with me a week
before I won the National Book Award for fiction in 1990), what
one sees is the life of a black American writer—a man in the

middle of his journey—who has been a college professor for fourteen years. He has two children, now ages fifteen and nine, and since the McCullough interview has published that crucial second novel, and a short story collection, *The Sorcerer's Apprentice* (1986), which was nominated for a PEN/Faulkner Award and contained several stories much anthologized ("China," "Moving Pictures," "Exchange Value," and "The Education of Mingo"). He has written numerous teleplays for PBS since 1978's *Charlie Smith,* as well as essays on aesthetics, and has given eighty-three lectures and readings in America, Germany, Czechoslovakia, and France on literature for the U.S. Information Agency. Added to this, he has published the aforementioned philosophical literary manifesto during a decade in which a divisive "identity politics" swept American culture, African American males were demonized, and black male writers deliberately marginalized. Furthermore, he has been fiction editor of the *Seattle Review* since 1978, has served as Northwest director for the Fiction Collective and as a fiction judge for the National Book Awards (1988), and has reviewed regularly for the *New York Times Book Review,* the *Washington Post,* and the *Los Angeles Times.* And, finally, he has reestablished his devotion to Buddhism and regular meditation as well as to the martial arts, which he teaches, and after six years has completed the novel that will in the next decade and a half be taught at colleges, high schools, and middle schools (as well as the Coast Guard Academy): a fiction, *Middle Passage,* often referred to as a "modern classic."

After the great success of *Middle Passage* there is a sea change. As a literary artist, my aesthetic position did not change, nor did my work methods, but from 1991 until today the workload intensified tenfold, and, hovering over each conversation, from "The Philosopher and the American Novel" (1991) through "A Man of His Word" (1998), is *Dreamer,* the in-progress, fictional re-imagining of the last two years of Dr. Martin Luther King, Jr.'s, life, which I told a *Publisher's Weekly* reporter was my next project. Looking back, and looking at these interviews, I now believe that was a mistake. Naturally, interviewers want to know—and report—what an author is working on. But during the seven years I researched and reworked and re-envisioned that 1998 novel, I couldn't go shopping without the checkout person at my neighborhood supermarket asking me, "How's the King book coming along?" The University of Washington's former president William Gerberding asked me to lunch just so he could tell me he was troubled by the novel's title and felt it might suggest to readers that King was an impractical "dreamer." Morris Dees at the Southern Poverty Law Center inquired, over dinner at his home in Alabama, if I'd be interested in writing his biography. The agent of the King family contacted my agent to see if I'd be interested in writing a "quickie book" (whatever that is) about where King's children were in their lives in the '90s. Perfect strangers mailed me sometimes useful material on King and *their* opinions about what the civil rights movement was all about. On and on it came for seven years: far too many cooks eager to contribute to this particular fictional concoction. And so I learned an important lesson: Never, never, never discuss publicly a complex, multilayered philosophical novel—or any creative work—when it is still in its tender, formative stages.

Readers will see, as I did, something else in these interviews conducted during the decade I devoted myself to King: namely, a deeper, more highly critical emphasis in my conversations on such matters as the state of black America in the post–civil rights period, the enduring and perhaps intractable problem of Eurocentrism in contemporary society, and my insistence that King be seen not simply as a political leader, but also as a spiritual one, like his inspiration Gandhi. Because I *do* write every novel as if it might be the last thing I ever do, as a kind of literary last will and testament, I am always changed profoundly by the creative process each book requires. This was true of *Dreamer* no less than *Oxherding Tale*. During the years I composed and researched the King novel, throwing out approximately three thousand pages, I watched my children grow into beautiful examples of young manhood and womanhood, but both of them encountered the same atavistic instances of white bigotry that I remember from the 1950s and '60s, and which the better members of my generation (the baby boomers) hoped would be consigned to the trash heap of human evolution; yet it was precisely the boomers and their children that practice, as I came to see, "liberal racism" and the glorification of all things produced by those of northern European descent. That my children should have to experience these ancient stupidities is something for which I am totally unforgiving, and because of that the tone of my recent work has noticeably changed, growing testier, whenever I discuss the illusion of "race" in America.

I watched from the late 1980s, when I first conceived the idea of a double for King and attempted that as a short story, the bloody, internecine inner-city gang wars of the Crips and Bloods, the crippling effects that single-parent households and the high incarceration rate for black males were having on the black family, and the battles over affirmative action. All these questions I addressed in other literary forms as I worked on *Dreamer*—in *Black Men Speaking,* which I edited with John McCluskey, Jr., in articles such as "The King We Left Behind," and in short fiction like "Executive Decision."

Furthermore, the seven-year meditation that was *Dreamer* returned me to the fundamental philosophical questions discussed in the earliest interviews: What is the self? The *white* self? The *black* self? Aren't these, after all, simply constructs or fictions—a Buddhist would say delusions—that only increase ignorance (*avidya* in Sanskrit) and suffering in the world? In other words, the post-*Dreamer* period, which is covered in interviews with Singapore-based critic John Whalen-Bridge and with Jim McWilliams, record the last and final stage in this particular author's development, i.e., my *complete* and public devotion to the Buddhadharma as a spiritual practice and way of life, a dimension present in my fiction from the beginning but not made wholly explicit in my writings until *Turning the Wheel: Essays on Buddhism and Writing* (2003).

So, as I said, I am deeply indebted to both Jim McWilliams and the University of Washington Press for assembling these interviews that, in a way, are both a window into the artist's life and a transcript of aesthetic and philosophical thought spanning a quarter of a century. And I must also thank the adroit and probing interviewers themselves, especially those who avoided the easy, stock questions you might ask *any* writer ("Do you work on a computer?" "Do you write for a certain amount of time each day?"), or the always irritating, generic "race" questions that have absolutely nothing to do with an author's specific, individual works ("What do you think of the controversy about the movie *Barbershop?*" "Do you support reparations for blacks?" "Do you prefer to be called black or African American?"), and avoided as well the all too easy tendency to disguise accusations of various kinds as questions ("Why isn't your fiction angry like other black writers?").

As with fiction and the essay, there is an art of the well-wrought interview, a "pushing hands" (as a martial artist might say) between both parties—the questioner and the questioned—that is almost Socratic in its spirit and, like Plato's dialogues, becomes for both members of the conversation a quest for truth based on careful listening and an openness to pursuing the unexpected. (Over the last three decades, I've interviewed John Gardner, Samuel Delany, Johanna Russ, Nobel laureate Gao Xingjian, and in 1992 I hosted the four-part KCTS public television series "Words with Writers," in which I interviewed Tom Robbins, August Wilson, Anne Rule, and David Wagoner.) The most memorable, perception-altering interviews are the delicate, dialectical creations of both interlocutors, of course, but

I believe special thanks is due those interviewers who through their generosity created a space in which the person questioned could relax and let his hair down. If the spirit of inquiry is distilled on these pages, as I believe it is, then much praise is due to the interviewers themselves.

*Seattle, July 2003*

# PREFACE

**F**IRST AND FOREMOST, Charles Johnson is a teacher. Not only has he taught creative writing at the University of Washington since 1976, and co-directed the Twin Tigers studio for martial arts in Seattle since 1986, but also, and more importantly, he has taught through his fiction. As he states to Nicholas O'Connell, "Fiction should open us up to new possibilities. It should clarify for us. It should change our perception." Indeed, Johnson's fiction achieves this difficult goal, for it never ceases to ask the tough questions about who we are and—even more significantly—who we could be. This is what is meant by "moral fiction."[1]

Three of Johnson's four novels have a protagonist caught between two competing philosophies, a strategy best represented

1. In many of his interviews, Johnson discusses how this phrase—coined by his friend and mentor John Gardner—has been misunderstood and trivialized. To locate those interviews, please refer to the index.

in *Middle Passage*. Here, Rutherford Calhoun must choose between the philosophies of Captain Falcon and the Allmuseri. Falcon, imperialism personified, believes that the strongest— physically and mentally—are destined to rule the weakest. Slavery, then, is simply another manifestation of the natural order of the universe. Moreover, Falcon is a "dualist," a man who believes that the mind and the body—as well as the self and the other—are irreparably split. For the Allmuseri, however, these notions are foolish. They believe that individual ownership of things is unnatural, indeed selfish. Furthermore, as Ngonyama demonstrates when he effortlessly carves a roast pig, the Allmuseri believe in an integrated mind and body. At the end of his arduous physical and spiritual journey, Rutherford therefore renounces his former life and becomes self-less when he decides to adopt Baleka and devote himself to her welfare. Rutherford has learned through the course of his journey the truth of the Allmuseri philosophy.

While his fiction has been his most significant instructional tool, Johnson has also taught us through his critiques of literature (*Being and Race: Black Writing Since 1970*); his essays about Buddhism (*Turning the Wheel: Essays on Buddhism and Writing*); his drawings (*Black Humor* and *Half-Past Nation Time*); and his television scripts (*Charlie Smith and the Fritter Tree* and *Booker*). He even taught us the rudiments of drawing in his PBS series, *Charlie's Pad*. More to the point of this collection, however, Johnson teaches us through his interviews.

Since 1978, Charles Johnson has given more than 250 interviews (this section of his curriculum vitae runs a few lines longer than six single-spaced pages). Most of those interviews were radio or television broadcasts, but many were for newspapers, magazines, scholarly journals, and chapters in books. This volume collects the most significant of those print interviews.[2]

2. For this volume, I have expanded the definition of "interview" beyond the question-and-answer format so that I can include four profiles for which Johnson was questioned at length. Also, I have edited all the inter-

The first three interviews in this collection—those by Ken McCullough (1978), Nicholas O'Connell (1987), and George Myers (1988)—show a relatively young writer, not yet famous. For want of a better phrase, we might call him at this early point in his career "a writer's writer," by which I mean he was well respected in creative-writing circles on American campuses— particularly because of his involvement with the Associated Writing Programs (currently the Association of Writers and Writing Programs)—but had not yet published a best-seller. Even at this point in his career, however, Johnson had already formed his aesthetics. As he notes in all three interviews, for example, after some early experiments with naturalistic fiction (which he decided not to publish), his attention turned toward philosophical fiction, a mode of discourse that would allow him to explore questions of identity and the limits of self-knowledge. As he tells George Myers, he wants his protagonists to wrestle with the "profoundly painful effort to answer the question, 'Who am I?'" Also apparent in these three interviews is Johnson's sheer love of language—its complexities, subtleties, and elasticity. He teaches us that every word counts when writing serious fiction.

Later in his career, interviewers would repeatedly ask him about his interest in Buddhism and the martial arts. Of the early interviewers, only Nicholas O'Connell asks about this facet of Johnson's life, and in so doing elicits a telling bit of analysis. After pointing out that Reb, the coffin maker in Johnson's second novel, *Oxherding Tale,* is essentially a Zen Buddhist, Johnson emphasizes the importance of selfless duty:

If there's an objective situation in the world that is not being fulfilled, you can fulfill it, not because of any egotistical reason, not because you think you're going to get anything out of it, not because you want to edify yourself, but because it needs to be done. You will perhaps alleviate suffering in some way, or maybe you will suppress the evil

---

views for stylistic consistency and have corrected typos, but I have not condensed them or changed a single word.

that exists, and make the good come forward a little bit more clearly. But you do it because it needs to be done.

Although he is talking about Reb, Johnson could also be describing himself.

Fame for Charles Johnson arrived in the summer of 1990, when he published the best-selling novel *Middle Passage,* for which he won the National Book Award. Quite suddenly, he was swamped by hundreds of interview requests as he traveled on one book tour after another. His vitae from July 27, 1990, to April 17, 1992, lists interviews in all sorts of media, from local newspapers (the *Greensboro News and Record* and the *San Mateo Times*) to appearances on network television (ABC's *This Week with David Brinkley* and NBC's *Sunday Today*). He gave at least sixteen radio interviews (from Los Angeles to New York, from Seattle to Dallas). And he was interviewed by Swiss, Dutch, and Nigerian television programs. The majority of these interviews are relatively slight and cover the same ground, but a few of the print journalists seem to have actually read *Middle Passage* and thus were able to ask some intelligent questions about Johnson's work. I have reprinted three of the many interviews from this period—profiles from the *Seattle Post-Intelligencer,* the *Chronicle of Higher Education,* and the *San Francisco Examiner*—to give a sense of just how big a celebrity Johnson had become in only a few months. In addition to providing some biographical details about Johnson, each of the three has something to recommend it: the *Post-Intelligencer* details the tremendous amount of research that *Middle Passage* required, the *Chronicle* expresses Johnson's strong objections to the ways in which the media wanted him to be a spokesman for black America, and the *Examiner* gives some background information about his year in San Francisco. While these interviews may not be essential texts for scholars, they are nonetheless interesting reading and provide a glimpse of how general readers see Johnson and his work.

On January 23, 1991, in the midst of the flurry of publicity for *Middle Passage,* Johnson paused long enough to deliver a lecture at the California State Library about his career.[3] Following his remarks, he took questions from the audience. This dialogue is particularly interesting because the questions are so varied, which means that Johnson discusses everything from his revision process ("I may do ten pages to get one") to his relationship with his agent ("They stood by me when I didn't make a penny for them") to Saddam Hussein's doubles ("So they stole my idea"). Johnson also talks at length about why he has chosen to write about Martin Luther King, Jr., for his next novel.

Following *Middle Passage* and its critical acclaim, Charles Johnson entered the first rank of contemporary American novelists, which meant that he became the focus of long, in-depth interviews in major scholarly and literary journals. Unlike most of the newspaper profiles from 1990 to 1992, these interviews are absolutely crucial for scholars of Johnson's work.[4] Jonathan Little's interview, originally published in 1993 in *Contemporary Literature,* should be considered one of Johnson's major statements. In it, he explains in detail his criticisms of the black arts movement, concluding that while it did produce some important ideas, its rigid ideology didn't lead to a significant body of lasting literature. He further argues that literature should never preach from only one point of view but,

3. This lecture is printed in the *California State Library Foundation Bulletin* 35 (April 1991): 1–16. I have reprinted the question-and-answer session.

4. As I was unable to secure reprint rights in two cases, I have reprinted eight out of the ten. Charles Johnson mentions in the foreword a 12 April 1991 interview with *Publishers Weekly* in which he discussed his next project, the novel that would become *Dreamer.* For the right to reprint that two-page interview, *Publishers Weekly* demanded $1,743. Fortunately, the magazine is available in most libraries and in full-text format through Info Trac, Expanded Academic Index. For a listing of additional interviews, see "Additional Interviews with Charles Johnson" at the end of this volume.

instead, should incorporate "all the available profiles of phenomena." Apparently not content with having already spoken so heretically, Johnson adds later in the interview that he objects to how Alice Walker and Toni Morrison have portrayed black men in their fiction, saying that those portrayals "just don't seem moral to me." Johnson's argument in his pointed criticisms is that authors need to look beyond their initial impressions if they are to grow as artists. As he tells Little, "Very often we only deal with surface images, the most easily graspable meaning, which is usually the meaning we've inherited, or somebody else's vision, now our own. For the sake of progress, we have to go much, much deeper." In yet another statement sure to be controversial, Johnson concludes that multiculturalism—if it is to mean anything at all as a literary force—should be held to high standards of intellectual excellence.

Like Little's interview, William R. Nash's interview—originally published in the *New England Review* in 1998—should be considered one of Johnson's major statements. After some background about family (with a particular emphasis on Johnson's father), the discussion returns to the problems posed by the black arts movement. Johnson concedes that some good ideas arose from the movement—"a people (black) long disenfranchised . . . finally have a voice"—but he immediately cautions that the dangers resulting from the "drum major instinct" far outweigh any benefits. There's nothing wrong with wanting to be first, Johnson says in paraphrasing Martin Luther King, but our goal should be "first in service to others, first in love, first in giving and generosity." Like Little, Nash asks about the importance of race in fiction. Johnson replies that being a Buddhist has taught him that "race" is nothing but an illusion ("I see it as *maya*"), something that is unimportant to him personally but has to be a theme throughout his work simply because contemporary America is preoccupied with race.

Another of the excellent scholarly interviews is that by Marian Blue for *The Writer's Chronicle*, the publication of the Association of Writers and Writing Programs. Johnson discusses his long relationship with the AWP and analyzes what he sees as the strengths and weaknesses of students learning how to write in a workshop environment. The two most interesting parts of this interview are when he stresses the necessity of imagination in writing ("But you can through empathy and sympathy try to transpose yourself over there behind another's eyes") and explains how he invented an African tribe, the Allmuseri ("I wanted it to be a whole tribe of Mother Teresas and Gandhis").

Irene Wanner's two-part interview for the *Seattle Review* (1993–1994) is the most detailed in asking Johnson about the craft of writing fiction. He explains, for instance, why he needs to outline extensively the plots of his novels and how he gets "inside" characters in order to make them believable. He analyzes plot construction and then shows how the conclusion of a story needs to follow logically from what the writer has set up in the first few pages. This interview has very much the feel of a graduate-level seminar with Johnson, and I have no doubt that it echoes what he says to his students over the course of a semester.

In striking contrast to Wanner's interview, Linda Davies's—published in *Glimmer Train Stories* in 1993—asks no questions about the art of fiction but, instead, focuses on Johnson's personal side, especially his social philosophy and his devotion to martial arts. Interestingly, these two passions overlap. After asserting, for example, that he believes in Dr. King's idea of "the beloved community," Johnson stresses that the sense of community fostered in a studio of martial arts leads to an understanding of others: "You become very bonded with the other people in the school. . . . It's really kind of nice, and it's everybody—it doesn't matter—blacks, whites, males, females, younger people, teenagers, as well as older people." Such studios, he adds, "train remarkably good citizens."

Jennifer Levasseur and Kevin Rabalais's interview—originally printed in 2002 in the Canadian journal *Brick*—focuses on the intersection between history and fiction, with a particular emphasis on the problems that Johnson faced in *Dreamer* and *Soulcatcher*. After he discusses his extensive research for those two books, he explains why—after a certain point—imagination becomes more important than research. Using *Crime and Punishment* as an example, he describes how fiction allows an author to ask philosophical questions about human nature that cannot be asked any other way. Among these excellent interviews is Michael Boccia's piece from a 1996 issue of *African American Review.*[5] This interview focuses almost exclusively on who has influenced Johnson and his art, which means that many of the questions are about his family and favorite authors.

The most curious interview is one from 1992 by Phoebe Bosché for *The Raven Chronicles,* a Seattle literary journal. The interview starts innocently enough, as Johnson discusses his script about the Tuskegee airmen of World War II and his career as a professor at the University of Washington, but when the questions turn to race and class, Johnson seems to become irritated, objecting strongly when Bosché suggests that "social forces"—such as poverty—can lead to people making bad choices since they see no alternative. In response, Johnson argues that people never have to be "victims" of their social or economic status, that everyone always has choices.

If the many interviews in scholarly and literary journals provide a wealth of information concerning Johnson's ideas about literature and philosophy, the three later profiles focus on his personal life. He becomes a real person and is not just the larger-than-life literary genius. The first of these profiles, "A Life of Balance Through Martial Arts" (1992), focuses on his Twin Tigers studio, while the second, "A Man of His Word" (1998), sheds some light on how Johnson teaches his creative-writing

5. Devoted entirely to Johnson, this volume (30.3) contains many excellent critical essays as well as several pieces previously unpublished by Johnson.

seminars. This latter profile also provides some important biographical material about Johnson's years at Southern Illinois University in Carbondale. We learn, for instance, that the research that eventually culminated in *Middle Passage* began with an undergraduate term paper. The third of these profiles, however, is the most interesting. Charles Mudede's "The Human Dimension" (1999) focuses on how Johnson's life and art reflect his passionate commitment to improving the human condition. Following an extended (and thoughtful) analysis of Martin Luther King's life and legacy, Johnson explains why he has committed himself in his writing to showing that King's vision for America is still possible. Why, exactly, does Johnson feel he must spotlight King's vision? The answer is simple: "I think everybody who is a compassionate, conscientious citizen should address the problems of our society in some way. It is appropriate to do."

Concluding this volume are two new interviews, one by me and one by John Whalen-Bridge. I intended my own interview to serve two major purposes: to be a capstone for Johnson's career so far and to be a sort of "catch-all" of questions that I had after spending so much time reading and thinking about all of the other interviews. After reading repeatedly about how important his family is, for example, I wondered why Johnson doesn't write autobiographical fiction. Similarly, after reading Marian Blue's interview, I was curious about how Johnson conducts his writing workshops and if he had ever considered publishing his own textbook for fiction. I asked Johnson a total of nearly fifty questions, and he answered each one with great patience and humor.

John Whalen-Bridge's interview—especially commissioned for this volume—is undoubtedly the most focused in the entire collection because it addresses only one question: How has Buddhism influenced Johnson's work? To this end, Whalen-Bridge (himself a Buddhist) asks Johnson many questions about his personal path on the Buddhadarma and how his faith offers an

avenue to escape conventional ways of looking at things. Johnson and Whalen-Bridge have a lively discussion about the connections between phenomenology and Buddhism, and I have
no doubt that non-Buddhist scholars will find this interview to
be a key document to help them understand Johnson's work.

In nearly all of the interviews in this book, Johnson argues
that we must examine something from numerous perspectives
before we can begin to understand it. We must scrutinize its
exterior from every angle in every type of light; we must systematically study its interior (and if we cannot get inside, then
we are obliged to imagine what is there based on our research);
and we must consider its environment so that we have a context for its being. This collection of interviews helps us begin
to understand Johnson: we see him as a young writer staking
out his territory, as a best-selling novelist enjoying his first major
success, as a veteran reflecting on a distinguished career; we see
him in a hotel during a book tour, in his martial arts studio, in
his university office, in his home; we see him as an author, a
professor, a family man. Have we now managed to fix him, like
a butterfly to the cork? Of course not. He is much too compli-
cated a human being to be so thoroughly explicated by one collection of interviews. But it's a start.

# ACKNOWLEDGMENTS

FIRST, OF COURSE, THANKS to Charles Johnson for allowing me to interview him so extensively and for writing the foreword to this collection of interviews. He has been very generous with his time, and I'm deeply grateful. Also, thanks to Carla Kraehenbuehl, my research assistant for fall 2002. Carla typed many of these interviews and conducted some key research into securing reprint rights for two of them. Finally, thanks to Lillian Crook, director of Stoxen Library at Dickinson State University, for being undaunted by my countless interlibrary loan requests. As always, my deepest appreciation and love to my daughter, Sophia. *J. M.*

# Chronology of Charles Johnson's Life

1948 Born April 23 in Evanston, Illinois, to Benny Lee Johnson
and Ruby Elizabeth Johnson

1965 Earned first paycheck by illustrating a catalog of magic
tricks

1966 Graduated from Evanston Township High School
Enrolled at Southern Illinois University in Carbondale
to study journalism

1967 Began studying martial arts

1968 Met Joan New, a student at the National College of Education in Evanston

1969 Worked part time at the *Chicago Tribune*

1970 Published *Black Humor,* first collection of cartoons
Began starring in *Charlie's Pad,* a fifty-two-part PBS series
about drawing
Married Joan New

1971 Received BS in journalism from Southern Illinois University

1972 Published *Half-Past Nation Time,* a second collection of
cartoons
Met John Gardner, a professor of English at Southern Illinois
University

1973 Received MA in philosophy from Southern Illinois University
Published first article, "Creating the Political Cartoon," in
*Scholastic Editor*

1974 Published *Faith and the Good Thing,* first novel
Taught at SUNY, Stony Brook, and began doctoral studies
in philosophy

1975 Son, Malik, born

1976 Accepted position as Acting Assistant Professor of English
at the University of Washington

1977 Promoted to Assistant Professor of English at the University
of Washington

1978 Wrote *Charlie Smith and the Fritter Tree,* first teleplay for PBS
Began serving as fiction editor for *Seattle Review*

1979 Received early tenure at the University of Washington
Began serving three-year term as Director of Associated
Writing Programs Awards Series

1981 Mother died
Made commitment to Buddhism
Daughter, Elizabeth, born

1982 Published *Oxherding Tale,* second novel
Promoted to Professor of English at the University
of Washington

1983 Received *Callaloo* Creative Writing Award for short story
"Popper's Disease"

1984 Wrote *Booker,* teleplay for PBS

1986 Published *The Sorcerer's Apprentice,* first collection of short
stories

1987 Received Prix Jeunesse Award (international youth prize)
for *Booker*
Named in a survey conducted by University of Southern California as one of the ten best short story writers in America
Awarded Guggenheim Fellowship

1988 Published *Being and Race,* a study of contemporary African
American fiction

1990 Published *Middle Passage,* third novel
Won National Book Award for *Middle Passage*
Named S. Wilson and Grace M. Pollock Professor
at University of Washington

1991 *Middle Passage* nominated for Chianti Ruffino Antico
Fattore, Florentine Literary International Prize
Received "Talented Tenth Award," given by Alpha Kappa
Alpha/Kappa Psi

1993 Won O. Henry Prize for "Kwoon," a short story originally
published in *Playboy*
Received the Langston Hughes Cultural Arts Award

1994 Provided initial funding for Charles Johnson Award for
Fiction and Poetry, sponsored by Southern Illinois
University

1996 *African American Review* devoted an entire issue to Johnson
and his work

1997 Co-edited *Black Men Speaking*, an anthology of literature
about the experience of African American males in America
*Charles Johnson's Spiritual Imagination*, first book about
Johnson's work, published
One of twelve African American authors represented on
stamps issued by the nations of Ghana and Uganda

1998 Awarded MacArthur Fellowship
Published *Dreamer*, fourth novel
Contributed to *Africans in America*, a companion book
to the popular PBS series
*Middle Passage* listed as required reading for all incoming
freshmen at Stanford University

1999 Contributed to *I Call Myself an Artist*, a collection of essays
by and about Johnson
Served on Modern Library's panel to select the 100 Best Non-
Fiction Books of the Twentieth Century
Received PhD in philosophy from SUNY, Stony Brook
(backdated to 1988, the publication of *Being and Race*)

2000 Published *Soulcatcher*, a collection of stories originally
written for *Africans in America*
Co-wrote *King: The Photobiography*, a book about the life
of Martin Luther King, Jr.

2001 Became contributing editor at *Tricycle: The Buddhist Review*

2002 *Charles Johnson's Fiction*, second book about Johnson's
work, published
Received Academy Award for Literature from the American
Academy of Arts and Letters

2003 Published *Turning the Wheel,* a collection of essays about
Buddhism and African American literature
Charles Johnson Literary Society organized
Elected to the American Academy of Arts and
Sciences

PASSING THE THREE GATES

*INTERVIEWS WITH CHARLES JOHNSON*

# REFLECTIONS ON FILM, PHILOSOPHY, AND FICTION

*An Interview with Charles Johnson*

## KEN McCULLOUGH

CHARLIE SMITH AND
*the Fritter Tree* is a film written by novelist Charles Johnson and conceived by producer David Loxton of WNET-TV and director Fred Barzyk of WGBH-TV. The film is a dramatization of the life of Charlie Smith, who, at the age of 135, is the oldest person in the United States. The film will be aired as part of the VISIONS series in the fall of 1978.

McCullough and Johnson met during the filming of *Charlie Smith*. This interview was conducted recently in Boston, where both were participating in editing the rough cut of the film.

McCULLOUGH: *Charles, when you started out, you were working in a primarily visual medium, cartooning, and then*

Reprinted from *Callaloo* 4 (October 1978), by permission of Charles Johnson.

*you went to the study of philosophy, which seems to be at the other end of the spectrum in terms of verbosity, then you moved into novels with a heavy philosophical emphasis. Now you're once again involved in a medium which is primarily visual, or at least a lot less literary than the other things you've written, and it's also a collaborative medium. First of all, how did this process evolve for you? And, secondly, what was the adjustment to screenwriting like for you?*

JOHNSON: When I was really young, I wanted to be a painter, but where I lived in Illinois, there was no one who could teach me painting. I managed to link up in 1963 with a polymathic artist in New York who wrote mystery novels, was a cartoonist, and had a broad artistic background. His name is Lawrence Lariar, and he's now retired. Whatever native talent I had as a painter Lariar subverted, happily, to comic art, which is what I did from the age of seventeen, when I first started publishing, until I was about twenty two, tired of it, and married. Along the way, since I wasn't thinking of anything other than visual expression, I published two collections of drawings, political satire, and about a thousand individual drawings in various periodicals, and did a television series when I was twenty-one and in college, which was called *Charlie's Pad*—a very, very early "how-to-draw" show for educational television. But working with images in such a limited way was frustrating. The expressions I wanted as I got older were impossible. Somewhere along the line I discovered I could do philosophy better than anything else—I flunked just about everything else because I was bored, so I did philosophy throughout graduate school and developed a style of thinking that I couldn't explore expansively in the form of comic art. This led me to the novel, which was rough going originally: I wrote six apprentice novels. I published nothing until I had the opportunity to study with a really good teacher, John Gardner. At that time I wanted to explore philosophical fiction; I wanted somehow to merge, in my own work, the black experience and about two thousand years' worth of

4

philosophical reflection. That's still the way I work right now, on the eighth and ninth novels—all of them are philosophical experiments.

The switch from literary art to film was a bit awkward, even though it circles back again to the visual medium and earlier television work. Because, as you say, it's a group project. When you write a novel, you are director, producer, costume designer, actor, make-up man, all that at once. But now it's all divided up, you have to make compromises, which I think is good. Every writer, in principle, should be able to write in as many forms as possible. Finally, all these forms of expression are unified in a personality, in the artist himself, because some things he can get to only through images, and some things he can get to only through imaginative uses of language, and some things he can get to only through conceptual approaches, or analysis. For me, then, each is a different order of expression and all are on a parity. It shouldn't, for the writer, be much trouble to switch—it's just a slightly different cognitive style for each, variations on creative expression.

MCCULLOUGH: *Coming into the experience of writing this screenplay, were you totally naïve as to what you were going to have to do?*

JOHNSON: Yeah, I'd never written drama for television. I was led by the hand in the beginning, out of the wilderness, by both directors, and that saved me from making lots of mistakes. I didn't know the grammar of film, and my approach was probably more novelistic than cinematic. Those were adjustments that had to be made.

MCCULLOUGH: *Technique-wise, the really excellent directors always seem to be a few leaps ahead of poets and novelists. You will see, for instance, something happening in a Godard film and be totally bewildered by it, but spot the same device creeping into fiction a few years later. Now, you not only wrote the screenplay for* Charlie Smith, *but you were on location and were able to work with the actors and the director in situ, and*

*now you are participating in the editing process. Do you antici-*
*pate that these inside experiences will alter your approach to*
*fiction in any significant way?*

JOHNSON: I want to be more categorical about this—I think
that there are certain things that you can do that approximate
in the novel the techniques and approaches and strategies of
film; and there are certain films that are perhaps very novelistic in their approach to storytelling, but I honestly believe that
you're talking about two different orders of expression. If it's
literary art, if you're really most concerned about the performance of language, then the entire editing process is focused
more on control of voice and rhythm. When you edit fiction,
what you want to achieve is a musical underpinning, for example, to the prose—you want to see language revitalized so that
its performance is startling throughout the story. Everything you
do is possible only because language is malleable and plastic
and waxy and flexible. But when it's a film—and this is a pretty
strong statement—language is not that important. It's rather
the logic of sound and the logic of images in conjunction, which
includes also a certain rhythm achieved between silence and
sound. That's what you're manipulating. We're talking about
two different orders of perceptual experience, and what's
exploited by the director and fiction writer is quite different. I
don't feel threatened at all by what Fred Barzyk and David Loxton do, and I don't feel any obligation to work an expression
possible in literature into film. There's an area where the two
overlap. But they're really different in terms of the aesthetic effect
possible in each.

McCULLOUGH: *When you read many people's novels or*
*plays, it's obvious that they were written with adaptation in*
*mind. There's certainly no indication, no trace of this in* Faith
and the Good Thing.

JOHNSON: You're right. What *Faith* does is appropriate
certain structural features from the black folktale. My own writing does not follow film technique—or anticipate adaptation—

as much as it does literary traditions, though the novel has been adapted as a play that we're still trying to produce.

McCULLOUGH: *How are you going to incorporate what you've learned from this particular experience?*

JOHNSON: Little things will show up in stories, not necessarily structural or strategic things from film, but a few smaller things I saw when we were on location in Texas. For example: when I wrote dialogue and, before, only suggested in a minimal way bodily gestures, the sort of interpersonal reaction that never fully occurred to me until I saw Glynn Thurman and Richard Ward (actors) read these things into the script to flesh it out—I'll be conscious of these nuances from now on, problems of characterization, concreteness.

McCULLOUGH: *On one occasion we were talking about the quality of haecceitas in certain works. I assume that this is what you've just been referring to. I think we were discussing Gerard Manley Hopkins's term "inscape."*

JOHNSON: Yes, it's this sense of radical particularity in each and every object in a poem, so that, in a poem, you encounter objects in a way you've never experienced them before—each has its particular essence. The terms derive, I believe, from medieval philosopher Duns Scotus, who spoke of haecceitas as that which is the particular, concrete essence of things, and quidditas as that which is the universal essence. Probably what you aim for in every literary work is a complete construction ex nihilo of an imaginative world that's coherent, consistent, and complete. This occurs automatically in film if the costuming and set designers have done their job well. It should be like that in every story, ideally.

McCULLOUGH: *I've just completed my first screenplay also, and, frankly, right now I'm bored with the prospect of writing fiction, because there are so many levels of things going on in a film that cannot be duplicated on the page. I'm coming to film via poetry, and what I've discovered in writing for film is that the same compression of image, experience, and time that hap-*

*pens in a poem goes on in film. The transition to film is a natu-
ral one for me—the grammar is the same, but for me fiction
has become a distant relative. The mystery and poetry inherent
in Cocteau's films, for example, and Buñuel's films erases the
boundaries and makes writing things out in a Jamesian manner
seem awfully elephantine.*

JOHNSON: Let me try to clarify what, as I see it, the creator
does. It seems to me that in all literary art, what you're really
interested in is someone's very special sense of the world. That's
what he's put before you. That's what you have in film, in sculpture, in painting, and in novels—an embodied expression, or
Weltanschauung, where style and sense, technique and vision
are coeval. James, therefore, creates James's *world*—his sense
of the world—which is not necessarily a paradigm, formally,
for fiction. All the representations in the work are at the service of this expression. Say you have a room like the one where
Rancher Smith dies (in *Charlie Smith and the Fritter Tree*), and
there are a bed, tables, and chairs. But these objects, as just
described, lack any sense of meaning until that room is, say,
darkened, until the creator's vision permeates every object, every
representation. The creator, then, is a lens that transfigures things
through language, through his unique voice. He coherently
deforms the world in an artwork. You get that sense in a film
often—a complete *Lebenswelt,* or "lifeworld" that the author
has created for his characters. But I believe that in fiction you
can achieve more levels of this kind than in film. Why? One
reason is that film offers us an *appearance* of the thing. You're
given the objects, and perhaps there will be a sense, a mood, a
texture that glows like a halo around it, suggesting that the object
is something more; but in a literary work, I suspect that you
can get seven, eight, nine levels of meaning very quickly. Somehow the literary work of art is closer to the life of consciousness; it can have, I think, a deeper effect on consciousness than
film, if it's true that language is bound up with whatever we
mean by thought itself. Consciousness grows and evolves with

8

its grasp of the word. This is an object (a cup) and it's here before us; it *appears*. If through language I say, "This is a cup," I've made a judgment in respect to it and the judgment is utilitarian—it allows me to pick up the object and use it to hold my coffee. If, on the other hand, I say, "Ah, this is a flower-holder," the object appears now with a different meaning, being. It's very much like the old Zen Buddhist parable, where three students are with their master and he says, "Describe this object to me." He holds up what appears, just then, to be a fan. One of his students, naturally, says, "Why, that's a fan." The master says, "Wrong!" The second student says something equally wrong. The master comes to the third student, and he says, "What is it?" The third student picks up the object, scratches his back with it, uses it as a fan, uses it to thwack another student on the knee, and suddenly the meaning, the being, of the object has opened up—language fixes the meaning of objects, nails it down, despoils and expands meaning, allows you to have several levels virtually at any point in a story, and so fiction is a philosophical enterprise for me: hermeneutics. If it's film, I don't know whether you can exactly perform that kind of deep, ontological archaeology on an object, or the world. You would have to profile one object in several different lights, that's about the closest you would come. We see it in one scene as a cup, in another as a flower-holder, in a third as something else again. If film can indeed come close to this kind of disclosure of the world, the viewer will grasp that the meanings of things are open-ended, constantly changing, evolving, and this will have an important philosophical impact.

McCULLOUGH: *Let's go into the collaborative aspect of making a film a little more. If you're working on a gestalt creation, isn't it probable that several consciousnesses, given that their egos are intact, have a much better chance of creating a transcendent work of art than one consciousness sitting in front of a typewriter yay-many hours a day?*

JOHNSON: Well, in reference to that, I *do* find myself sitting

in my study, staring at a page I've just typed, trying to reconstruct from my own perspective, or point of view, a coherent
piece of the world. But in film it is more than just one perspective
or way of seeing because film is an intersubjective product—
not a single vision, which means that you must convince someone else that what you see is there by constantly hammering at
him until he sees it; but you have to give a little bit of the totality of your vision, because he's hammering at you for things
you've missed. In the end, it's overwhelmingly democratic.

McCULLOUGH: *The sixties programmed most of our generation of writers into believing that the majority is always
wrong* . . .

JOHNSON: [Laughter] I can give, I can give. Especially in a
project like this, where we worked almost from scratch. I didn't
come to the directors with an original script. Rather, they asked
me if I wanted to do a story based on the life of the oldest man
in the country. Our problem was that we had certain facts that
somehow had to be incorporated into the drama, or altered.
You can look upon these facts in two ways—as stepping stones
or as obstacles. We got together and tried to understand what
this man's life was like—what it meant. For one director, the
sense of his life was that he was feisty, crusty, individualistic.
He never really looked upon himself as being a black man living through what may have been some of the worst years of
black American history. For me, I saw something different. What
I saw was that by living through all those years, his story is more
triumphant, not because he's feisty, but simply because he
enshrines it all. And, of course, someone had a third opinion,
someone had a fourth. Well, what that really boils down to is
that if I had gone ahead and written this thing without consulting anyone, I would surely have missed part of what his life
meant. But working collectively on it, I think we managed to
take the shards and fragments of his life, from the written and
videotaped interviews we used, and reconstruct a sense of his
world that has at least a family resemblance to his own life.

*Reflections on Film, Philosophy, and Fiction (1978)*

McCULLOUGH: *What effect did looking in on the editing process of this film have on you?*

JOHNSON: What struck is what strikes anyone new to film—the possibility of restructuring, re-envisioning the entire thing, of going back to the beginning, even after all the performances have been turned in. That's trivial, of course.

McCULLOUGH: *I'm not so sure it is. I think that most writers who are new to film would have a tendency to think that there's one way to do it, the right way. In my limited experience with television, I've seen projects in which the content was there, in the can, but no one knew how to assemble it. There are a number of genius editors who can come in and in a few days construct a really knockout film. I'm thinking of Charlotte Zwerin in particular—she has rescued many a film.*

JOHNSON: What the editor does, I guess, when he comes in and looks at this mass of material, and no one can figure out what the connections are between episodes and shots, what the editor does is simply what any good hermeneuticist does—he comes in and, on the basis of his experience and a certain cognitive talent, conjures meaning out of all the chaos, which is to me the heart of the creative act. That's what art is about, it's enriching experience by organizing the pieces such that some sense that was embodied there, buried, but not clearly seen, is bodied forth.

McCULLOUGH: *Going back to the fact that you were led through the process from the beginning by the hand and didn't have to do much research into how to write a screenplay, do you feel that you're better off not having taken a screenwriting course or approaching it in some formal way?*

JOHNSON: I have a friend who writes screenplays for a living, and he unloaded a lot of scripts on me. I looked them over so I could see the formal variations. Having seen what they were—or, rather, that there *was* no definite form—I sat down and simply wrote a story, as a story, with description, everything, and didn't think about it specifically in terms of the grammar of film. I don't think that at the early stage of creating the primary concern should be thinking now as a writer for film, or thinking now as a writer of short fiction, or now as a writer of novels. I think it's basically having some intuitive grasp of what goes into storytelling—I think that's absolutely crucial, that one understands, for example, the theory of storytelling in Poe's "Philosophy of Composition," or in Aristotle's *Poetics,* or, in Shakespeare, the evocation of character and event. After that, you can make adjustments to a particular medium. Basic elements of storytelling—situation, plot, creation of a world— cut across all forms. I think later one can become more sophisticated and, if he wants, suggest shots to a director, but telling a story, and a story of importance—where man is grappling with meaning—is the writer's first concern. Knowledge of film history is valuable, but not crucial.

McCULLOUGH: *In terms of making allusions to other films, in particular, or in avoiding allusions?*

JOHNSON: That might be helpful, yes. But on the other hand, a writer who comes to film may do too much of that. He might straitjacket a creative director's ability to take his story and translate it into his own very special understanding. Writers and directors have two different kinds of imagination, different *styles* of thought. But it shouldn't hamstring a director if the writer does what he feels is necessary to tell a good story.

McCULLOUGH: *In the early days of film the writers were the shamans; now it's the directors who have top billing. The writer has become a secondary force in the field.*

JOHNSON: From my perspective, that's not true. Take the *Charlie Smith* movie. I didn't realize until we were looking at the material today that my particular, quirky way of looking at things—the way I live the world—had made a larger impression on the story, on the meaning of his life, on the characters, than I'd imagined earlier. Pearl, Charlie's wife, is straight from my imagination. To my knowledge, he never had a wife named Pearl, or a wife quite like her, but the drama called for her creation, for the sake of coherence, poetic consistency. This is a crucial point. Anyone can sit down at a typewriter, and write, "This happened, then this happened, then this happened," but the creative artist—he or she achieves what phenomenologist Maurice Merleau-Ponty called "a coherent deformation of reality," you know, a world that is lensed through his perspective. That's what animates the story. That's why I don't believe that in the case of the writer and the director working together the writer must be subordinate. Their subjectives *merge.*

McCULLOUGH: *Do you find that your analytic background in philosophy gets in the way at all when you're writing?*

JOHNSON: Friends of mine in philosophy say, "Johnson, you're a novelist and, therefore, will never be a great philosopher—*no* novelist has ever done philosophy." People I know in fiction say, "Man, your head gets in the way." I think both these groups cancel each other out. I will say, right now, for the record and just to infuriate them, that I'm the only black, systematically philosophical writer of fiction on this planet. [Laughter] This means that, as a phenomenologist, my focus in fiction is narrower than that of most writers. The subjects that interest me are the ones that require philosophical archaeology. I wrote six novels that were heavily influenced by James Baldwin, who I greatly admired, but somewhere along the line I wanted to write stories that were more ambitious in terms of digging deeper into the life of consciousness and dealing with the ambiguity of the world, because that *is* the way the world is given to us all, as ambiguous. Too rich in meaning. Out of this chaos you forge sense, and there are surely as many ways of making sense as there are subjects in the world. Every one of us is right, every one of us possesses a truth. This is, obviously, Hegelian. You bring together as many people as you can, and they tell you, "This is what I think, this is what I feel, this is my judgment about the world." That way, you get maybe a piece of the world, only a piece. That's why working with a group like this one is important for a writer. In other words, philosophy doesn't get in the way because all creative work can be seen as a philosophical project; it is the art of interpretation. It is trying to conjure sense out of the world, and if a story isn't doing that, then I don't know what it's doing.

McCULLOUGH: *Say some more about what it's like to start from scratch on a project like this.*

JOHNSON: Well, the first time Fred Barzyk and David Loxton told me about the project I was skeptical. I said, "Gee, you know it doesn't look like there's enough stuff here to work into a first-rate drama." But when we looked hard at it, we saw that Charlie Smith, who was born in Liberia, tricked onto a slave ship in 1854, sold in New Orleans at the age of twelve to a rancher who made him a Texas cowboy—we saw that Smith was a fantastic yarn-spinner, a fabulist for his own life. Then it became interesting for me because we had ample room to fill in the gaps in Smith's memory, even exaggerate his life with the degree of humor that characterizes the old man himself.

McCULLOUGH: *After the film had already been shot, a few of us made a pilgrimage down to visit the real Charlie Smith in Florida. I was watching you very carefully when you sat and talked with him. There was a certain confusion that registered on your face. You went through a range of expressions which were very ambiguous.*

JOHNSON: They were ambiguous?

McCULLOUGH: *Yeah, I could see that you were not sure what to make of what you had done, what you had extrapolated from this man's life.*

JOHNSON: It was a frightening moment for me. First of all, because he's the oldest man in the country, black, maybe one of the oldest men in the world. For me it was like falling into a fairy tale, going to visit one of those fabulous characters described in fairy tale terms: the *oldest* man in the world, the *youngest* son, or the most *beautiful* princess. Like that. On the other hand, the ambiguity was there, too, because although we had made a complete articulation of what we conceived his life to be, here he was in the flesh, outstripping us! Running beyond us, beyond the reach of our understanding. It's like what Sartre says in *Saint Genet:* "After you have explained Racine by his environment, by the age, by his childhood, there remains *Phèdre,* which is inexplicable." It must be this way. Ours is only one expression of the life of Charlie Smith, which we hope is *a* truth, not *the* truth. Another story will be *a* truth. If you keep hearing stories about the old man, you may get the whole truth some day, but don't count on it.

McCULLOUGH: *What are your plans in relation to screenwriting?*

JOHNSON: We're presently nursing two projects—one is a PBS miniseries adapted from Ralph Ellison's *Invisible Man,* which terrifies us, but we hope to see it completed; and the other is an ongoing series adapted from a radio drama I wrote for Earplay Productions in 1976. As I said before, writers should be able to write everything, anything. You should be able to write novels, radio plays, operas, short fiction, gags, manifestoes; you should be able to write philosophy, epic poems, screenplays, and charms to raise the dead, blight your enemies, and kill rats, everything.

# CHARLES JOHNSON

## NICHOLAS O'CONNELL

C
HARLES JOHNSON'S
novels, short stories, and television scripts explore classical problems and metaphysical questions against the background of black American life. His approach to writing is phenomenological, in the style of philosopher Edmund Husserl, but he also draws inspiration from the entire continuum of Asian thought, from the Vedas to Zen Buddhism. His work brings together Eastern and Western philosophical traditions, with the hope that some new perception of experience, especially black experience, will emerge.

Johnson was born in Evanston, Illinois, in 1948. He demonstrated an early talent for drawing and began a career as a cartoonist at seventeen. After graduating in journalism from

Reprinted from *At the Field's End: Interviews with 22 Pacific Northwest Writers* (University of Washington Press, 1998), by permission of Nicholas O'Connell. First published 1987 by Madrona Publishers.

Southern Illinois University at Carbondale in 1971, Johnson went on to write and co-produce the PBS series *Charlie's Pad.* He received his MA in philosophy from Southern Illinois University in 1973, and while there met novelist John Gardner, who guided him in the writing of the novel *Faith and the Good Thing* (1974). Johnson did graduate work in phenomenology and literary aesthetics in the PhD program at SUNY-Stony Brook before becoming a professor of English at the University of Washington in 1976.

He is the author of the novel *Oxherding Tale* (1982), a collection of short stories entitled *The Sorcerer's Apprentice* (1986), two collections of cartoons, and television scripts for the PBS series *Booker* (1984) and *Charlie Smith and the Fritter Tree* (1978). He is currently at work on the novel *Rutherford's Travels* and has recently completed *Being and Race: Black Writing Since 1970,* a book-length essay which will be published by Indiana University Press. He is the fiction editor of the *Seattle Review* and received a Guggenheim Fellowship in Fiction in 1987.

In 1970, Johnson married Joan New, an elementary-school teacher. They and their two children live in Seattle.

The interview took place in the spring of 1985 in Johnson's office on the campus of the University of Washington. Surrounded by the works of Hegel, Kant, Marx, and Heidegger, and equipped with several packs of cigarettes, Johnson talked long into the night about his approaches to fiction and philosophy.

O'CONNELL: *You've been a cartoonist, a student of philosophy, a television producer, and a photojournalist. Why did you choose to write fiction rather than continuing in one of these other fields?*

JOHNSON: I still do all of those things. It's not like one got left behind and another was picked up, but when you're talking about language, you have the possibility of multiple levels of meaning. If I shifted at all from the image to the word it's because the word is polymorphous and you can create a work of fiction that has more dimensions than a drawing or even a film. Film, of course, is wonderful, but I can't think of a single film, even the ones that I love, that are as rich and complex, and have the same vision and depth, as the greatest novels.

O'CONNELL: *Do you think that you will keep writing fiction, or will you use it up and go on to something else?*

JOHNSON: Right now, fiction is at the center of my work: telling stories in many different forms. I just do the film because it's fun, and because I like to work with producers and creative people who extend my own imagination, and because I want to make some money. But fiction is the basic thing. When you write a story, you have to do everything that the entire film crew listed in the movie credits does, which is work as a scriptwriter, producer, prop person, costume designer—the whole thing. You have far greater freedom as a writer of fiction, and you're challenged to force your imagination into all these different roles.

O'CONNELL: *So fiction is a more aristocratic art form, whereas film is more democratic?*

JOHNSON: More aristocratic, yes. Every film is a celebration of the crew. Every book, no matter what the writer might have drawn upon, is ultimately the product of a single consciousness.

O'CONNELL: *Did writing come easily for you?*

JOHNSON: Writing came easily, yes. I enjoyed writing. I enjoyed writing papers in college, because I enjoyed expressing myself in language. So when I started writing novels it seemed to me to be an extension of what I was already doing.

O'CONNELL: *Why did you start with a longer form of fiction like the novel?*

JOHNSON: Because the novel, of all the fictional forms we have, is the most expansive. It has the greatest room for exploring experience, for character development, and creating a coherent, consistent, complete world.

O'CONNELL: *What did drawing do for your writing?*

Charles Johnson (1987)

JOHNSON: My concern with commercial objectives got exhausted early through drawing. When I was in high school I did six drawings for a magic-magazine company in Chicago; I thought my life had changed. I still have that first dollar framed. I was obsessed with publication. I think I published a thousand drawings.

By the time I got to fiction I was more patient. I didn't have the hunger to publish that I did when I was a cartoonist. That was good because it taught me to let the story develop as long as it needed to. I care about the process of fiction now more than the egotistical joy of seeing my name in print.

O'CONNELL: *How did you develop your writing style?*

JOHNSON: The first six books I wrote were heavily influenced by three writers—Richard Wright, James Baldwin, and John A. Williams—all of whom I admired a great deal. The books were very naturalistic. They were about racial politics for the most part. They were dark, grim, murder-filled novels. I couldn't read any of them after I was finished.

I started feeling that a change was necessary after the sixth book. There were levels of meaning that I wanted to achieve, philosophical questions that I wanted to raise, and naturalism as an approach prevented that. It was at that time that I met John Gardner, who changed my life and literary approach. He had twenty-five years of experience as a writer behind him. I looked at his work very carefully, even to the extent of reconstructing scenes to see if they could be done differently. And he taught me two things that I couldn't get a handle on as a young writer: voice and prose rhythm. He was very helpful with that because he was a very gifted stylist. Also he was a polymathic writer: he could write in several different forms. He had a strong philosophical background. He was passionate about fiction, not just his own, but good writing by other people.

So my writing changed under the influence of Gardner. I found the outlets I needed for philosophically interesting fiction in respect to the black experience. I still write some stories that are naturalistic, but only if the meaning of the story demands that approach.

O'CONNELL: *And so naturalism is just one of many approaches?*

JOHNSON: Naturalism is one approach to interpreting reality. It came into its own a hundred years ago with certain writers who wanted to achieve the illusion of objectivity, but it leaves out any number of experiences people claim they have had in this world, experiences that don't fit within the narrow confines of the naturalistic method. So instead of being the only approach a writer has at his disposal, it's one of many. Every novel that I do has a strong realistic element, a naturalistic element, but not only that. There are other aspects of experience, of conscious life, that come in and create a more rounded picture of reality.

You see, naturalism is very Greek in its structure. The Greeks have gods manipulating the destinies of man. Naturalism hasn't a god anymore, but it has a modern equivalent—social forces. The social forces operating within a naturalistic story are pretty much the equivalent of the old Greek gods.

It's a strange form of literature. It's social determinism, which I don't particularly like. I think people are free and in control of their destinies, if they really want to be. Naturalism is a literature of victims, as far as I can see. Most of the characters are moved by internal forces or by social conditions or by the age, and are not free to choose how they're going to act. And that's one of the reasons I had to move away from naturalism because I just don't believe that's true of people. I don't think we're puppets. I don't think we're marionettes, whether you're talking about Greek gods, or the economic state of the United States at the moment. Even people who are radically poor and down and out still manage, if they wish, to be self-sacrificing, to care for others, to love and be compassionate, to rise to all the great virtues that we consider to be most human. They are not victims.

# Charles Johnson (1987)

O'CONNELL: *Does naturalism rob them of their dignity?*

JOHNSON: Yes, it does. It gives them no dignity. I don't like that. It's one of the problems I have with a lot of black literature. I'm not knocking naturalism. Everything I've written for television has been naturalistic. It's a very good discipline to make you think about ideas in a particular way and people in a particular way. But you can only get to certain aspects of experience through that. If you look at the life of the spirit naturalistically, you would have to conclude that there is no life of the spirit, there's only a psychological life. If you had to write a story about some of the great saints, Thomas à Kempis, Thomas Aquinas, you would have to think about them not in terms of what they said about themselves, but in terms of modern theories of psychology, Freud down through Maslow. As much as I like Maslow and Jung, I don't think they give a full account of the subjective life. And yet within the framework of naturalism, psychology is all we have in terms of talking about the life of the spirit. It psychologizes it. It makes it mechanical, just a series of causes and effects.

O'CONNELL: *So it's too limited an approach for you?*

JOHNSON: The great fight in life and in literature always is to prevent some form of idea or situation from enslaving you. It's to keep your mind open and your eyes open and your life open, to find ways of not being limited. Fiction should open us up to new possibilities. It should clarify for us. It should change our perception.

O'CONNELL: *Why has black literature for the most part been written in a naturalistic style?*

JOHNSON: One reason is because Richard Wright, who had the first bestseller as a black writer in 1940, selected this as his mode of expression. Wright set the style for the literary approach of a generation of black writing.

Now there are exceptions. There were writers in the past who tried other approaches, for example, Jean Toomer in the '20s. There's a little bit of Eastern thought that creeps into his writing. His work is extraordinarily surrealistic and hallucinatory, very different from the naturalistic tradition. But he didn't set the style for other imitators. His work is just unique.

And then we have Ellison's *Invisible Man,* another unique work which is, by God, more surrealistic, larger-than-life, allegorical and metaphoric than probably anything in black American fiction. But he did not create a body of imitators either.

Naturalism remains the primary style, up to this very day. The main reason for this is that most black writers are interested in social realism, addressing social questions, and naturalism gives you access to that maybe better than other approaches. Wright is rightly understood as the father of modern black fiction, but his approach is a cramped approach; it leaves out a lot.

O'CONNELL: *Are you trying to extend the range of black fiction in your own work?*

JOHNSON: I'm not going to limit myself to a particular form. As a story suggests itself to me, I look for two things: I look for the fictional form to express it that's most appropriate, I look for the voice that's most appropriate, and then I let the story bring in as many aspects of prismatic sides of reality as it needs to.

When I was a philosophy student reading fiction, I would look at black American literature and be impressed by what I didn't find there. I didn't find a philosophically systematic body of black fiction—black fiction addressing some of the perennial problems of Western man, taking up questions of value, ethics, meaning, the good, the true, the beautiful, the self, epistemology—right on down the line. There was none of that.

My work basically addresses those philosophical questions. For example, if you're going to talk about the assault on black identity in a culture that is primarily white, primarily Christian, then you must talk about the higher question of identity in an intelligent way. You must take up the question and follow it through as methodically and systematically as you can.

## Charles Johnson (1987)

In a work of fiction it means dramatizing that question against the backdrop of black American life. Say you start out walking around today, and you're black and you're thinking about how somebody just denied you a job and you feel that there was bigotry involved, or you go to the counter and give the woman your money and instead of putting the change in your hand, she puts it down so that you have to scrape it off the counter. You wonder, "Why did she act like that? 'Cause I'm black? What does that mean?" Your feelings are murky.

Most people only get to the first level of describing that. They don't take the issue further and begin to explore the question of what it means to be a self. Suppose this person made the decision, "Well, all right, they're bigots and I'm black, and my identity is black." You wind up like George Hawkins. That's exactly the decision he makes in *Oxherding Tale*. He's hurt by this incident and he becomes a cultural nationalist. He's trying to find some way to make himself feel good, and does it by denying everything that the white world represents, and by elevating everything he feels the black world represents. And even that's a joke, because he says, for example, it means "emotion and not reason, passion and not thought."

But, if you think about it, and you go back and look at other things that other men and women have said about identity, and the great sweat they put into trying to figure out the question, then you have something you can use as fuel for your own investigation. It's like somebody else did a report on it, and now you can use their report. You don't have to agree with it. You don't have to buy their conclusions, but at least they covered some of the territory that you yourself are murkily involved in. And you can come up with something maybe that nobody has ever said, but yet includes what they said. At the heart there will be a philosophical question applicable to all people, but as it takes on the particular form of black American life, we understand something new about it because the universal has to be realized or embodied in the particular.

23

O'CONNELL: *Are you a practicing Buddhist?*

JOHNSON: I would call myself a practicing Buddhist, but not a very good practicing Buddhist. I was raised in an Episcopal church in Evanston, then later fell away in college from a belief in institutional religion. But the study of Eastern religion gave me a deep appreciation for the mystical core at the heart of Christianity—the similarity between Meister Eckhart and the twelfth-century Zen Buddhists, the parallel statements from Christ and the Buddha—so that I still have my roots in Christianity, but have a deep involvement in all forms of Asian thought and meditation. I meditate and I read the literature, and I do other related disciplines because it feels right for me. For a long time it has. From the time I was nineteen and first in the martial arts, the teacher I had said, "You don't have to study Buddhism to make progress in this martial art, but it will help." So I did. Since I was in philosophy already it was easy to do. But I didn't really get serious about meditating until 1979 or '80. Now it's a large part of my life. I do it every day, twice a day sometimes. It's clarifying. It helps to clear my head, get rid of a whole bunch of ideas and just experience things, sometimes with a great deal of immediacy. Right after meditation, language is not operating, I'm just looking at things. It's later that language comes into it and I start making judgments. I say, "What's in front of me is a flower vase." Well, just after meditation it's only this object. I'm just looking at it. It may appear as a particular kind of image that I've never seen before. It's after language, and after you get into the course of the day, that you begin making easy judgments, and don't see things clearly anymore.

O'CONNELL: *What influence has Buddhism had on your fiction?*

JOHNSON: It amazes me that some people have never pointed out one very simple thing about storytelling, and that is the nature of desire whenever we talk about a conflict for a character. Handbooks on writing, even John Gardner's, say, "To have a story, the character must have a conflict." There must be conflict, because if there's no conflict there's nothing a character can act upon; there's no plot. And the conflict is either something in the characters' world that they don't want and they have to get rid of it, or it's something not in their world that they desire to bring in. Well, all fiction which operates on that basis defines part of human nature as involved in desire. It's implicit. It's saying, "This is universal for all men. Desire is fundamental to all of our experience."

Now I wonder if that's true. I'm not entirely convinced of that. I know that there are people on the planet who do not live that way. Buddhists, for example, do not live that way. The first two noble truths of Buddhism are "Suffering is universal" and "The cause of suffering is desire." The Buddha was an incredible empirical psychologist, because I do think those ideas are universal. As I look at the world, I see suffering. Being alive is suffering in a certain sense, even for insects. And for human beings, the cause of suffering is desire.

*Oxherding Tale* brings this forward in a way that has not been brought forward in any other book that I've seen, certainly not in black American literature or within American literature. Reb is the Zen Buddhist in the novel, and a lot of reviewers don't realize that. They don't know enough about other cultures to recognize him as such. He doesn't operate out of desire, he operates out of duty. It's duty that is the foundation for all his behavior.

O'CONNELL: *But isn't there something else behind this sense of duty, such as a god or deity that helps him to decide what his duty is?*

JOHNSON: The novel never says that. I never mention God. I never even mention Buddhism, as a matter of fact, and that was the hard thing about the novel, because I knew that as soon as I did, people would have a knee-jerk reaction, they would shut down on it. So there's a line that says, "Something acted upon him. A push, a shove, a finger on the spine, only then did he move." You could say it's instinct if you wanted to. But I don't pin it down with God and the universe because modern readers just wouldn't be able to deal with that.

But there's another line, "Reward he did not expect, nor pleasure, desire was painful, duty was everything." That's almost strictly the description of a true Brahman out of the *Bhagavad-Gita*. It's duty, not desire, that makes Reb do what he does.

If there's an objective situation in the world that is not being fulfilled, you can fulfill it, not because of any egotistical reason, not because you think you're going to get anything out of it, not because you want to edify yourself, but because it needs to be done. You will perhaps alleviate suffering in some way, or maybe you will suppress the evil that exists, and make the good come forward a little bit more clearly. But you do it because it needs to be done.

And that's what motivates Reb. Man does not have to operate out of the basis of desire, so that when people describe it as fundamental to conflict and character, there's a presupposition operating that they haven't really thought about. They haven't thought that they're presenting a view of man metaphysically, and that they are also not thinking about other alternative ways of existence.

O'CONNELL: *Do you agree with John Gardner's thesis that fiction should be moral?*

JOHNSON: I agree with that absolutely, but in a slightly different way than John. I think that he's right, but I don't believe you can ever successfully argue for moral fiction. It's a faith in man that Gardner had. It goes all the way back to his first book, *The Forms of Fiction,* where he says that man is one step lower than the angels. He sees a nobility and dignity in the species, but you will never be able to argue that philosophically and convince all the modern readers who have suffered through the tragedies and disasters of the twentieth century.

O'CONNELL: *What did Gardner mean by moral fiction?*

JOHNSON: Moral fiction has nothing to do with preexisting moral precepts that the writer brings to the page. That leads to

*Pilgrim's Progress,* which no one is going to be convinced by in 1980. When Gardner says "moral," he means that the writer is responsible for the kind of fictional world that he puts onto the page. A lot of writers try to cop out by saying, "I'm just trying to tell it the way it is." But whenever you have a fictional work, you have an interpretation of reality that immediately refers back to the consciousness of the writer. If the writer sees only gloom, despair, entropy, then we have to ask that writer, "Why is this all that you see, when there are other people out there whose experience is somewhat different, who can argue this is not a complete portrait of reality?"

The second thing is characterization, which Gardner was very concerned about. You must approach characters with the same empathy, identification, and effort at understanding that you do with people you care about in the world. To slight characters, to set somebody up as a tool, a device for a story, is to perform in a fundamentally immoral way.

Gardner once raised the question of whether you had to be a good person to be a good writer. And in a sense you do. You have to care about how other people see the world, in order to create a rich, complex fiction that has the feel of the real world where other people's interpretations are in conflict with your own. In the final analysis, the conflict of interpretations may be what fiction is all about, because this is one intersubjective world, a world of multiple interpretations.

O'CONNELL: *Do you strive to write moral fiction?*

JOHNSON: Yes, I strive for truth and accuracy of character. If you look at a story, what you have is the writer presenting an interpretation of experience that should clarify your experiences for you. We read fiction not just for entertainment, but for clarification, for greater knowledge of who we are and why we behave the way we do. The plot of the story is in effect the writer's equivalent of the philosopher's argument. You say this kind of person is in this situation, and this happens because of that. You're saying in effect: this is the way life works, given these conditions and premises. So plot is extremely important. And if a writer is to abandon plot, it means he's abandoning the responsibility to make sense out of the world and his own experience. Plot is crucial and intimately related to character.

O'CONNELL: *Do you think that a novel should be as tightly constructed as a philosophical argument?*

JOHNSON: A novel or story should be as tightly constructed as a logical proof. There shouldn't be anything superfluous in it. There should be no narrative slop. There should be no excesses that get in the way of exploring the characters, the issues; and at the same time entertaining the reader. Readers want three things: they want to laugh, cry, and learn something. If you forget any one of those, your fiction is a bit slim.

O'CONNELL: *Are you consciously aware of the theory behind everything in your fiction?*

JOHNSON: I may be different from other writers in this respect. I have to understand the story philosophically before I can write it. Coming out of philosophy is helpful because I understand two thousand years of philosophical arguments and positions on different issues in the West and East. So it allows me to get to the major aspects of the problem quickly, but it may still take a while to get to an aspect that is new or original. The process of writing the story helps to do that. It uncovers things. It is a laboratory. You go into the story not knowing the answer, but you know a lot of other theories about the experiment that you're going to do. You've seen other attempts to resolve it. By the end of the story you may be startled by the conclusion that you come to.

O'CONNELL: *So language is the laboratory where the fiction writer works to discover truth?*

JOHNSON: Language is something that we find ourselves in the midst of. Before my kids were able to speak they found themselves surrounded by all these words and babbles and sounds, till one day magically they made sense and the kids were able to imitate and repeat the sounds and live within language. It was at that point that the child's very consciousness was structured by the structure of language.

Language has a capacity to rigidify and calcify our seeing; we think only in terms of certain words and certain experiences, and don't break through to anything else. The writer of fiction has to break through that. As Heidegger says, it's language that covers over our perception. And it's language in the hands of an artist that uncovers our perception. It's the same phenomenon that conceals and reveals. This is why I think fiction is exciting. When I'm writing, things happen, and I don't quite know where they came from. I'd like to attribute them to the language itself, to its unpredictable possibilities. It's like a trap door, the language drops you down to this whole other level of seeing.

O'CONNELL: *And by rearranging the language you create new perceptions?*

JOHNSON: It can only happen through words. Heidegger's famous phrase for this is, "Saying is showing." To say is to show, which is why the language of newspapers, television, and the media basically covers over our experience. We get used to talking in shorthand terms; people become incapable of seeing.

It's really hard in writing to free yourself from clichés, ideas minted in the media or other people's minds, so you can see the issue clearly, not thinking in terms of social formulas, social clichés, but really trying to look at the subject with radically unsealed vision.

O'CONNELL: *How does this phenomenological approach apply to writing?*

JOHNSON: It's very easy. It's something that writers and painters use all the time. If you go to an art class, you see people drawing a figure. The people who are not truly seeing will look at the figure on the stage, and something will happen between the time they look back at the page and draw because they won't draw what they see, they will draw what they think a figure looks like—it will have nothing to do with the real person on the stage.

Phenomenology is basically forgetting what you think the human figure looks like and looking at the human figure in front of you. Every artist does that. You have to divest yourself of the prejudices, the comfortable preconceptions about what you're dealing with. That's hard to do. It makes the process of writing exhilarating but at the same time exhausting.

O'CONNELL: *How does the final result of this process, a work of art, convince us?*

JOHNSON: A lot of people seem to think that a work of art boils down to being only a matter of taste, subjective difference, and finally fashion or whatever the hell it might be. That's stupid. That's dumb. If somebody is trying to describe a particular character, they can achieve greater and greater accuracy, so that they can come up with a description that nobody will be able to deny.

Art can be looked upon in very objective ways. One of the reasons that art in this country, and particularly in writing programs, is so sloppy is that writing people think art is not serious, that it doesn't have the rigor, the rules of science. But if we're talking about truth and accuracy, then art does have objective standards. We can say, "This story is replaying stuff that the writer has seen in other stories, and is not advancing the form of the novel or the short story." Or we can say, "This writer has written about things that have never been written about before, or has written about things in a way that's deeper than any other writer."

You can say many things about how art objectively can advance. But you must know cultural and intellectual history and the history of literature to make these judgments. Most writers write totally off the top of their heads. They don't know how their work fits within the tradition of literature, they don't know really what their objectives are. But art, like science, has rules, objectives. It's only on the basis of having a sense of tradition that you can say that something fits within the continuum and advances it.

O'CONNELL: *Do you enjoy the process of writing?*

JOHNSON: I love the process of writing. I am at my fullest when I'm writing. I can think of no activity that brings so much of everything that I am—everything I've learned, everything I feel, all the techniques at my disposal—into one suspended moment that is the work of art. So it's very exhausting when it's working exactly right.

O'CONNELL: *Do you think there will come a time when you will not need or want to write any more?*

JOHNSON: Every writer should leave that possibility open. There was a time before I was a writer when I did other things. There may be a time after which I don't write but do other things. Art is part of life, it's not the whole of life. It's not the reason for existence. It takes a writer of courage to admit that he has said all that the universe has given for him to say, and after which he would only repeat himself, fall into formulas, imitate other writers, or just basically destroy what he has built if he continues. I don't think a writer should just babble on and on. If you have something to say, you should say it as effectively as you can, then you should shut up.

O'CONNELL: *In his essay "Poetry and Ambition," Donald Hall says he sees no reason to spend your life writing poetry unless your goal is to write great poems. Do you agree with this approach to writing?*

JOHNSON: When it comes to the crunch, the only two worthy goals are to serve this discipline you have entered into by contributing something great and to make a place for yourself in the literature of the age. The ambition of the writer should be to be one of the great American writers. That's the highest ambition, to leave behind a work that will be meaningful to people many years after you're dead.

O'CONNELL: *Who do you measure yourself against?*

JOHNSON: Most of the writers I read on my own time are pre-twentieth century—Dickens, Hawthorne, Poe, Chaucer, Shakespeare, particularly Homer. That's about it. Those writers and also the philosophers—I read a lot of philosophers—who have stood the test of a millennium or five hundred years. Those are the ones I think most about, whose works I return to most often. I won't go into all the problems I have with contemporary literature, but I have a lot of problems with it. I don't think that most writers write out of the deepest sense of seriousness that Donald Hall talks about. We have an apparatus in America that will give awards and grants and fellowships and a little money to writers. And you can work that game for a lifetime, and never do anything important. You can also find publication, because there are literally hundreds of literary quarterlies, so getting published is nothing really to crow about. And I think that apparatus, which had a good intention, mainly to support the arts, can become a way of degenerating into supporting second-rate writers with very limited ambitions.

I think a real writer simply has to think in other terms. Not, "Will I get in this magazine? Will I get this NEA next year?" but whether or not this work is something he would do if a gun was held to his head and somebody was going to pull the trigger as soon as the last word of the last sentence of the last paragraph of the last page was finished. Now if you can write out of the sense that you're going to die as soon as this work is done, then you will write with urgency, honesty, courage, and without flinching at all, as if this were the last testament in language, the last utterance, you could ever make to anybody. If a work is written like that, then I want to read it. If somebody's writing out of that sense, then I'll say, "This is serious. This person's not fooling around. The work is not a means to some other end, the work is not just intended for some silly superficial goal, this work is the writer saying something because he or she feels that if it isn't said, it will never be said."

Those are the writers I want to read. And there are not many twentieth-century writers like that. Writing is a "career" in the twentieth century. It's a "profession." And I use those words pejoratively. I think writing is a passion. I don't think you choose writing, I think writing and art choose you. I think you write because you have no other choice, not because it's a celebrity thing.

I got a letter many years ago from a woman. She told me that she read *Faith and the Good Thing* on the verge of committing suicide and after reading it decided to live. You're left with the feeling that you can do some good in this world through what you do, as if art in the old religious sense were good works, or in the Indian sense, *karma yoga*. You do it because someone's going to benefit from it: that's why you do it.

# BEING AND RACE

*An Interview with Charles Johnson*

## GEORGE MYERS, JR.

M YERS: *MARTIN HEI-degger's* Existence and Being . . . *is that the echo you want readers to hear with the title you picked for* Being and Race?

JOHNSON: Yes, I specifically wanted to place this book within the tradition of phenomenology, which was my chosen "style" when I did PhD work in philosophy at SUNY-Stony Brook. The title should echo other works, such as Heidegger's *Being and Time,* Sartre's *Being and Nothingness,* and Marcel's *Being and Having.*

MYERS: *What specifically about Heidegger is a key to your critical book, or your fiction?*

JOHNSON: Heideggerean phenomenology, and the entire tradition in general through Mikel Dufrenne, provided a theoret-

Reprinted from *Gargoyle* 35 (October 1988), by permission of George Myers, Jr.

ical framework for reexamining all the uncritical terms we use—
especially in the media—when talking about black life and literature. Generally, such terms as "race" and "experience" and,
on the literary side, even "story," are used with no effort whatsoever on the speaker's part to clarify what they mean.

If the phenomenological method has any credibility, it should
allow us to examine these experiences without our usual presuppositions and without explanatory models, so that what we
achieve after the eidetic reduction, *epoche* or "bracketing," is
a new fresh encounter with the phenomenon of "race" or
"story."

MYERS: *What moved you toward generally philosophical
issues in your fiction while other black artists and writers of
your generation, or those maybe a little older, moved more
toward ideological concerns in their art or books?*

JOHNSON: I've always enjoyed the work of my black con-
temporaries and predecessors, especially Jean Toomer, Richard
Wright, and Ralph Ellison, but, when I was much younger—
about nineteen or so, and at that time a comic artist and philosophy student—I realized that we did not have in the tradition
of Afro-American literature anything that might be called
"philosophical fiction." Our writers have always been pressured
to limit themselves to racial and social issues, usually defined
by white and black critics in the most narrow of terms.

What I'd hoped to do when I started writing novels in 1970
was "fill the gap," so to speak, by exploring those philosophical and scientific questions other black writers had blinked
away, ignored, or dismissed, because I believed then, and
believe even now, that they are crucial to our understanding of
culture and consciousness.

MYERS: *Where did your basic interest in philosophy come
from, Southern Illinois?*

JOHNSON: My formal study of philosophy began at Southern Illinois University in 1967, by which I mean the course work
leading to a degree. But, as I mentioned, I was a comic artist.

35

I started publishing drawings in Chicago when I was seventeen and was obsessed with everything related to the visual arts. The result was that a love of doing art forces one to think about art, which leads to aesthetics, and that ultimately forces an artist to consider all the philosophical questions in epistemology, metaphysics, ethics, ontology, and so forth. In effect, an early involvement in art prepared, I think, the foundation for philosophical study.

MYERS: *Was that when you apprenticed yourself to novelist John Gardner?*

JOHNSON: I met Gardner my last year, and his, at Southern Illinois when I was finishing a master's degree.

MYERS: *Did you seek him out for your instructor, or was he the only writer there for you?*

JOHNSON: I sought him out. He'd just published *Grendel,* which meant he had a good reputation, but not yet *Sunlight Dialogues,* which meant he hadn't become a national celebrity short on time.

I'd written six apprentice novels, all bad imitations of Baldwin, Wright, and John A. Williams, although one of them—number four—was accepted for publication by a small New York house. I asked them to give it back to me. The reason was because, under Gardner's direction, I was writing *Faith and the Good Thing,* which was radically different in style from the other naturalistic novels and closer to my own vision.

I asked John for his advice on the book accepted for publication, and he said something very wise. He said, "If you think it'll come out and you'll have to climb over it, then ask for it back. The first book should be a strong debut. If the critics and reviewers get the wrong idea about what you can and can't do, you'll have to fight in future books to change their minds." I'm paraphrasing what he said here, but I took his advice, and I'm glad I did.

MYERS: *Why Gardner and not, say, Donald Barthelme or William Gass or someone like that?*

JOHNSON: Gardner was an admirer of Bill Gass, and so am I. The difference among these authors, and a fortunate one for me, was that John and I were remarkably alike. I think we recognized that when we met. He took me under his wing, so to speak, and didn't mind seeing himself as my literary father.

More than anything else, I suppose, I admired the musicality and prose mastery of his earlier works, like the opening pages of "John Napper Goes Sailing Through the Universe," and Gardner's capacity to shift competently from one literary form and tradition to another. He was, after a fashion, a "philosophical" writer, and had an aesthetic—that of moral fiction—that I perfectly agreed with in principle, although I don't think John argued this well. For example, I spoke with him by telephone when he was working on *On Moral Fiction,* and asked him how he was handling methodology. His reply was, "When method breaks down, I bang on the table." So I sent him two books I thought might be useful: Mikel Dufrenne's *The Phenomenology of Aesthetic Experience* and *The Main of Light,* the latter a wonderful book on poetics by one of my Stony Brook profs, Justus Buchler. Both appear in the footnotes to *On Moral Fiction.* Still, John went through them too late to do anything other than mention them after the book was in galleys.

MYERS: *You've said he helped find a way to work through philosophical issues in your novels. How?*

JOHNSON: The tradition of naturalism I was entangled in for those first six novels presented a barrier to me because in all those novels I admired, with the exception of a few things by Richard Wright, the authors fail to present blacks as intellectually vigorous people. I'm thinking of Chester Himes, John A. Williams, and a score of their imitators. Gardner's deep sense of the theory and practice of great fiction, which comes through in everything he said about realism, the eighteenth-century English picaresque, the parable—all of which as forms were inherently better able to embody broad philosophical exploration.

Naturalism is pretty much tied to a late-nineteenth-century vision of the physical world and human psychology. It's fine, for example, if you want to write novels of social protest. But other visions and interpretations of the world require other fictional means.

MYERS: *You had written six novels before working with Gardner?*

JOHNSON: They were written quickly, between 1970 and 1972. No one told me you couldn't write a novel in three or four months. So I did. I was used to organizing everything in my life in terms of academic quarters. You know, starting a class in September and finishing it in early December. I didn't see any reason why I couldn't do a novel each term. I wrote about ten pages a day in the beginning, three drafts for each book. Gardner slowed me down to writing *Faith and the Good Thing* in nine months, which struck me as a slow period of time then. I threw out about 2,400 pages on it. The point, I guess, is that a background in journalism made me learn to write fast.

MYERS: *Can you say you have one Chuck Johnson book, say, for example, the PEN/Faulkner Award nominee* The Sorcerer's Apprentice, *or some other book, that seems more complete to you, or like a favorite son?*

JOHNSON: The book I care most about is *Oxherding Tale*. I dreamed about it for ten years and took five years to write this thing. Actually, it was prefigured in the first bad novel I wrote, which was about a black martial artist who finds himself thrown into a world of Eastern thought. Later I managed to use the same situation for a story, "China," which turned out better.

Everyone speaks of how important the slave narrative is to black fiction. I knew I wanted to work this [in *Oxherding Tale*] but to open it so that all the larger questions of freedom and slavery could be explored on a metaphysical level and in terms of Eastern and Western thought. Also, I wanted a narrator as intelligent as Frederick Douglass, a story which—as a story—

would be highly entertaining. To be honest, I think I was born to write this book.

MYERS: *What makes a good novel good?*

JOHNSON: Imaginative storytelling reinforced by massive technique. I think it should be entertaining and present vividly rendered characters, original portraits, who have problems we care about. Problems which, as the characters work through them, uncover deeper levels of thought and feeling in our own lives.

Like philosophy, a good story clarifies some dimension of our lives and leads us to reexperience the world with unsealed vision. I know I'm asking for a lot. The old literary virtues of plot and meticulous detail, and also philosophical objectives— a revelation of disclosure in fiction of who we are and why we behave as we do. But if we can't meet these objectives, if our work is anything less than the greatest fiction we inherit, then we should quit and do something else.

MYERS: *How do these qualities or characteristics of a novel relate to "being" or "race"?*

JOHNSON: This is a tough question. The easiest thing for me to say is that every work of human expression, the novel included, presents an interpretation of the world. And, in the most microscopic ways, the image itself is a workshop of a vision, of reshaping a reader's perception. Of each work of art, we must ask, "What has this writer, through his interpretation of experience, chosen to show us? What has he included or profiled or represented? And, more importantly, what has he left out, and *why* has he left it out?" Every plot is an argument. Every story is not the imitation or representation of something in the world, but rather an experience the writer has created for a reader to live through. If this sounds credible, we can ask, "What meaning emerges for the racial world in this work? Is the writer simply offering us the racial world as he or she has seen it portrayed in *other* novels and stories, or is there something new here?"

MYERS: *In* Being and Race *you say black fiction is about the "crisis of identity"* . . .

JOHNSON: Black fiction has always been about the crisis of personal identity, the profoundly painful effort to answer the question "Who am I?" in a culture that constantly portrays blacks as different—as inferior in racist literature, as comic in the minstrel tradition, as exotic during the 1920s, as dangerously violent in the 1960s, and, in the 1970s and 1980s, as morally superior by virtue of being victimized. Look at almost any work by an Afro-American author. It's there—the quest for selfhood.

Recently, at a colloquium devoted to *Being and Race* [March, 1988] at SUNY-Buffalo, one of the panelists, historian T. J. Davis, remarked how shocked his students were when they read a nineteenth-century document that had slaves on a farm enjoying a moment characterized by laughter. The students refused to believe it. They couldn't imagine slaves having anything to laugh about, to be happy about, because, well, they were *slaves*. The anecdote sticks in my mind: Our idea of what a slave is, what a phenomenologist would call his essence or eidos, categorically rules out the possibility of laughter. Isn't this strange? This is precisely the reason I felt I needed to write *Oxherding Tale*—to broaden the vision of black being, black identity, and black selfhood.

MYERS: *Then, is fiction by WASPish New England Calvinists or Abenaki Native Americans about something else, other concerns, entirely?*

JOHNSON: When it comes to the crunch, the quest for identity may underlie all American literature. Americans are all transplants from somewhere else, except for Native Americans, but their "world" has been shattered sufficiently to make identity a question of crucial importance, too. Finally, all the philosophical questions involve one another. "Who am I?" is related to "What am I?" And to other questions, such as "What can I know?" "What are others?" Indeed, "What does it mean for something to *be* other?"

MYERS: *Does the American literary canon, that is, the approved or sanctioned canon taught in schools and offered on bookstore shelves, exclude black literature?*

JOHNSON: Yes and no. There really is no "canon" these days. Wright, Du Bois, and Ellison have been taught for decades. An awful lot of black women writers are also taught these days, and my own work, too, I guess.

# AUTHOR NAVIGATES
# UNCHARTED WATERS

Middle Passage *Takes Readers*
*on Spirited Journey*

## M. L. LYKE

F OAMY-MOUTHED DOGS
chew fingers off human captives. Sailors thrashed by seas as high
as mountains succumb to oozing boils and chancres. A dwarf
of a captain who makes William Bligh look like a saint brags
about barbecuing a cabin boy for dinner. Mutiny is afoot.

Sound like serious fiction? Serious black philosophical fiction?

Charles Johnson, University of Washington professor, novelist, essayist and literary critic, is quick to describe his fast-
paced swashbuckler *Middle Passage,* a book that's up for an
important National Book Award next Tuesday, as "accessible,"
especially in comparison with earlier, more complex works such
as *Oxherding Tale* (1982).

Reprinted from the *Seattle Post-Intelligencer* (20 November 1990), with
permission.

"It's more entertaining, more fun, more spirited in some ways," says the forty-two-year-old writer, who plays with literary form and tone the way some painters play with pigment.

Yet only a dimwitted, high-seas mongrel would describe this adventure, told through the eyes of a thieving scoundrel who stows away aboard a nineteenth-century square-rigger, as simple entertainment.

That's too easy. And Johnson, a front-line warrior in the battle against simplistic thinking, is not into easy. Highly praised as a "novelist of ideas," he's one of the major players helping to redefine contemporary black American literature with complex, thoughtful fiction based on character, not ideology.

"There's an attitude about black writing in this country," he says, "that if it's not the protest novel, then what is it?"

Consider: The scoundrel in *Middle Passage* is black, a former slave freed by a master who schooled him in deep philosophy. The reason he's fleeing? The woman he loves wants to marry him.

The ship, unbeknown to him, is a slaver. As the sole black crew member, he's in a moral pickle.

But that's not all. The buyers and sellers of the ship's human cargo, a tribe of mythical African sorcerers whose shape-shifting god has been trapped and carted aboard, are not necessarily white.

All of which can lead a young black thief whose soul is adrift to some serious philosophizing.

Aye, matey.

"Art should be a form of discovery," says Johnson, relaxing back into a chair in the small University of Washington office he has occupied for fourteen years. "If you only see what you think you would see, art is not doing its job."

He looks positively professorial in this room of free-flowing ideas. His hair is frosted gray, his glasses are the quarter-inch variety, and his speech is thick with literary references, historical anecdotes, statistical revelations. Sentences sometimes end with a questioning tone, as if to ask a student, "Do you get it? Understand?"

But look again. This teacher-writer is as unpredictable as the fiction he writes. An Episcopalian-turned-Buddhist, he meditates an hour every day, teaches Chinese martial arts at a school he co-owns on Phinney Ridge and, despite the incredible discipline he brings to his work, confesses to writing in binges. "I get onto something and I'll write for twelve hours. I'll binge write, then I'll go to sleep, get up, and I'll binge write some more," he says, lighting up an Old Gold Light.

A cigarette?

"It's my writer's habit," he says with an easy chuckle.

Johnson started writing at twelve when his mother gave him a diary. His home was Evanston, Illinois, a place he has described as a "progressive 'Leave It to Beaver'" town. And his goal was cartooning, not writing.

But by the age of twenty-six, he had published his first novel, *Faith and the Good Thing,* showing the rich characterization and heady mix of the real and the surreal that would quickly bring him critical acclaim. By twenty-six, he had also established careers as a political cartoonist and a journalist, and had launched a television career that has continued into the '80s with such gems as *Booker,* the 1984 PBS show he co-wrote on Booker T. Washington.

Under his belt, he had two degrees from Southern Illinois University—one in journalism and one in philosophy. He would nearly finish a third—in phenomenology and literary aesthetics—before being wooed west by the University of Washington at age twenty-eight. He is now one of two black professors in the English department out of a staff of sixty-five.

When he decided at twenty to devote himself to writing, Johnson did it with drive, producing six novels in two years. They weren't good novels, he's quick to tell you—just novels.

"One wouldn't work for one reason, so the next one I'd try to improve what didn't work—plotting the curve, working on characterization.

"I was training myself to be a novelist."

Helping him along in the process was novelist John Gardner (*Grendel, The Sunlight Dialogues*), who taught his young apprentice about literary music and rhythm. He also taught him to continually challenge himself, changing voice, language, and form from one piece of writing to the next.

"Sometimes I would pass my stories by Gardner, and I still remember his remarks. He'd say, 'You did this before. You're relying on what you figured out in the last story.'

"I'd say, 'You're right. I'm ashamed of this. I'm sort of coasting on last year's work.'"

Those challenges are something Johnson passes on in classes at the University of Washington, where colleagues say he has become a major drawing card for creative-writing students across the country. Students describe him as one of the most respected teachers on campus, also one of the most intent.

"I learned from him a certain perspective about fiction writing—one of the great seriousness about the task at hand," says former student David Guterson, who has published his own book of short stories, *The Country Ahead of Us, the Country Behind*.

"He taught me that if you want to write well, you have to devote yourself to it the same way a monk devotes himself to a spiritual task. You have to take all the vows and enter the monastery."

*Middle Passage,* Johnson's first novel-at-sea, is as salty and gritty as *Moby-Dick*. Yet the only boat he has ever been on is a Puget Sound ferry.

How did he do it?

Six years of writing and nearly two decades of research.

"In 1971, I did all the slave trade research. I knew exactly what someone paid for a small child, or a woman, or a man of a certain age. But I didn't know the ships, the language and lore of the sea."

He immersed himself in the literature.

"I went back and read every story, from Apollonius of Rhodes and Homer all the way to Melville, Conrad, and the Sinbad stories. I also read slave narratives, and I read dictionaries of the sea to learn the language. I read at least one book on cockney slang, to get the sailors' dialogue."

If Johnson wins the $10,000 National Book Award for his efforts next week in ceremonies in New York, he'll be the first black male writer to do so since Ralph Ellison was given the award thirty-seven years ago for his *Invisible Man*.

"I'd be very pleased about that, because his book has meant a lot to me over the years. It's so rich, so multileveled, so exhaustive, so rich in ambiguity," says Johnson, also nominated for the PEN/Faulkner award in 1987 for a collection of short stories, *The Sorcerer's Apprentice*.

Don't go hanging any mantles on Johnson if he wins, though. He's a black writer, not *the* black writer. The difference is important.

"It's always what people do to black writers," says Johnson, who wonders aloud how one black writer is supposed to represent the experiences of thirty million black Americans.

"It's impossible for one person to represent so much diversity in the black community, between the experience of the blacks who are southern, the blacks who are northern. Between those whose great-great-grandfather was a slave, and those whose families have been free since the Revolutionary War.

"Then you have Africans in the country, then West Indians. You have black people who are millionaires, you have black people who are absolutely poor and have been on welfare for three generations.

"That's a big burden to put on one spokesman," says Johnson.

"No one would think of doing that with a white writer, with Updike, asking him to represent all of white America."

Johnson has several projects brewing that will continue pushing literary limits—including a novelistic take and double take on Martin Luther King that represents another stylistic leap for the author.

"We've been told that Stalin and Hitler had doubles, men who looked just like them. They'd be rounded up and dressed like the Fuehrer and sent to public functions in case of assassination.

"What if Martin Luther King had a double?"

Also in the offing is a new book of essays by twelve black writers who explain how they got to be writers, what their aesthetic objectives are, and their opinions on contemporary fiction.

Johnson finds the growing support for such projects—and such thinking—promising.

"What's encouraging now is there is a new openness among the reading public and publishers about what black writers do.

"They do what white writers do, which is a great many things."

# WINNER OF NATIONAL BOOK AWARD WON'T BE A "VOICE OF BLACK AMERICA"

## PETER MONAGHAN

CHARLES JOHNSON is finding that winning the National Book Award for fiction—one of the publishing world's most prestigious prizes—can make for much exhilaration, and some trepidation.

Since his novel of seafaring and slave running, *Middle Passage,* was honored in November, Mr. Johnson, a professor of English at the University of Washington, has been juggling a hectic schedule of interviews, readings, book-signing parties, and other public appearances. Patiently—and happily, he points out—he has been answering all of the reporters' questions.

While his reputation among readers of contemporary American fiction has been steadily building since the 1970s, the award

Reprinted from the *Chronicle of Higher Education* (16 January 1991), with its permission.

has attracted scrutiny of a kind new to him. "I don't know what to think about it," he says.

One aspect of his sudden renown, however, he certainly dislikes: the danger that he will be cast as a "voice of black America," as other successful black writers often have been.

To that, he objects: "The whole notion of being a spokesman—being *the* black writer—is ludicrous. We have many writers, in the same way that there's no one 'Great American Novel.' No. There's a family of great novels by American writers."

Some fault lies with publishers, Mr. Johnson argues. "If you promote a book as being representative of young black males today, or of the black situation," he says, "you've already packaged in such a way as to say, 'This is capturing the experience of millions of people.' I think that's an insult, really, to black people—to assume that our experience is so simple that one book can do that."

Mr. Johnson's book does not attempt that. But *Middle Passage*—an allegory-laden work—does address many aspects of the life and history of black America.

The book, which was published by Atheneum, is set in the 1830s. It is the story of Rutherford Calhoun, a recently freed slave who flees responsibility by stowing away on a clipper. What he discovers too late is that the ship is bound for Africa, where it collects slaves. The captives, members of a mystical tribe, eventually mutiny and slaughter most of the crew.

One irony of Mr. Johnson's attempts to avoid being cast as a spokesman for black America is that in saying why he is not a spokesman, he has in a way become one. Sensing he is in a spotlight, he has tried to use the opportunity to call attention to the work of other black writers. "So few black writers are known to the American public," he says. "At any given time it might only be three or four."

Mr. Johnson has been working to spread the word about black writers for some time. He wrote his 1988 book, *Being and Race: Black Writing Since 1970* (Indiana University Press), he says, "because I believe in the promotion of African American writing, and minority writing, and simply great writing—I don't care where it comes from."

In *Being and Race* Mr. Johnson set out to dispel the impression that most recent works by black writers have been novels of protest and to show readers "that black writers, each and every one, have a different aesthetic position."

His own fiction has been as idiosyncratic as any of the works that he has championed. In addition to *Middle Passage,* he has written two other novels—*Faith and the Good Thing* (1974) and *Oxherding Tale* (1982)—and a collection of short stories, *The Sorcerer's Apprentice* (1986). The publication of those books followed six "apprentice novels" that Mr. Johnson wrote before becoming a published author.

His works are philosophical, reflecting Mr. Johnson's academic training. He has a master's degree in philosophy from Southern Illinois University and was close to his doctorate and a career in philosophy when in 1976 the University of Washington offered him a position in its creative-writing program. He directed the program from 1987 until last year.

The hero of *Middle Passage,* well educated by the clergyman who inherited him as a slave, speaks like the star of a philosophy graduate program, but the novel is also a rousing seafaring yarn. What he wanted to write, Mr. Johnson says, was a book that was "an entertainment and an adventure story," but one that also worked as "a novel that was philosophical."

His books all revolve around such issues as race and freedom, but as much as any of the writers he discusses in *Being and Race,* he demonstrates a lack of bitterness about the legacy of racism. It is not, he says, that racism does not gall him. Rather, his response is to celebrate black American life and achievement and to ask, in a philosophical mode, what gives rise to prejudice and what response is most worthy.

"I like to be sensitive to political issues when I write," he says. "But I think—this is going to be a radical statement, maybe—I think moral questions precede political questions. They logically precede them."

*Middle Passage*'s political element can hardly be overlooked—a mad, imperialist captain enslaves an ancient, deeply spiritual people and then sails a ship named the *Republic* to its ruin. "But," says Mr. Johnson, "what is most important, I think, are the more fundamental questions that give rise in the novel to political issues"—questions concerning slavery, personal responsibility, and society.

Mr. Johnson says the reason he chooses to depict characters who are heroic, rather than smothered by oppression, is simple. In reviewing the place of African Americans in U.S. history, he says, "The negative is obvious. We have spoken a lot about it. But I think we have in some cases forgotten the remarkable triumphs of black people."

He mentions a few—Mary McLeod Bethune, the educator; Gordon Parks, the photographer; and the Reverend Martin Luther King, Jr. "These," he says, "were remarkable human beings who understood racism but stepped over it the way they would a puddle."

Mr. Johnson says he plans to treat aspects of King's life in a fictional way in his next novel. In an emotional acceptance speech at the National Book Award ceremony, Mr. Johnson predicted that African American writing in the coming decade would broaden beyond political statement to address more fully "what it means to be a human being who is black." That would entail, he said, "a fiction of increasing intellectual and artistic generosity, one that enables us as a people, as a culture, to move from narrow complaint to broad celebration."

Mr. Johnson's growing literary stature suggests that he will be prominent in such a movement. And he appears to have the energy for the task. In addition to his fiction writing and teaching, he remains a frequent contributor of reviews and essays to national publications.

Next fall he will return from a leave to assume the Univer-

sity of Washington's first endowed professorship in creative writing. Between now and then, he will be busy writing—both fiction
and his autobiography.

The opportunity to meet some of his readers face to face while
on the book-signing circuit is an aspect of his celebrity that Mr.
Johnson says he enjoys and finds useful. In part, he says, it is
because he always has considered the idea of the "audience"
for his writing to be too abstract.

"The more immediate faces I can write for," he says. "I still
write for my friends."

# THE PHILOSOPHER
# AND THE AMERICAN NOVEL

O N JANUARY 23, 1991,
Charles Johnson lectured about his career and the writing of
*Middle Passage* to an audience at the California State Library.
Following the lecture, he fielded questions from the audience.

QUESTION: *Can you talk a little more about the actual time
when you decided to abandon the first epic [an early draft of*
Middle Passage] *you described?*

JOHNSON: My agent said to me, "This doesn't work." I sent
her a copy. And she said, "No way." I wrote a draft to basically map out the general parts of the story for myself, and I
passed it by her. I always pass stuff by people. As a matter of
fact, as I was doing the final drafts, I was sending them chunks

Reprinted from *California State Library Foundation Bulletin* 35 (April
1991), by permission of Charles Johnson.

of fifty pages and getting responses back. There is a section in the book in which Rutherford—some people like this section a lot—in which Rutherford has to help throw the dead body of an African overboard; it's just two pages. The reason that's in there is because I was conversing with Anne Borchardt about this, and she said, "I don't think Falcon's evil enough." She said, "He seems twisted and pathetic, but I really don't think he's evil enough." So, I said, "Okay, Anne, I will show you something that will really convince you that he's evil. I will turn your stomach." And so I wrote that description with all the stops pulled out. This is decomposition, and it's just awful. By the way, I do know about decomposition of bodies. Long ago, when I was first starting writing, I had a friend in college who was studying to be a policeman. I looked at one of his textbooks, and there was a chapter that told policemen what signs to look for in the decomposition of a body—what it looks like after six hours, after twelve hours, after eighteen hours. I take notes on everything—I have my high-school notes shoved in a drawer. So, I built that scene basically to show you what happened with slaves who didn't make it over, but also to nail down the malignancy of the captain.

QUESTION: *I think it's interesting that you chose a riskier way of writing this book because it's highly romantic, and it works very well. And the other solution you mentioned is more like a classic resolution of a tale. Why did you select the highly romantic?*

JOHNSON: Well, there is a reason for that, too. Actually, there were a couple of reasons. If you look at the first novel I published, *Faith and the Good Thing,* the main character, Faith Cross, meets a man whom she marries, and it doesn't work out. They separate, and they're not together by the end of the book. In *Oxherding Tale,* the main character meets a woman whom he marries, and it does work out.

One of the things that I began to realize after I had been married for about thirteen years is that I do believe in marriage. I really do. I believe in family. And as I came to this book, I wanted to do a romance between a black man and a black woman that worked out. It may be romantic, but I figured they deserved some happiness by the end of the book. Why not? It could go either way. Why not go that way, which I think is more positive. When a reporter was doing an interview with me recently, he said, "Well, this is basically boy meets girl; boy loses girl; boy gets girl." Well, I guess so. Why not?

QUESTION: *I'm really into research. In 1965, I had a black professor, Otis Kravitz, and had a book that he assigned for undergraduate classes.*

JOHNSON: Oh, I read that book long ago. That's the book that proposes the idea that the slave plantations were like concentration camps.

QUESTION: *I thought it was one of the best primary sources on slavery. Do you think everything you did, all this research, was right on?*

JOHNSON: Did I think Elkins's book was? Well, I didn't go back and look at that, but I do remember reading it. Everything that I could get my hands on that had to do with African American history or culture I read. I was reading that ever since the late 1960s. The first time I ever read Richard Wright, it was because of my mom. She had a copy of *Black Boy* on the shelf because we sure didn't get that in high school. It wasn't there. I just pulled it down one day; I opened this thing, and I was shocked. This was unbelievable. In the late 1960s, more things were being reprinted. So I came across the Elkins book and read a lot of Eugene Genovese at that time because he was very popular. Everything I could get. It would be hard for me to sort out all the research I did for *Middle Passage* because it's been happening for at least eighteen years or better.

I always tell my students this, and they never listen because they don't need to. If I read a book, I like to laugh and cry; I like to learn something. And sometimes I'll just settle on learning something if I don't laugh or cry, but if I can get all three in a novel or work of fiction, I'll be very pleased with it, you see. And so, I like to do research. I think it adds something.

There's another factor, too; let me throw this out. I have a friend who's a writer I recommend very highly, and you may know his work already: James Alan McPherson. He teaches right now at Iowa and got a Pulitzer Prize, about 1978, I want to say. Jim said something very interesting once, and he said this in print. He felt that black writers have the obligation to try to do something with black American history in fiction because so little of the history is known. I don't want to try to put a burden on everybody—to try to lard it in, knife it in somehow into the text—but if you're writing about the cultural world, the historical world of people of color, if the history can work its way in, then I think we perform a service that needs to be performed.

QUESTION: *What is your obvious audience?*

JOHNSON: I think about my friends. If you go to a movie and you're standing in line, they'll give you a little card to fill out, your age, your economic group, because they think of movies in terms of targeting them to young adults. Some people do that with books, and they're thinking, okay, this is my audience. I don't do that, because with every book I try to do something different. But I do think about my friends. If I write a particular passage, I know that if a friend so-and-so from ten years ago reads this, he's going to light up because we talked about it. So, there's usually a concrete image in my mind of who I'm writing for.

I've been reading from this novel for a long time—since it was in progress for six years. Once I gave a reading in Chicago, and there was a woman in the audience who was just wonderful. She came up afterwards and she said, "Well, listen, you've got Isadora in there, and let me tell you how women handled cosmetics a hundred years ago." Seriously. And she told me that they used berries to redden the lips and they used charcoal from the hearth to darken their eyes. That's in the book. I was very grateful to her for that. When she reads that, I would hope that she would say, "Ah hah, I made a contribution to this."

QUESTION: *It's clear from your story that you have liberated yourself from the tyranny of the first draft, that when you get engaged in a project you will carry it through and complete a draft, knowing that it doesn't have to be perfect because you have the ability to go back and do subsequent drafts.*

JOHNSON: That's the fun of it.

QUESTION: *How could you avoid trying to save all the good stuff that's from the first draft to such an extent that you just keep rewriting the first draft without really getting to a second and third draft?*

JOHNSON: One of the things that I learned from Gardner was how to revise. When I did those first six books, it was, like I said, about ten pages a day. I could do three drafts in ten weeks; I'd simply go back to the beginning of the book and start writing over again, looking at what I had. I didn't know how to revise.

This is very important. I started taking my pages to Gardner, and he'd do things that would shock me. He would take out his pen and he would start doing scansion on my prose lines, stressed and unstressed beats. I would say, "Why are you doing that? Isn't that for poetry?" He answered, "Yes, it's for poetry, but it's for prose, too." I actually went through one of his stories doing that, and I noticed that every story he had at that particular time ended with three stresses, just like that. It's like slamming a door at the end of a story.

There's a level of music here that you cannot get unless you revise heavily over and over, until the line is so tight, so tight, that if you pull that one line out, the sentence in front of it and the one in back of it will collapse into that hole, and that will cause the previous paragraph and so forth to collapse into that hole. It's got to be so tight that you cannot substitute a word or change a rhythmic beat.

Now, that doesn't come with the first draft. I know that for a fact. I would never send a first draft out, because a first draft is like saying, "Let me put down what I think and feel to see if it's worth going on with, and if it is, let's take out the junk and try the second draft." But in the third draft—just maybe—I've added the detail I need, and it's sort of there. But, usually it might be the third thought, or second thought, it might be the tenth thought; so, I just expect that I may do ten pages to get one.

I have no problem with that at all if I'm writing fiction. If you're writing journalism, you've got to be a little bit faster. It may be a first draft. Even for a book review, because the deadline is so quick. But I was a journalist many years ago, so I came to regard my drafts as not written in gold. The editor would change things, and so forth.

Let me tell you a quick story about this, too, because I think it's very illuminating—something I learned about Gardner. He gave a reading once, then talked to people afterward. A woman came up to him, and she said, "I think I like your books, but I don't think I like you." And he said, "Well, that's fine. That's okay, because I'm a better person when I write than I am in person." Seriously. And the reason is because he can revise. What you've got to say you go over until you've got just what you want, and it sounds right, and no problem. Maybe the only time we ever have a chance to get it right is when we write, just maybe. At least, that's for me what's exciting. I can go back and scale away the gunk in my thought until it gets a little better. And it's always a kind of horizon. You never really reach that completely, but it's always a goal that's a little bit ahead of you.

QUESTION: *The first time in reading the book, I had the sense of the real grabber story. I just loved the story. But then I started thinking, this is using the slave trade to talk about the lack of experience in America today. I got a little further, and then I started thinking, he's using this whole situation to talk about the situation of man in the world at anytime. (I shouldn't say "man" but "humans.") How conscious of*

# The Philosopher and the American Novel (1991)

that are you when you write, or is that something that sort of comes out after your characters have created the story for you?

JOHNSON: No, that's really important. This is true of this book, and the one that preceded it, *Oxherding Tale*, in the sense that I guess I use history as metaphor. This is not a strictly historical novel. It has a lot of historical research, but it is a drama about race and cultural vision. You've got the vision of a captain, which is radically opposed on every level—epistemologically, ontologically—to the vision of the Allmuseri, to the Africans. And you have what happens when you throw all these human beings with different values and visions together on a ship.

The consequences in this book are cataclysmic: The ship goes down because they can't figure out a way to live together. It's me versus thee as opposed to a harmonious vision-of-connectedness, which the Allmuseri have, so yeah, it's clearly about humanity; but at the same time it's about contemporary relationships. You've got this gangster, Papa Zeringue. And to me, he's like a drug lord today. He's somebody who feeds his own people poison. And on one level, I'm thinking that he's not a totally bad guy because he's trying to help; but on another level, he's a gangster, and he's profiting from this, and that is fundamentally wrong. So, it's a story that maybe collapses past and present and is a philosophical novel. It's a drama of ideas at the same time. At least, I hope so.

QUESTION: *Just a couple of things. What are you writing now? What do you want to write?*

JOHNSON: What do I think about writing? I have a couple of things that are really important to me. Even before all this happened [the National Book Award], I had been talking to my friend, John Gallman, in Indiana. Ever since *Oxherding Tale* he's been asking me to do books. Basically, he asked me to do *Being and Race,* which is a critical study of black writing, because he wanted to publish a book that talked about the landscape of black writing for twenty years. And I didn't want to take all

59

that on. But I had read the books over twenty years. I had them, so I did it.

He came back to me two years ago with a couple more books that I wanted to do. One is called *Black Writers on Writing,* and we have twelve black writers: Terry McMillan is in there; James Alan McPherson is in there; Al Young is in there; Doris Jean Austin is in there; David Bradley is in there. It's twelve people talking about their development as writers, their aesthetic, what they think of contemporary black literature right now. It gives twelve people a chance in thirty pages to do what I tried to do in this whole book. So you get multiple viewpoints on African American literature and aesthetics. That's called *Black Writers on Writing.*

The other book is going to take longer, and I'm co-editing it with black writer John McCluskey of Indiana. It's called *The Black Male in America.* That's a tentative title because there was a book in the mid-1970s with that title. But our hope is not to get writers now, but social anthropologists and historians and other people to talk about the situation—which is very critical— of young black males between the ages of sixteen and twenty-four. I think about that all the time because my son is fifteen years old, and we talk about things: all the things that pull at a fifteen-year-old. That will take a little longer, because we will really have to work with the writers to come up with the essays. One film producer—Avon Kirkland, a black film writer in San Francisco who I've worked with before—is doing his in the form of a screenplay. So they will be very formally different and from many different disciplines. Those are two books I'm working on.

The next book I want to do is one on Martin Luther King. I keep talking about that as a way of convincing myself to get it done. I have a stack of books on King at the house. What I want to do is bury myself in the minutia of King's life. I want to know what he took in his coffee, if he drank coffee. I already know how he shaved. He shaved the same way my dad did. He used a depilatory, a powder that stinks so bad, because his skin was sensitive; he couldn't use a razor.

I want to bury myself in this guy's life, and then I want to write a story about a man who is his double. Just hypothetically, suppose somebody looked just like Martin Luther King, and it might even be three people. And suppose they made public appearances for him. And what happens to those three people, all of whom latch onto different parts of King's life and personality after his death. What happens to them? And I would really like to play with that idea.

One thing that shocked me the other night is something said by a friend of mine—a writer I work with named Art Washington, who's now a story editor on *MacGyver*. He's up in Vancouver, where they shoot this show. Art and I worked on *Up and Coming*, which was a black show set in San Francisco in 1981. He called me to say he'd seen a television program on Saddam Hussein, and apparently Saddam Hussein has a double. I was blown away. I was thinking about Churchill and Hitler and Stalin. I didn't know somebody in the contemporary world had a double who sounds just like him, apparently, and who appears in his place.

So they stole my idea, but that's okay, because I'm still going to do it. I'm still going to do it, because when I finish the book, I'll know King much better. I really think we need to think about him for the 1990s, and do what we can to reinterpret the significance of the civil rights movement for the next decade and into the next century. So that's a book I'm real excited about.

QUESTION: *I'll tell you, I really encourage you to do that, because if there was ever a man for our country, it was Martin Luther King. He was killed at such a young age. He had things to tell us, to write to us, and get us together that didn't get published because he was killed in 1968, and I hope you do get inside of him and "wear his moccasins," if you will, and do that.*

JOHNSON: Well, thank you. I'm really interested. You say he

was killed at such a young age. It amazes me that I'm forty-two years old, and I look at those pictures of King, and he didn't make the age of forty. He was thirty-nine. That was hard for me to get through my head, that somebody lives a life like that and never got to be forty? That's astonishing to me.

QUESTION: *How do you work with your agent?*

JOHNSON: I've had the same agent for seventeen years. They stood by me when I didn't make a penny for them. They just sort of believed that this was worth doing. They're a good agency. They don't pressure me. They don't tell me what to do. Their attitude is, "Well, when you've got it done, send it to us, and we'll make sure we find a place that will take it." Quite literally, they will go through twenty publishers, if necessary, to find a place for it. So, I usually tell them what I'm working on. I might send them one-hundred pages, after I figured out what I want to figure out.

QUESTION: *Do you write before you start talking about it?*

JOHNSON: I usually have to wait awhile. As I said, I run perhaps fifty pages by my agent, or one hundred maybe. There was a time when I would show my stuff to three people I trusted, and one was John Gardner, because he knew so much about the theory and practice of literature, and he could come back at me with, "Read this book," or whatever. And one was my wife because she reads all kinds of popular fiction. She could tell me if it was boring or not—just what the ordinary person would tell me. And then there was my agent. I would give it to them and they could tell me if they could sell it or not. That's their angle. They very rarely give me back a "change this, change that" kind of thing. They're just not like that. They're very respectful of their authors. They would never say what some agents I've heard would say: "Your last book didn't make much money. You need to write a bestseller." There are some agents like that, and I would be very uncomfortable with them because I really feel I need to pursue whatever is most interesting to me at the moment and not just worry about making money. That's not the purpose of art.

QUESTION: *Was there someone who has discouraged your writing?*

JOHNSON: You see, that's virtually the worst thing you could tell anybody. I've known people who teach creative writing—a couple of people I've known, and I won't mention their names because they're friends of mine—who told students, "You haven't got it. You can't do fiction." And as it turns out, some of the people they told that to later became friends of mine and told me these stories. And you can't say that to anybody. You don't know what they're going to do in five years.

I've been in workshops. I teach creative writing. We impose deadlines on people. That's the value of a workshop. That's the value of a creative-writing program: It makes you do something within a set period of time, and you also have people to talk to who are doing the same thing you are doing. But if you impose deadlines in a creative-writing class—well, there may be a star who amazes everybody. His or her work has strength of voice, and the imagery is beautiful, but then you've got the class turtle who works a bit more slowly. Once the class ends, many of the stars stop; the story isn't there, the deadline isn't being imposed. And it is the slower person usually who keeps going and plodding along. And that usually is a person who earns it, I think, and that's the one who has a story collection that comes out two years later. The worst thing anybody could ever do to other human beings is tell them they can't do something. I don't believe them; you have no idea what this person may go through, positive or negative, in the next two or three years. They may change their entire life, their vision of the world, and open up their capacities. I just don't believe in doing that.

QUESTION: *Do you ever see yourself doing workshops versus teaching at the university?*

JOHNSON: I do go to the conferences and I do workshops

regularly; I've done that for about ten years now, I guess. And they are enjoyable They are usually about a week long; they are very intensive, of course. You can't get as much done, but I like the experience very much. I get to meet a lot of different people that I wouldn't otherwise, just teaching in one city. You form lasting friendships that way.

QUESTION: *You are involved in so many things. What are your hobbies?*

JOHNSON: I don't really have a hobby. Long ago I got involved in the martial arts—when I was nineteen years old. I was in six or seven different schools, and I finally settled on one school. I began working out in San Francisco, in 1981, and I am now co-director of a school for that system in Seattle, with a friend of mine. We work out at the studio two hours, three times a week, and my son comes on Friday, because Saturday he doesn't have school, and that's sort of what I do when I'm not writing. Or I do things with my family; we'll play chess or whatever, or watch a movie, but I can't watch movies without being critical. I'm saying to myself, that's a lousy line of dialogue, or that character is flat.

It's interesting: I got a call a couple of weeks ago from Spike Lee. He has a book coming out called *Five for Five*. He's got five writers writing about his five movies; the fifth coming out this year is called *Jungle Fever*. He got several people to write about his movies—Terry McMillan is one; Toni Cade Bambara; Henry Louis Gates is another—and he got me to do it, and a fourth guy, whom I don't really know. And the interesting thing about that is that I have always been really hard on Spike and some of these movies. But when I finally looked at this movie he wanted me to write about—*Mo' Better Blues*—I found stuff in it that was really quite interesting. His intent in it is to say something about the black artist's relationship to his community; this is really quite good. But I can't turn the critical apparatus off, I really can't, when I watch a movie. It's rare when something sweeps me up and I weep. The only time that happened recently was with *Glory,* because I wept about three times. My son was with me; it was embarrassing. Here's this grown man with tears, but there are certain moments when Denzel Washington is trying to tell the other members—what was it, the Fifty-fourth?—why he loves these people for what they are doing. I just get choked up. Also, I really like Morgan Freeman, too.

As one final footnote: He was in that movie that I mentioned earlier, *Charlie Smith and the Fritter Tree.* I'm sure he would never remember me, because this is 1977. He had a minor role. He had just come off *Electric Company.* In the movie, Charlie Smith, a bounty hunter, has to bring in a criminal called Railroad Bill. Well, they give the role of Railroad Bill to Morgan Freeman. Because the guy has a peg leg, Morgan had to have his leg strapped behind his back. So he was grumpy; he really didn't want to talk to people, he didn't want to socialize, so I didn't get to meet him. I just said I'm not going to mess with this guy, because he looks like he's in pain.

What he's done is work hard over all those years to become one of the preeminent actors today. I mean, he did it all; it was the long road, the hard road. That's something I respect profoundly—never giving up. You do what you gotta do, and you do it the best you can, and you have faith that you will get better and that someday people will recognize it. I think that's what Morgan's all about, so I was really happy to see him in *Glory,* too.

QUESTION: *I would like to know who your top three African American male writers and African American female writers are.*

JOHNSON: All right, I'll tell you. In the fall, Atheneum has a new novel coming out by Paule Marshall—it's called *Daughters*— and I think she's wonderful. I met her once. She is one of the most spiritual people I have ever seen in my life. I'm looking forward to that book because Paule Marshall has been writing since the 1950s. I think that book is going to do a great business, I think it's going to be a celebrity. I like her an awful lot, and I like a lot of people for different things.

I like the way Morrison handles a poetic prose line; I like the way Terry McMillan has a real inborn sense, I think, of story-telling; that is to say, she switches voices well when she's writing about her male and female characters.

Among the men, I like a lot of people. I really think Jim McPherson is a genius; I really do. Whenever I hear him speak, things come out that nobody ever thought of, and they are unerringly accurate. I could go down the list. I have so many writers that I really admire. I like John Wideman. Again, I admire the length of time that he has devoted to the practice of literature, since the late 1960s. He published his first book when he was about twenty-six years old. What he's done, I think, is very important.

I like a lot of different people for different aspects of their fiction, but I will tell you one thing. I have a great deal of interest in newer writers, names I could give you, but you probably don't know them. A guy named Louis Edwards has a book coming out called *Ten Seconds,* from Greywolf Press. I saw it in galleys—his first novel. He's a jazz musician; he has a radio program, and I want to say it's in New Orleans. This remarkable book about a young black man is almost all interior. What he's looking at are the hurts and pains and the inner life of a black male, and what I thought was interesting about that was that for a long time people didn't think black males had inner lives or hurts and pains. And yet it is so subtle, things you wouldn't expect. I was very, very impressed by that. That's a book I highly recommend; it's called *Ten Seconds.* It ought to be out by spring-time. A lot of interesting younger writers are coming along.

QUESTION: *What do you think of in terms of the longevity of King and the so-called plagiarism; how does that fit at your juncture right now?*

JOHNSON: I don't know; there was a lot of press about that. It's his dissertation, or whatever it was, and people would connect that and talk about his infidelity. It's just knocking the guy down. Human beings are flawed, but the overall effect of his life far outweighs—in terms of significance, I believe—these moments of weakness, or mistakes.

This is one of the main reasons that I want to do this novel. When you get somebody who has streets named after him in major cities, who school kids get to see the image of all the time, the image gets rigid; it doesn't seem human anymore. And in the King story, it's interesting to me, you have a human being like the rest of us—like Gandhi, if you want, like Mother Teresa—and somehow, out of all the weaknesses and flaws we have there comes something that is a major contribution to the rest of the community defined in a broad sense. That's what interests me: the moments when we transcend our human fallibilities and manage to do something that might be for the common good.

So I'm not worried about the plagiarism charge. I mean, I might have it in the book, or I might not—probably will because it's part of the record, but that's not what's really important about the guy.

QUESTION: *I understand. The only other question I have for you concerns your comments, if any, about the war.*

JOHNSON: I wish this war was over; that's my comment, I wish it were over. Thank you very much.

# THE SORCERER'S APPRENTICE

## CYRA McFADDEN

About to meet the multifaceted black writer Charles Johnson, one wonders if he'll manifest himself in a puff of smoke. The man is a novelist, a former cartoonist, a philosopher, an academic, and the co-owner of a kung fu studio. His writing is equally hard to categorize. Johnson's specialty as a novelist is slipping back and forth over the border between the fantastic and the real, taking the reader along as willing hostage. His mind plays on the page, spinning off images, and his prose is so rhythmic, you could dance to it.

In San Francisco to promote the Plume paperback edition of *Middle Passage,* a book that won him the 1990 National Book Award for Fiction, Johnson turned out to be a self-possessed man

Reprinted from the *San Francisco Examiner* (17 November 1991), with permission of Florence Fang, Publisher.

in a conservative navy-blue suit. His dark-rimmed glasses gave him a serious, scholarly look. Except for his scuffed maroon cowboy boots, he could have passed for a corporate CEO.

Striding athletically into the lobby of the Clift Hotel, he apologized for a case of jet lag that didn't seem to be slowing him down much. An international traveler, Johnson was just back from Japan and Indonesia, where he lectured on multicultural issues for the U.S. Information Service.

He's got one of those minds that can cover a lot of ground in a hurry. A few minutes into lunch in the hotel dining room, where he was relegated to the smokers' ghetto, Johnson had mentioned the rich culture of Jakarta ("It's gone from the Stone Age to the modern"), why he likes living in Seattle (the city is more diversified than people tend to think, with a 10 percent black population and a black mayor), and his great respect for San Francisco kung fu grandmaster Doc Fai Wong.

Wong taught Johnson Choy Li Fut, the 125–year-old kung fu system that he practices. Johnson described him as "a gentle teacher" and, as he spoke, he inclined his head in a slight bow. A trim, fit man, the writer gives the impression of simmering energy even while sitting still—just as well, given his busy life.

Johnson and his wife, Joan, have two children. Daughter Elizabeth, ten, is a fledgling cartoonist. Son Malik, sixteen, is a high school student, "interested in writing and the martial arts." The writer tries to spend as much time as he can with his family, but he could use more hours in the day.

Since 1970, Johnson, who's forty-three, has published three novels, a collection of short stories, an anthology of black writing, and two books of cartoons, as well as writing and producing for public television. Just so he doesn't wind up with time on his hands, he's Pollock Professor of English at the University of Washington, holding the first endowed chair ever in the creative writing department. And his literary reputation keeps growing.

One critic ventured that *Middle Passage*, an account of the voyage of a slave ship, "may just be" the Great American Novel. In the *New York Times Book Review*, novelist Thomas Keneally compared it to *Billy Budd* and *Moby-Dick*.

Only 209 pages long, *Middle Passage* is both an adventure at sea and a fable about good and evil. Its cast includes a ship's captain who's a moral monster, the stowaway who tells the tale, and a mysterious African tribe, the Allmuseri. The narrative rips along and the language showcases Johnson's rich vocabulary; it is a rare reader who will grasp all the classical references and not have to look up words: "thalassic," "choriambs," "melic," "litotes," "contrapletes."

Yet the scholarly author has more than a little in common with the Swamp Woman, the conjurer in his first published novel, *Faith and the Good Thing*, and with Falcon, the villain of *Middle Passage*. All three are storytellers whose subject is no less ambitious than what it is to be human. They all love to kick ideas around. You can imagine the three of them arguing about the Platonic ideal over a beer—in Greek.

Johnson was born and raised in Evanston, Ill., the only child of a father from South Carolina and a mother from Georgia. His father left school after fifth grade because, with twelve children to support in a depression, his parents needed his help on the family farm. A man who sometimes held three jobs to support his own family, he reminds Johnson of the character Hoak, the dignified and practical chauffeur in *Driving Miss Daisy:* "Morgan Freeman captured a certain kind of black man at a certain time in American history."

Although Johnson's mother's education ended with high school, "she was a big reader of books," and the household was full of them. "Sometimes we'd read the same books together and then talk about them." In addition, she "had an artistic sense, a kind of flair. We didn't have much money, but my mother would make things, shelves for bric-a-brac out of cardboard boxes, for instance, that made the apartment more attractive."

She encouraged Johnson to read, and later to draw. He thinks that she would have made a very good teacher. But at the time, he remembers her telling him, prospective teachers had to pass a swimming test. That ruled out his mother, who had asthma. Her son became her only pupil. "She sort of took out her artistic sensibility and her pedagogical sensibility on me," he told the audience at a lecture at the California State Library in Sacramento, not long after receiving the National Book Award.

In the same lecture, an informal talk about his life called "The Philosopher and the American Novel," he told how at age twelve or thirteen, he decided to be a commercial artist. "I could sit in my parents' apartment—it was really a tenement at the time, 1959—in front of a chalkboard that my parents got me for a Christmas present, and I could sit there and draw in the kitchen for hours. . . . My knees would be covered with chalk by the time I got through.

"And, usually, some kid would beat me up at school or something, so all afternoon long I'd draw me beating him up. You know? It gave me a place to go with my imagination. And as an only child, I had friends, but really the world of the imagination—the books and the drawings—became a very dear friend to me."

His father worried that Johnson would starve; black people didn't become artists. Johnson sent off for a mail-order cartooning course anyway, in response to an ad that he found in *Writer's Digest*. For two years he sent his teacher drawings. The teacher, a prolific writer and artist named Lawrence Lariar, corrected these drawings and sent them back. Eventually, the pro and the novice met and became friends.

By then Johnson had started Evanston Township High School, rated the second best in the country while he was there. "People in Evanston were well off. They spent lots of money on the schools, so even if you didn't have much money, you got the benefit of that. We lived a couple of blocks away, in the first house that my dad bought," a major step up in the world. "Owning your own house is very much part of the American dream. My grandmother scrubbed floors on her hands and knees to buy her house."

Already selling a few drawings, Johnson framed the first dollar that he made as a cartoonist. He still has it. He took a creative writing class at Evanston Township and liked seeing his stories in the school paper, but cartooning remained his first love. In the next seven years he published one thousand drawings and sent each one to his father. About to be buried beneath a paper landslide, the elder Johnson finally approved his son's career choice: "Yeah, you were right, OK?"

At Southern Illinois University, Johnson majored in journalism and produced and starred in a TV show on how to draw for the local PBS affiliate. He drew political cartoons for the college paper. In his junior year, the poet LeRoi Jones (later called Amiri Baraka) appeared on campus, electrifying him. "I thought he was talking right to me." Clad in a dashiki, as were the two guards flanking him, Baraka read his poems and urged black artists to bring their talents back to the black community. Johnson left the event "in a daze," cut classes for days and did nothing but draw "black people, black history, black culture."

His book *Black Humor* was published the following year, 1970, while Johnson was working as an intern at the *Chicago Tribune*. That same year, he married Joan, a former elementary school teacher who's now a full-time wife and mother. The couple met when she, too, was in college, and in defiance of the odds, they have stayed married for twenty-one years. Says Johnson, "We were meant to be married. Our birthdays are seven days apart."

*Black Humor* was followed by another cartoon collection, *Half-Past Nation Time* (1972). Although Johnson was moving away from drawing and into writing, he'd found his subject: his heritage. Words poured from him so abundantly that although he was taking a master's degree in philosophy at the same time, he wrote six novels in two years. "I was used to organizing my life in ten-week blocks. . . . So I'm writing a novel in ten weeks. I'd sit down and do ten pages a day."

About to charge into his seventh, as obsessed with writing as he'd once been with drawing, Johnson realized that he needed help. Again fate sent him a mentor, this time the brilliant writer and teacher of writing, John Gardner. A man with a longtime interest in Eastern philosophy himself, with whom Johnson felt an instant rapport, Gardner was living in southern Illinois then.

Johnson heard about his writing class and telephoned him. When Gardner agreed to look at his work, he drove to the senior writer's house in a rainstorm with his six novels under his arm. Gardner must have been impressed with his industry as well as his prose. He took Johnson on as a pupil, handing out rigorous criticism, imparting the secrets of the craft and guiding Johnson through the book that established him as a bright new talent. The opening sentence—"It is time to tell you about Faith and the Good Thing"—suddenly came to him, Johnson told the audience at his Sacramento lecture, and the rest of the book followed. "I didn't know who Faith was; I didn't know what a Good Thing was. But I sat down and I wrote these twenty pages until seven in the morning."

In *Faith and the Good Thing,* which was published in 1974, Johnson explores the ground that he continues to explore, the black experience from slavery to the present. Faith Cross is an innocent young woman who, when her mother dies, leaves the rural south for Chicago in pursuit of "the good thing." Her pilgrimage is really a search for self-worth, one that subjects Faith to terrible trials. In that respect, although her story is contemporary, she represents all black people who came to America as slaves. "Listen," Johnson urges on the first page, launching into a tour de force of a death scene:

"The Devil was beating his wife on the day Faith's mother, Lavidia, died her second death. The first, an hour-long beating of bedsheets pierced by grating breaths, had been the day before, but a country doctor, Leon Lynch, came to the farmhouse where they lived and massaged Lavidia's heart. She returned from wherever it was she had been, both her legs pumping beneath the covers, her white eyes wide with terror. Lavidia raced like that the entire night, into the next day, and would have broken all long-distance records if she had not been flat on her back. Finally she rested, counting her breaths."

Faith Cross encounters the Swamp Woman, who owns a large machine that hums and plays music, "its gears powered by the frantic racing of a green Gila monster along a treadmill." She also lives the brutal life of a prostitute in a squalid Chicago hotel. The book reminds one of the South American "magical realists," but because of Johnson's wit and his ear for dialogue, it stays firmly grounded in the everyday. When Faith gapes at the reptile-powered machine, for instance, the werewitch tells her breezily, "I'm gonna patent that."

Gardner advised his protégé to keep breaking new ground, instead of repeating his first success. Although Johnson's second published novel, *Oxherding Tale* (1982), is also about a journey, it's not set in the modern world. Instead, Johnson "naturally went to a form that was native to black people, which is the slave narrative." Because of his long interest in Eastern philosophy, he "wanted a novel that would appropriate all that material from that tradition and would also approach questions of freedom and bondage, not just in the physical sense, but in the psychological sense, in the sexual sense, and in the spiritual sense." The parable took him five years to write—after he read every book that he could find on slavery in the library of Stony Brook University, where he'd taken a low-paying job. "That was my chore after I finished with my T.A. class at Stony Brook; I would sit there for three or four hours and speed read."

One gets the sense of someone strongly imbued with the work ethic, for whom idleness is sloth. But in this case, his efforts were for a good cause. The same research later served him in good stead for *Middle Passage*. Between the writing of the two novels, Johnson left Stony Brook for Seattle, where he was offered a better job, and published a collection of short stories (*The Sorcerer's Apprentice,* 1986) and an anthology of essays (*Being and Race: Black Writing Since 1970,* 1988). The former introduced the Allmuseri, the African tribe that continues to haunt his imagination and to figure in his work. The latter won him a Guggenheim Fellowship.

"The discussion of black American culture has opened up remarkably since then," Johnson noted while he was in San Francisco, citing recent books by Stanley Crouch and Shelby Steele. He hoped that the Clarence Thomas nomination would lead to further discussion and to increased understanding. "I think the controversy has been healthy, because it's made people realize that black Americans are as diverse as any other Americans."

At the time we talked, it should be noted, the Supreme Court nominee hadn't been charged with sexual harassment. Johnson said that Thomas deserved a chance, adding, "I think I understand the sort of cultural and intellectual world that he passed through." All of which sounded evenhanded to the point of obscuring Johnson's own political views; did he, for instance, consider Thomas a brilliant jurist, qualified for the highest court in the land on merit alone?

"The debate isn't about Clarence," he continued, before I could ask the question. "It's about culture. Derek Bell of Harvard, for instance, saying early on that he's 'offended that a man who looks black but thinks white should be nominated.' He assumes that Clarence 'thinks white' because of his Harvard education. When the truth is that his views just happen to differ from those of Derek Bell." A man who weighed each word of this discussion, taking pains not to be pigeon-holed, Johnson broke into a wide smile.

On the way to the Maritime Museum, where he was to be photographed for this article, Johnson reminisced about the six months of 1981 that he spent in San Francisco. "I look back on that time a lot because so much happened to me then, and it's all intertwined with the city." With Art Washington, he co-wrote and produced the KQED-TV series *Up and Coming,* about a middle-class black family. The series won prizes and Washington became a good friend. In fact, the two men had sat up talking until 2 A.M. the night before.

It was here, too, that the kung fu enthusiast studied Choy Li Fut with Doc Fai Wong, who has a studio on Taraval Street. When he went back to Seattle, he and a friend, Gray Cassidy, opened their own kung fu school to teach the same system.

But it is a sorrowful event that is most vividly imprinted on his memory. "When I was down here, my mother died. I went back to see her in the hospital and promised her that if she pulled through, we'd name our second child after her. Our daughter Elizabeth—my mother's middle name—was born two or three months after mother died." Johnson looked out the car window, remembering.

At Aquatic Park, he bounded out of the car. When he reached the *Balclutha,* the landmark sailing ship moored there, he took the stairs two at a time. The *Balclutha* is smaller than the slave ship in *Middle Passage,* he mentioned, pacing the length of the deck. The ship is also in better shape. Here's the way Rutherford Calhoun, the ex-slave who stows away on her, describes the *Republic,* a seagoing nightmare, on its way to collect its human cargo:

"She was stinking and wet, with sea scurvy and god-awful diseases rampant. . . . She was perpetually flying apart during the voyage, falling to pieces beneath us, the great sails ripping to rags in high winds, the rot, cracks and parasites in old wood so cancerously swift, springing up where least expected, that Captain Falcon's crew spent most of their time literally rebuilding the *Republic* as we crawled along the waves."

The hold is "darker than the belly of Jonah's whale," a maze of tiny compartments. The forecastle cookroom swarms with cockroaches and rats. The "head" is unspeakable: What did Calhoun expect, the captain demands when the stowaway is discovered. "'Tis a *slaver,* Mr. Calhoun, and the cargo awaiting us at Bangalang is 40 Allmuseri tribesmen, hides, prime ivory teeth, gold and bullocks. . . ." According to Johnson, "Twenty percent of the crews and slaves on such ships didn't make it back. They died of diseases and in storms." Of "ten or eleven million Africans taken to the new world, roughly 80 percent survived."

Falcon speaks of blacks as "mudmen." The white-supremacy movement still uses the term, says Johnson. His interest in the history of slavery isn't mere scholarly curiosity. It's visceral, you realize reading *Middle Passage.* While Johnson's rollicking humor keeps the book from sinking of its own weight, his is an impassioned treatment of the subject.

The slave trade is the ultimate human degradation, and Falcon is "the devil in a way." Asked if he believes in pure evil, Johnson replied that he doesn't know, but that "the Nazis and Hitler come pretty close. Evil is when you know what is right and wrong and deliberately choose to pursue the wrong." That's what the Falcons of the world did when they subjugated the Allmuseri.

The captured tribesmen of *Middle Passage* are "shackled in twos at their ankles." Even so, their nobility is obvious. "About them was the smell of old temples. . . . Cities lost when Europe was embryonic. . . . A tall people, larger even than Watusi; their palms were blank, bearing no lines. No fingerprints."

Johnson's next novel will be about Martin Luther King, Jr. It's "not a biography, but the story of a man who's Martin Luther King's double—like Saddam Hussein's look-alike—and who appears in public for him when he's got scheduling conflicts." The novelist is thinking of making King an Allmuseri "because King's vision is so anchored in the spiritual," the black leader himself such an old soul. There goes Charles Johnson the historian/Eastern philosopher/word wizard again, changing history into myth, fact into fiction and scholarship into art.

# AN INTERVIEW
# WITH CHARLES JOHNSON

## PHOEBE BOSCHÉ

## PART I

O

N A RECENT, RATHER
brilliant May afternoon, I spoke with writer and critic Charles
Johnson in his office on the campus of the University of Washington. He had just returned from viewing a film as a juror for
the 1992 Seattle International Film festival. Along one plain-
looking wall a row of his own books was lined up smartly, like
good little soldiers, English and foreign translations intermin-
gled: *Faith and the Good Thing, Oxherding Tale, The Sorcerer's
Apprentice, Being and Race: Black Writing Since 1970,* and *Middle Passage,* winner of the 1990 National Book Award.

BOSCHÉ: *As far as judging films, you once said that "film of
course is wonderful, but I can't think of a single film, even*

Reprinted from the *Raven Chronicles* 2.1 (1992) and 2.2 (1992), by permission of Phoebe Bosché.

*the ones that I love, that are as rich and complex, and have
the same vision and depth, as the greatest novels." So when
you're judging films, what are you looking for?*

JOHNSON: I guess two things. One is I want to experience
it the way that I believe the producer wants it to be experienced,
which is as art, as an entertainment. Just as a common reader
or viewer. That's how I approach either a book or a film. But
after that, after I experience it on that level, I want to think crit-
ically about it and see how good the film is.

BOSCHÉ: *These are literary things, aren't they? Narrative,
plot. . . .*

JOHNSON: If it's a low-budget production, you really have
to emphasize what you've got, which is usually a few locations,
okay. It might all be primarily interior, like a thing I was looking at today, 'cause you don't go out on location a lot. You might
have two or three central characters and what's really going to
matter is the depth of development and exploration of character. The sense of story. I look, in many ways, on the level of
narrative and story and character, for the same things I often
look for in fiction, but then when you step back you have to
look at the film's technical achievements or lack thereof.

BOSCHÉ: *Have you seen trends or patterns emerging in any
of the new films?*

JOHNSON: What I've seen is a real focus on telling the story
in mostly all of them . . . an emphasis on character, on very, very
quiet moments in lives that would be marginalized or that you
wouldn't necessarily know anything about. The one I just saw,
*Confessing to Laura,* takes place against the background of revolution which is happening in the streets but which forces, and
this is very interesting to me, which forces this rather lonely
government worker who has problems with his wife, who is
very overbearing, to stay in the apartment, across the street, of
his wife's friend, to whom he takes a birthday cake. This is just
when all the stuff begins to break out in the revolution. So he's
stuck there and his wife is watching him from across the street.

It's about the revolution in their lives, in that apartment, because they can't go out because they'll be shot in the street.

BOSCHÉ: *So you do look at films the same way you do novels. . . .*

JOHNSON: Storywise, storywise. These are not terribly filmic films, that is to say basically they are carried by narrative, character, and plot. They are not carried by a sequence of images, for example, or techniques that are somehow coming together to create some kind of gestalt in your mind by the end of the film. They don't have the money to do that. You go back to fundamentals when you have a very low budget.

BOSCHÉ: *Are you still working on the script about the all-black World War II air squadron?*

JOHNSON: I finished that. That was done in January. I was the second scriptwriter to come on.

BOSCHÉ: *So it is being produced?*

JOHNSON: We'll see. I wrote it for the head of Columbia, Frank Price. The most recent thing I've heard, that bankrupt Orion is about to be bought by three people and he's one of them. So this may end up at Orion.

BOSCHÉ: *How was it being in the world of that script?*

JOHNSON: They gave me absolute freedom to do this the way I wanted to do it, and I had a great deal of fun. I got flight manuals, books on how to fly. I went back and dug up stuff that I wanted to do in terms of black Americans. Basically it is an epic story about young black pilots who had to overtrain, that is to say, they had to do more in the way of study and performance to get into the military . . .

BOSCHÉ: *. . . than their white counterparts.*

JOHNSON: . . . to prove that they could fly. And then the story is played out, first at Tuskegee Institute, which is where they did their first early preliminary training and basics, and then in the European theater. So it is played out against the entire background of the war. And these were remarkable flyers. They had records that you would not believe. They were the first to sink a destroyer with just fire, you know, from their plane. They flew something like 15,000 missions and never lost a single bomber.

BOSCHÉ: *Really? I never heard that. Did you read mainstream newspapers published at the time? Did they publish their exploits?*

JOHNSON: The black press knew about it. I don't know about the mainstream press, but people have been feeding me all sorts of articles about them. The person who brought this project to Columbia is one of the flyers. He conceptualized the story. I came on basically because they had the story mapped out more or less but the characters were not interacting, nor did they have the depth that was necessary. So it was a rewrite, but also a re-envisioning in lots and lots of ways. It's a very satisfying story to me. I really enjoyed it.

BOSCHÉ: *If it's finally produced, maybe by Spike Lee, I wonder how multidimensional the characters will still be.*

JOHNSON: No, it wouldn't be Spike Lee, it's not his type of film. But if they stick with my script, these characters will interact with each other, grow because of each other, grow because of their situations in the military (it was called the Air Corps then) and they grow once they are in the European theater.

BOSCHÉ: *What happened to them after World War II?*

JOHNSON: What happened to them? Oh, many of them did like other people did. They went into civilian life and became all kinds of professional people, in most cases.

BOSCHÉ: *I have a friend in Seattle. His father was a high-ranking officer, black, and traveling around the U.S. after the war, he couldn't get rooms, etc.*

JOHNSON: Oh, you're looking for things like discrimination?

BOSCHÉ: *I just wondered how these guys, after this incredible experience, fared.*

JOHNSON: Well, when they came back to America, they certainly got Jim Crow in the South, but not in certain parts of the North. My flyers all come from different parts of the country, from New York and from Mississippi and from Iowa. The story ends just before they go on to the bombing of Berlin. I take them through a couple of missions, but this film has to be brought in somewhere around $30 million, so you can't have too much going on in the way of massive World War II destruction.

I think the important thing about this picture is that it breaks a lot of stereotypes and misconceptions and preconceptions about black Americans. These flyers were the *best* intellectually, physically, morally, emotionally, of any people you could possibly find, anywhere, in the Army Air Corps. There were hundreds of people who tried out, right. These were the ones who succeeded. These were people who basically looked at racism as something like a puddle that you step over if it's in your path. They did not allow anything to stop them. A friend of mine says that if they make this movie, it will revolutionize black films in Hollywood. These are not men like we've seen. These are men like Colin Powell; these are men like Benjamin O'Davis. They don't trip over stuff like that.

BOSCHÉ: *Well, I hope the film gets produced. There is a line in your novel,* Faith and the Good Thing, *about taking many paths—journalist, teacher, writer, cartoonist, philosopher, father—and picking up the pieces along the way. Have you gotten the whole thing yet? The good thing?*

JOHNSON: [laughter] There are lots of little good things, according to the Swamp Woman, right, and they all have to be appreciated for themselves. And they're all the same. It's all an expression of the same thing, which is creative expression.

BOSCHÉ: *But you still teach. Why are you still teaching, when financially you probably don't have to?*

JOHNSON: I don't have to teach, but I enjoy it. I've been in school my entire life, since the age of five. I like my colleagues and, in a *good* class, the intellectual exchange and the dialectic that goes on. That is a very rewarding experience.

BOSCHÉ: *And it does help your writing, doesn't it? If you do hit the right people to talk to?*

JOHNSON: I think so. Yeah. I admire writers who are full-time freelances and sort of go off by themselves but I think they probably hunger after a certain point for intellectual engagement with others and a social life. If it is a bad quarter, that's another matter. If all this stuff is miserable, no, I don't enjoy it. That's awful . . .

BOSCHÉ: *I remember where you once said, you were shaking your head after reading class papers, all these students are just thinking about getting laid, why can't they ever think of themselves in someone else's skin. Something to that effect.*

JOHNSON: Sometimes it is just difficult for undergraduates who are still trying to figure things out. The grad students are always a delight to work with. I think I've never had a bad graduate class, and even the upper division undergraduate classes have been very good. *Except,* I've had this same conversation recently with people, I think the skill level that students bring in now is somewhat lower in the upper division and undergraduate classes than it was ten to twelve years ago. They've read less. They seem less ambitious in a certain kind of way. It's just very odd. I've seen it this year in the undergraduate classes, and it rather surprised me because only two years ago the 300-level had people with all kinds of backgrounds and knowledge and the wonderful things they would bring in. Not so much that, any more.

BOSCHÉ: *You've said that you have problems with a lot of contemporary fiction, so do you read much of it?*

JOHNSON: Oh, I do have problems with it, but I read a lot of it. I was a judge for the National Book Award in 1989, and for two years I've been a judge for the *L.A. Times* Book Prize. I see whatever the publishers consider their best offering for the year. It doesn't pass by me.

BOSCHÉ: *I got the impression you still read mostly the old greats, to get something for yourself, for your own nourishment.*

JOHNSON: Well, I do, to learn. There is a level of technical performance, I think, and even a way of envisioning that has been lost. I come out of philosophy where the whole thought process can be different at times. So I usually am very demanding of the things that I read. I want clarity; I want coherence; I want completeness. I want thoughtful works. I want, basically, works that are capable of changing my perception as well as moving my heart.

BOSCHÉ: *What was the first book that did that? That changed your life, your way of seeing.*

JOHNSON: My mother had lots and lots of books of all kinds. Books on yoga and Richard Wright's *Black Boy*. She was in a book club. Philip K. Dick. I remember exactly when *Man in a High Castle* was published because it was a Book Club alternate at the time. So I guess it was science fiction when I was young because that tends to be intellectual fiction to a certain extent. It is full of ideas, it dramatizes. A lot of it is extremely imaginative, too, so you're not just getting the surface of life. It's not just the ordinary. There's something more going on that reflects back on the ordinary.

So my tastes are very eclectic. An example is *Invisible Man* by Ellison. That is a magnificent performance. It is a purely literary experience that really does help us determine what goes on in our world. He gave the language a way of describing the condition of people, just through the title of the book, and he's working with consciousness and perception. It's original. In many ways it's exhausting. That is the kind of fiction that engages me most.

Right now for example, I have to review for the *New York Times* a book of philosophy by K. [Kwame Anthony] Appiah, an African philosopher. It's called *In My Father's House*, and he is going at—in this absolutely amazing way—every presupposition that we have operated off of in terms of the conflict of race since W. E. B. Du Bois. Basically he's really looking hard at this and saying what does this mean, and when does the conflict of race arise, and how do we use these terms. This is very, very difficult work and, it seems to me, extraordinarily valuable.

BOSCHÉ: *Well, I do think that much of the writing in America about multiculturalism seems shallow.*

JOHNSON: A lot of it is. For example, Appiah, who is African, really does take a hard look at how it is that black Americans came up with the notion of Pan Africanism that violates all the diversity of language and cultural difference in Africa itself.

BOSCHÉ: *Reading your books, and this may be a controversial statement, your characters, Faith and Calhoun, for example, didn't seem to be of any particular race. To me, that is a good thing.*

JOHNSON: Well, they live in a world that had racial kinds of signatures . . .

BOSCHÉ: *Yes, but they could be anybody. They're just human beings. Like the great books I read as a child, many of them written by men, mostly male characters, but somehow I never thought of them as male or female . . .*

JOHNSON: I didn't think of them as white. I was interested in the story and what was going to happen next and, basically, that what is going to happen to this person can potentially happen to me. Their emotional lives are not that different: love, hate, fear, desires of various kinds. You can't read literature that way and benefit at all from stories.

BOSCHÉ: *You're a storyteller.*

JOHNSON: I think that is personally fundamental.

BOSCHÉ: *In a way you're an entertainer. Do you think that is a negative thing?*

JOHNSON: No, no, no. I think all great art entertains, but all entertainment isn't great art.

BOSCHÉ: *But you don't have great, dark tragic elements in your work that, say, Faulkner does.*

JOHNSON: I don't really have a tragic vision.

BOSCHÉ: *You don't. Yours is humorous.*

JOHNSON: Well, no. In *Middle Passage,* there are awful things that happen to human beings.

BOSCHÉ: *But still, somehow, there isn't that darkness . . .*

JOHNSON: Because that's not all that happens to human beings.

BOSCHÉ: *Well, it's strange. In a way it's like Mark Twain . . .*

JOHNSON: Mark Twain? There's things I like about Twain.

BOSCHÉ: *I love Twain, but he's going out of style. Some are saying he's a racist.*

JOHNSON: That's an easy way for finding an excuse for not reading Twain, right. For there is very interesting stuff in it. But a book like *Middle Passage,* for example. The vision that operates in that novel, when it's not, say, phenomenological, is very Buddhist, particularly the last line in the novel: "Isadora drifted toward rest, nestled snugly beside me, where she would remain all night while we, forgetful of ourselves, gently crossed the Flood, and countless seas of suffering."

BOSCHÉ: *Even the character Papa, as bad as he is, you don't make him seem evil. He's a human being. What amazes me about your writing is that it is almost like you are not human; you are so understanding. There is too much tolerance.*

JOHNSON: What? I'm just human.

BOSCHÉ: *I don't see any hatred, real hatred, in your work at all.*

JOHNSON: I didn't grow up in an environment in which there was hatred. Hatred is not an emotion that I can hang on to for very long or feel. I think that hatred is very often based upon fear. And hatred . . . what is the cause of that? Other people have said that to me, in Indonesia and I think recently in Amsterdam. I don't know why that would be an expected thing of a black writer.

BOSCHÉ: *I think it is. Other black writers might want to see anger in your work that's not there.*

JOHNSON: What for? If they want to see anger they can go

to Wright. Or they can go to Baldwin. But, on the other hand, what I want is art and beauty and goodness and truth. That's what I want.

BOSCHÉ: *What you've said about moral literature, what John Gardner said, about how at the heart of things, you want beauty, it strikes something in me—it feels real. But I also hear the other voice and I think it is legitimate, too—that the anger needs to be heard, too.*

JOHNSON: I think an angry novel can be powerful; I think it can be an indictment; I think it can call your attention to some problems in the world. That doesn't mean that it is art, though. That's not going to make it art.

BOSCHÉ: *Richard Wright's novel is angry and beautiful.*

JOHNSON: I like Wright a lot. *Native Son* is a remarkably complex book; in fact, I think it is more complex than most people have actually wanted to acknowledge and talk about. But see that's not the question, the anger to be used. There is a quote by William Gass I thought very amusing and interesting. He said he needs hate's heat to warm his art. That is totally antithetical to why I write. I much prefer the quote of Alex Haley, who said if you are wondering what you're going to write, find something that you love and praise it. I think Alex is a deeper and wiser man in that respect.

# PART II

JOHNSON: Back to the issue of race. If you go to Africa, you are going to find so many different peoples, even so many different races, that there is no oversimplified, generic way to talk about all of them. And yet, once they've been talked about that way, some Africans, according to K. Appiah—and he is talking about African intellectuals trained in Europe—to react against Europe, will adopt the characteristics that they feel are most tribal, particular to their nation. But those are characteristics that were *originally* outlined by the Europeans and their anthropologists, right, who were trying to sort out and carve up Africa.

BOSCHÉ: *Are you also talking about what is happening with black Americans, trying to adopt those same tribal characteristics?*

JOHNSON: Appiah's talking about African writers and intellectuals, but you could say that it's true here in America too. What is there, in the way of racial essence, about black people that you would identify as universal? What *is* there? You know? Tell me one thing—you can come up with physical stuff—that all black people have in common. One thing. That's a hard call.

BOSCHÉ: *I thought I read where you said that everyone, in America anyway, is a mongrel. Looking at myself, that is certainly true.*

JOHNSON: I think it is. You know Alex Haley had a book, which he was going to do, which he didn't live long enough to do, about gene pools—the mixing of gene pools in people in this country. And Appiah even goes through this long thing with genetics in his book—this is remarkable—dealing with chromosomes in the genes and pointing out how at any given point there are more similarities and common ancestries between two people who live on the planet than differences.

We talk about things we want to believe, but I'm suspicious of why we want to believe some of these things. Why we have a stake and an investment in somebody really believing there is an essential difference between me and the other. There has got to be some element of ego involved and a misunderstanding of the other if you can't inhabit, if you feel it is impossible to inhabit, their world.

BOSCHÉ: *In Lucy Lippard's book,* Mixed Blessings: New Art in a Multicultural America, *she asserts that it is "the universalist concept that refuses once again to come to grips with difference," and that universalism acts as a filter, intimidating marginalized groups "into veiling themselves and their images in order to be acceptable in the dominant culture." For her, to approach art with universal standards/motives is to decontextualize one's work, abdicating responsibility to one's self and to one's art and thus to the community which spawned it. What do you think about that?*

JOHNSON: That's foolish. When I say "universal" what I mean is phenomenologically shared meaning. If there are no universals, we're back in the same position that Plato was in 427 B.C. If you remember Protagoras, who said, "Man is the measure of all things." What he meant was not that men are the measure of all things, he meant that every man has his own logic, everybody had his own subjective truth. That is what the Sophists were arguing. Plato was up against a world in which there was no shared meaning at all. The question was, how to find a common public truth. That is the whole basic argument of *The Republic* and his other works. Whether he succeeded or not, by putting it in forms, for example, is another matter, but the universal basically means shared meaning, at least in phenomenological terms. You see one thing, and you describe it to me and I say, "Oh, yeah, I see that." What happens, using language, is that you cause this to be disclosed in a particular way to me—you make a profile of it.

So I think the assault on universals is arguing something stupid, which is arguing against the European idea in literary criticism—that there are things that apply to all people. What that assault comes down to is arguing that since Europeans created these ideas, they apply only to them. But if we do not have universals as I've described them, what we have is subjectivism, and we fall finally into solipsism. Without universals there is no reason why I, being black, can go to the Caribbean, and talk to somebody, say a Haitian. We've got nothing in common. We're black, but we have absolutely different cultural worlds and there is no common basis for us to talk. Now if we are human beings, that is a different matter. But this is foolish talk and deflects us from the real questions of literature.

BOSCHÉ: *You don't think it is relevant to examine individual/community differences?*

JOHNSON: What will enrage me is if somebody goes to my wife, or, particularly, to my son or my daughter, and fails to see them as radically individual and unique and not like anybody who ever lived on this planet before or will ever live again. If they come at them with some umbrella term, some *bullshit* about who they think they are without asking them—that's ridiculous. I don't want them to do that to them. They've got to figure out who these kids are. That's the novelist's job as well. You don't deal in types or stereotypes. You've got to give up all presuppositions if you're going to have any success.

BOSCHÉ: *Going back to the novelist's job, do you write with an ideal reader in mind?*

JOHNSON: Yeah, in a sense the ideal reader is a literate reader; a curious reader; a reader without prejudices; a reader who likes the things that I hope are in my books, which are characters that I hope are interesting and suspense and philosophy and the taking up of some perennial questions that are the human condition, in respect to the black world, because that's the realm where it's played out.

BOSCHÉ: *Take one of Wright's characters, Bigger Thomas. Isn't he powerless in his world? Manipulated by outside events?*

JOHNSON: No. He achieves his sense of freedom through murder. He sees that as his only possibility for a creative act . . .

BOSCHÉ: *But isn't that an act of powerlessness?*

JOHNSON: It's a powerless world, but there's other people in his world who are not portrayed as being powerless. Again, going back, one of Wright's big contributions to our literature is the victim theory of black life, and I have enormous problems with that . . .

BOSCHÉ: *I know. You've talked about that a lot.*

JOHNSON: I talk about that a lot because I didn't grow up with people who were victims. I didn't perceive myself as a victim.

BOSCHÉ: *None of your characters are like that either.*

JOHNSON: No. None of my characters feel that somebody else has control over the choices in their life. They can always make choices.

BOSCHÉ: *Do you think that is true in real life?*

JOHNSON: Yeah, I do. I think you can always make a choice.

BOSCHÉ: *Many people don't agree with that. They see social forces manipulating . . .*

JOHNSON: What social forces? What's a social force?

BOSCHÉ: *Poverty.*

JOHNSON: Oh, I've been poor. I mean, so what—you get hungry. But you see, these great big capitals, Poverty, Racism—the victim theory takes away dignity from black people . . .

BOSCHÉ: *From everybody . . .*

JOHNSON: . . . . it takes away dignity from anybody. And you cannot move out of the victim position into any position of power, that just does not work. What you get when you portray somebody as a victim—one of my best friends is so strong on this, we talk about this a lot—what you get is pity for that person, but you don't get respect for him. That's one of the problems. Shelby Steele was quite right about this, too. When your entire mode of operation is based upon making somebody else feel guilt and pity, they're never going to feel respect.

I think, because I grew up in a family where my dad worked three jobs, and my great uncle was a construction worker who built, all over my home town, churches for people to worship their God in, residences for them to live in, apartment buildings, I didn't grow up in a world in which I felt black people were powerless.

BOSCHÉ: *But you had the right models. What if you don't have those?*

JOHNSON: I saw friends of mine who didn't. Not *all* the members in my family either, for that matter. I had an uncle who went to jail for killing a guy who he caught in bed with his wife. With his bare hands he killed him. Every family has all kinds of mixes of people. But when one puts that rap on black people: powerlessness, victim, crawling on your knees, begging the white man. What is that crap? I've never believed it.

BOSCHÉ: *Take the recent riots in Los Angeles, the violence. Violence seems to have to come out when people don't have other options. I'm not saying they are victims, but they perceive that they don't have other options.*

JOHNSON: Why do they perceive themselves as not having other options? Now I think that the inner city of South Central L.A. is pretty bad, okay. But if you listen to black people who are on the money these days about this subject, a lot of what we have to do is on us. It's that simple. It's on us. The government can't make a man stay with his family forty years or love his wife or love his kids and stay with them. Can't make somebody decide that they're going to loot. The government can't do that.

# A LIFE OF BALANCE
# THROUGH MARTIAL ARTS

## TIM ALLEN

T'S FORTY MINUTES
into the martial arts class being held in a classroom of the Phinney Neighborhood Center, and perspiration is pouring from
Charles Johnson's brow. A mirror runs across the north end of
the classroom, and Johnson, a lanky, forty-four-year-old black
man dressed comfortably in gym shoes, sweat pants, and shirt,
spars fiercely with the reflection that matches him move for move.
Johnson is focused on this particular moment: All the world's
concerns, all the day's annoyances have been left outside, transforming this classroom into what he calls a "privileged space."

This is not quite the image Charles Johnson's creative writing students at the University of Washington might expect of
their English professor, winner of the National Book Award for
the novel *Middle Passage*.

Reprinted from *Phinney Ridge Review* (Summer 1992), with permission.

Johnson is one of four co-instructors in the Chinese martial art of Choy Li Fut, along with Gray Cassidy, Dave Sawin, and Tim Frisino, that meets at 8:00 P.M. every Monday, Wednesday, and Friday in the Center. And though this is a serious class based on a four-thousand-year-old tradition of rugged combat and gentle philosophy, the four instructors conduct it with the camaraderie of old friends who have studied together since 1980.

A unifying theme in many martial arts is "balance" in all things, both physical and spiritual. Visiting Charles Johnson's home office, you can see that he tries to attain that balance in his own life. One end of his office is devoted to the martial arts, and is outfitted with weights, a kickbag, and pictures of revered masters of the martial arts.

The other end is devoted to writing, with a computer; framed plaques and awards; wild stacks of books, notes, and journals; contracts; research papers on his next novel about Martin Luther King, Jr., screenplays for Columbia Pictures and Home Box Office; and correspondence from friends and fellow writers.

Scattered here and there are figurines of Captain America and Batman; an incredibly detailed model slave ship like the one in *Middle Passage,* fitted with miniature brass and rigging; old photographs of family back in Illinois; a model of a P-51 Mustang fighter plane like those flown by the all-black Ninety-ninth Pursuit Squadron that Johnson has written about in a screenplay for an upcoming HBO movie; and a hand-drawn comic book by his daughter, Lizzie.

We're back in the classroom in the Phinney Neighborhood Center. The students are stiff from their daytime activities; the chilly night air doesn't help. Gray Cassidy, a sandy-haired, barrel-chested man who looks about as easy to push aside as an oak tree, loosens up the class members by leading a series of formalized stretches and exercises, called *kuen.* The class is always small on Friday evenings, so students have plenty of room to spread out. Gray counts off each movement in Chinese, and soon the air smells of honest sweat.

Charles Johnson grew up in Evanston, Illinois, a suburb just north of Chicago, and attended his first martial arts class while in his late teens. He was excited to hear about an interesting karate class being held in Chicago and faithfully commuted to the city every weekend. But different martial arts espouse different ideals, and though Johnson did well in the class, he found the class harsh both physically and philosophically. He sought something else.

Charles is a man with a love of learning. As a student at Southern Illinois University, he double-majored in journalism and philosophy, and even had a program on the college PBS station teaching cartooning. In 1965 he sold his first cartoon; five years later he had sold over a thousand. But by 1970 his interest in philosophy and fiction started to take precedence.

The class in the Phinney Center has warmed up now, and Charles is practicing his *kuen*. His movements are smooth and fast; his breathing deep and steady; and his arms snap like whips as he channels the power of his entire body through his fist.

Each student's style is modified by his unique musculature and body shape. Though he is moving all the time, Gray seems solid as a rock. He says the class is suited to anyone from sixteen to sixty-two who is sturdy and in good health.

Tim Frisino, a much smaller man, moves like a cat slipping through the tall grass. He trades off with Gray and takes a moment from coaching a beginning student to say "everyone is like each other's big brother" and everyone in the class works to make sure that all practice correctly and safely.

Charles discovered Choy Li Fut during a sabbatical from the University of Washington. He went to San Francisco for six months to write and produce a PBS television series. Naturally, he looked for a good local martial arts class. At the time he was interested in kung fu (which means literally "hard work" or "effort") and discovered that the Choy Li Fut style was being taught by the highly revered Doc Fai Wong.

Charles testifies that Doc Fai Wong's warm philosophy and style was what he had been seeking for many years. He says it was the difference between going to a "teacher" and going to a "boot camp." That approach is what the co-instructors have tried to project in their class since 1989.

Charles seems to have found a balance between his work as a professor of English; his art as an acclaimed author; his study of martial arts; and his family of wife, Joan; daughter, Lizzie; and son, Malik.

Charles Johnson is one of our neighbors.

# AN INTERVIEW
# WITH CHARLES JOHNSON

## JONATHAN LITTLE

LIKE HIS NARRATOR
in *Middle Passage* (1990), Charles Johnson charts a course
through the vexed and volatile issues of multiculturalism and
racial politics in America. The rush of publicity Johnson received
after his best-selling novel *Middle Passage* won the National
Book Award in 1990 drew attention to his versatile and prolific
career as a cartoonist, novelist, short story writer, essayist, and
screenwriter. Whatever the medium, Johnson continues to
address the charged philosophical questions surrounding culture and individual racial identity.

Johnson began his artistic career with two collections of political cartoons lampooning American race relations, *Black Humor*
(1970) and *Half-Past Nation Time* (1972). His interests then

Reprinted from *Contemporary Literature* 34.2 (1993), with permission.

turned to writing. After completing six unpublished novels, Johnson published *Faith and the Good Thing* (1974). The novel reflects his primary interest in blending philosophy and fiction as he depicts Faith's search for the truth or the meaning of life, the "Good Thing." His next two novels, *Oxherding Tale* (1982) and *Middle Passage*, both set in the nineteenth century, also show African American characters struggling to define themselves as they search for spiritual and metaphysical happiness in the face of difficult odds.

Johnson explains the link between philosophy and fiction in *Being and Race* (1988), his phenomenological study of African American writing since 1970. In it he argues for the need for "aesthetically venturesome" and "wickedly diverse" philosophical African American fiction that is not tied to any single genre or motivated by any single ideological or political agenda. Johnson's collection of short stories, *The Sorcerer's Apprentice* (1986), illuminates his range as he experiments with realism, allegory, fable, fantasy, and science fiction. His novel in progress concerns Martin Luther King, Jr., whose ability to draw from many different spiritual and cultural traditions has impressed and influenced Johnson.

Johnson's publishing career has coincided with an equally prolific career in television and film screenwriting. His credits include *Charlie Smith and the Fritter Tree* (1978), a dramatization of the life of a 135–year-old African American for the PBS Vision series, and *Booker* (1988), a program about the childhood of Booker T. Washington for the Walt Disney channel. He has recently completed a screenplay adaptation of *Middle Passage* for Tri-Star Productions.

Johnson was an energetic and engaging host during my stay from July 31 to August 3, 1992, in Seattle, where he teaches creative writing at the University of Washington. He showed me around the city he calls "the social correlate of my soul," with its African American mayor and harmonious mixture of Asian, African American, white, Native American, and Latino

American populations. It seemed strikingly appropriate to Johnson's eclecticism that during our wanderings we toured an amphibious assault Navy vessel, a downtown bookstore where he has given several readings, a local artist's backyard studio, and, at Johnson's home, which was being remodeled, the boarded-up entrance to his home gym; he has for eleven years practiced Chinese Choy Li Fut kung fu, and he now teaches it in a neighborhood center. As we walked, I had the uncanny feeling that I was momentarily participating in one of Johnson's fluidly polymorphic and international fictions.

LITTLE: *In all your novels it seems that your central characters are questing after some kind of enlightenment and that during this process they have to work through a variety of options embodied in other characters in the novel. Is this an accurate interpretation of the structure of your novels?*

JOHNSON: In each one of the novels there is a progression from ignorance to knowledge, or from a lack of understanding to some greater understanding. Certainly that's true of *Faith and the Good Thing*. I know it's true of *Middle Passage*. The last chapter is "Moksha" in *Oxherding Tale,* meaning "enlightenment" or "liberation." Yes, you're right. That is the structure of the books, probably the short stories, too. There's usually a moment of awareness, an epiphany if you like, a place where the character is smashed into a larger vision under the pressure of events. Usually he goes through a lot of positions that other people hold, which are partial. It seems kind of Hegelian in that way. Not that the final position synthesizes all of them, but that the character goes through several moments.

LITTLE: *What happens to individual identity during the process of development your main characters go through?*

JOHNSON: I think it dissolves. "What is individual identity?" is a central question for me. I personally don't believe in the existence of the ego. I think it's a theoretical construct. There's no empirical verification for it at all. And if there is such a thing

99

as identity, I don't think that it's fixed or static; it's a process. I think it's dominated by change and transformation, more so than by any static qualities. It is many identities over the course of a lifetime. That identity, if it is anything at all, is several things, a tissue of very often contradictory things, which is why I probably have a great deal of opposition to anything that looks like a fixed meaning for black America. I just don't believe it. It's ridiculous as a thought.

LITTLE: *Is this process of development similar to Ralph Ellison's statement, "Thus because jazz finds its very life in an endless improvisation upon traditional materials, the jazzman must lose his identity even as he finds it"?*

JOHNSON: That's a nice quote. I'm not sure what it means, but I'm certainly willing to give credit to Ellison for anything. It's very interesting to me where we get the notion of the self. Hume, with his radically empirical approach, looks into his experience to see if there's anything that corresponds to the idea of a self. What he finds are memories, impressions, sensations, but no self. For Hume the self is inferred as a thing that holds all of this together. It's much the same in Buddhism, where the self is an illusion. In Buddhism all you have is this flow of impressions and sensations. The self is one of those objects we talk about without having fully examined it. For me, if there's any way to talk about it, it's as a verb and not a noun. It's a process but not a product, and never is a product, unless it's dead, and then there's no more possibility for action and change. Once dead, it becomes somewhat like Whitehead's idea of the eternal object.

LITTLE: *So at the end of* Middle Passage, *Rutherford becomes a model for these ideas?*

JOHNSON: Andrew Hawkins's identity in *Oxherding Tale* is that of a free-floating creative force. That's true as well for Rutherford. What he's done is apprehended or taken so much from all the people who are already on that ship, from the Allmuseri to the various members of the ship—but he's done that his entire life. That sort of tissue of world experience is what he is. He's become much more humble in terms of making assumptions about objects and others. He's more willing to listen and wait for them to speak, which is a very phenomenological position in the world. It's very simple. It's not a difficult idea.

LITTLE: *His identity, though, I would say, isn't lost; rather, there's an accretion.*

JOHNSON: It's cumulative, if you like. It's Whitmanesque in a particular sense. I'd like to talk about it in the same sense that Toomer does in the poem "Blue Meridian." Let's be more specific. When you say "his identity," what do you mean?

LITTLE: *Maybe I'm looking at calcified perceptions of identity, but I was thinking in terms of his development as a character. Does he lose himself, as Ellison would say, in the process of finding himself?*

JOHNSON: I like that formulation, yeah. There's a line by Husserl that's really very nice: "I lose myself in the objects and the others." Yes. I do think that's what it is. What he finds is not a fixed notion of the self. It's something that's very expansive. You've seen, for example, the Necker's cube? When I show it to my students, they always see the initial kinds of variations, tilting left, tilting right. We write them down, and we do this for about half an hour. Then someone begins to see things that nobody else did in the room. The others don't see them until that person has narrated and described it—"I see a . . ." Everybody else is looking and straining, then, "Oh, yes! I see that now too."

We go through this, and we get maybe thirty possible disclosures of that one simple object in class, each based upon everybody's different backgrounds—where they're coming from and where they were born, how they grew up, the kind of mother they had, the father they had, the objects they looked at. All of that's brought to disclosing the object. But somebody will say, "I see a paper bag," and nobody else is able to see it.

Only if that person describes it will the other people see it. So at one point, what is entirely subjective becomes intersubjective. We share an image. When we go down the line, looking at profiles of the Necker's cube, you can never really get two of those images at once.

One of the things that's interesting is that people are sure in the beginning when they first look at it. "Oh, it's got to be this, it's got to be that," they say. Then they become more humble as they get to the thirteenth profile, the fifteenth profile, the twentieth profile, and then if somebody new comes in the room, there may be yet another disclosure of the object. If you said "What is it?" which is the final question I ask them, they know they can't answer that question, because it's a box leaning left, *hyphen* a box leaning right, *hyphen* a box leaning up, *hyphen* a box leaning forward; it's *hyphen* a fish tank, *hyphen* a paper bag, *hyphen* a stage, *hyphen* looking down at a pyramid. Its being is a hyphenated being, always open-ended. It is all of those perceptions, but only one of them can exist at a time before consciousness. Using Husserl's idea of consciousness, we must say that consciousness is always consciousness *of* something.

In much the same way, that is how I talk about every phenomenal object. Things are given to us in profiles. Sides, angles, but not the entire thing. We have to walk around, for example, that wall. That's given to us there. But empirically, we have no sense at all that there's a room on the other side. This all could be like a Hollywood movie set. Until you walk around and see the other side and confirm or refute that, you just don't know. That is much like where we find Andrew Hawkins and certainly Rutherford Calhoun at the ends of *Oxherding Tale* and *Middle Passage*. There have been so many profiles disclosed and revealed for the meaning of the world that one has a very humble attitude about making existential claims about it. You know that even if you've exhausted all the possible meanings at this moment, the next generation, given its experience and what it brings to that object's revelation, will find something new. Being is historical. I'm in agreement with what Merleau-Ponty says of perceptual experience, that the more revelations and disclosures and profiles you get for the object, the more ambiguous it's going to become, the more hazy. That's what interests me. The easiest images to get are the first two or three. Box left, box right, box forward, box back.

When I think about how we write, it seems we always go with the first two or three perceptions. We don't go with the fifth or the fortieth, because you have to dig to get to those. You have to force the imagination. You have to go to the trouble of confirming with somebody else, "Did you see that?" Of course, all science begins that way too, with a first person seeing—the scientist looking into the microscope. It's one person, one consciousness and this object. He has to say to a colleague, "Come here, look at this, do you see that?" Then you have intersubjectivity. If you have three people, it's even better. That's what I believe in far more than objectivity. Intersubjectivity is shared meaning, a shared vision.

But the problem with our writing is that we reach for the first one or two meanings. The reason we don't dig deeper is because the resistance is so great. In other words, you may have to free up all your presuppositions, all the prejudices, all of your background to be able to get to the thirtieth or fortieth profile or disclosure of the object. Usually, I think that happens in the social context. Somebody else on the other side of the room coming from another part of the world, or world experience, will through language, as Heidegger says, allow this object to be disclosed for somebody else. If you do it by yourself, you have to fight against all the presuppositions and prejudices. I think that's what fiction ought to be about. It ought to be about getting beneath those sedimented meanings, all the calcified, rigid perceptions of the object.

For the average person, doing this, letting meaning flower in this way, can be frustrating. It doesn't allow them to *use* the object as they'd like to. For utilitarian reasons, they say, "That's a Necker's cube leaning left, or a Necker's cube leaning right." But that's not good enough for the artist or the philosopher. I think we have to bracket the whole idea of utility if any object—or the world—is going to disclose whatever meaning it has. I think the same thing is true of racial phenomena. Very often we only deal with surface images, the most easily graspable meaning, which is usually the meaning we've inherited, or somebody else's vision, now our own. For the sake of progress, we have to go much, much deeper. Metaphor allows us to do that.

LITTLE: *You seem heavily postmodern in your emphasis on parody and intertextuality. There's a sense of creative theft or borrowing in your works, Rutherford perhaps being the best example of this, as he "trespasses" on other identities and becomes interpenetrated by them.*

JOHNSON: What do you mean by "borrowing"?

LITTLE: *In terms of the structure—Homer's* Odyssey, *for example. You not only borrow structural elements but historical detail from sea narratives, slave narratives. You obviously spent a lot of time doing research for* Middle Passage.

JOHNSON: I did, in fact. Let me see if I can make sense of that in terms of where we just were in our discussion. What I didn't have when I got to *Middle Passage* was knowledge of the sea, so I spent six years reading every book and rereading every book I could on that subject, anything relating to sea adventure. I read Homer, Apollonius of Rhodes, the Sinbad stories, slave narratives, Gustavus Vasa, and some material that was sent to me from Werner Sollors at Harvard. I looked at all of Melville again, Conrad. You name it, anything I could.

Why do that? Well, for two reasons. One is very writerly. I needed to know the parts of ships; I needed to know what that whole universe was like. But I needed to know the literary universe of the sea as well. What I needed to know were the profiles, again, the disclosures, the meanings that other writers for two thousand years have had for this particular phenomenon, the sea. I needed, in so many words, to look at that Necker's cube and see the phenomena of the sea disclosed over and over again. If one looks, and this is a simple matter, I guess, at any author who's written about the sea, whoever it is, the sea means something quite specific in the way that it is disclosed and experienced.

But why, why did I do that? Is that borrowing, is that stealing, is that intertextuality? I think it's something else. I think it's the fact that all knowledge, all disclosure, all revelation from the past, from our predecessors, black, white, and otherwise, is our inheritance, and most of the time we just don't know it. Seriously, we just don't know it. That's why we do research. Any sense that other human beings have made out of the world, any sense that they have pulled out of this universe of nonsense as Merleau-Ponty would say, any judgments—all that is what we have inherited as human beings. And, in a way, that's how I have to write. I have to know that. We are perpetually indebted to our predecessors for that. It's not something I can ignore or something I can abandon. I may come upon a disclosure of the object that's different from anything that's come before, but I think it's predicated on all that came before. In the same way, I don't think you can get the Einsteinian universe without first the Newtonian universe. It's all a long conversation, and the writer does not come into this discussion ex nihilo, born with nothing behind him.

Does that make sense in terms of how *Middle Passage* came together, and why research? It isn't just to do a historical novel. It's not that. It's to understand what others have brought to the rendering and disclosure of the subject. You could call it borrowing, I suppose. My intention is somewhat different, a very synthetic technique.

LITTLE: *I think you install the reference, but you also subvert it, or you do something new with it.*

JOHNSON: Yes, if I'm doing it, it's again much as we discussed that Necker's cube. I'm trying to say, "Yes, the sea is this, as so and so said, yes, the sea is that, as so and so said, but it's also *this."* It keeps opening up, I hope, as we progress through the book. The same thing happens with the major characters. We're seeing sides of them disclosed in dramatic situations in the course of the novel as they interact with different people. They learn things about themselves that they could not have known except through these encounters.

LITTLE: *In terms of African American fiction now, where would you come down with Toni Morrison when she seems to rework the black aesthetic and the black arts movement? She seems to reject political prescriptiveness but at the same time holds on to the aesthetic principles of black art. She identifies them as non-Western and oral.*

JOHNSON: Let me say a few things. I don't want to be unfair to Toni. I understand what the black arts movement was and why it came about. It was very interesting and very exciting. It had a big impact on me when I was a cartoonist. But in *Being and Race,* I try to trace through some of the limitations that are imposed on creative freedom by that particular orientation, and also on intellectual freedom. If we were going through our Necker's cube and all those profiles, we would probably have to stop at a certain point if we had a black nationalist orientation or a black aesthetic position. That's why I had to move away from it. It just wasn't answering enough questions. It wasn't going deep enough in terms of investigating phenomena. People in the black arts movement do not seem to be widely interested in questions that are crucial to all of us. Our relationship to the environment, for example, our relationship to technology. All the human questions. I do think it's a narrower focus.

Morrison is an extremely talented prose stylist. I happen to think that the earlier books are better than the later ones. *Sula* is a very interesting book. And in *Beloved* she achieves something I would talk about this way: I would say it is the penultimate or final fruit of the black arts movement. It's extremely poetic. You can look and see that for six years she spent time revising and rewriting those lines. And she's very good at that.

But, on the other hand, I have real problems with the vision that animates that book. Again, it has the problems that you find in the black arts movement. I could take you through the book step by step and say why that's so. It's an interesting, middlebrow book. I don't think it's an intellectual achievement, because I'm not sure where the intellectual probing is going on. The last book, *Jazz,* is really—I don't know what to say about it. There are no characters, there's no story, there's no plot, and even the poetry which Morrison is so good at is not there. It just isn't there. I'm not sure why she released that book at all.

We still have to address the black arts movement as an ideology and speak about it in those terms. There are wonderful things that came out of that period, and important things, but I'm not sure it led to very much literature that we would consider to be lasting. I've got first editions on my shelf of books from that period that I'm sure most people have never heard of. I found them to be interesting when I read them, but, unfortunately, they did not meet the standard that Ralph Ellison set in 1952 with *Invisible Man,* or the standards set by Albert Murray with his remarkable essay *The Hero and the Blues.*

The question is this: Are there two aesthetics? Is there a white aesthetic and is there a black aesthetic? What constitutes a black aesthetic? The oral tradition? What's that? Take call and response, for instance. Everybody says that. Where is call and response in the novel? This is my question. I know what it is. It occurs in the black church when the minister and the congregation respond back and forth. Sure. As my friend Stanley Crouch points out, you can tell a story orally, but when you get to the novel you have to do things that are particular to the novel as a form for that story to come to life.

There's a lot of easy, simplistic thought that goes on in our discussion of black literature. A certain voice is supposed to represent the oral tradition. Well, there are lots of voices in the black community, lots of voices. Why is one selected over another? We have the voice of Du Bois, we have the voice of Douglass, we have the voice of Harriet Tubman, we have the voice of Malcolm X. Why is one voice chosen to represent the oral tradition? I also get really tired of people saying, well, black people have been telling stories for years and years. *Everybody's* been telling stories for years and years. Some of those are wonderful stories, such as when Julius Lester collected black folktales. They are beautiful, wonderful stories that were told orally and finally set down. But when you compose them on the page in one of the literary traditions that we inherit, you have to do things to those stories to make them effective as literature. Character development, connections, transitions, all kinds of things.

We have a way of talking about these so-called differences between the white and black aesthetic that do not make a great deal of sense. Skip Gates has this idea of "signifying" as somehow being a part of this. But again, if that's a general aesthetic proposition, then you should be able to go to any black literary work of art and find that it signifies in the way that Skip is talking about. You can't do that. All these works will defy that very simple notion of how you go about it. And the same thing with the oral tradition. I just don't believe it. I don't believe that there are two aesthetics. It cannot be universally demonstrated for all black literature.

LITTLE: *So you would also reject Morrison's idea that literature should be used as a means of African American empowerment?*

JOHNSON: What does she mean by that? What does that mean? African American empowerment through literature? How does a book do that? Does a book empower me to vote? I don't get it. How do you interpret that?

LITTLE: *It seems to me that she and others feel that you can maintain connection with a heritage, an ethnic identity that might be lost or appropriated by mainstream culture. Writers can use literature as a means of counteracting oppression and historical conditions.*

JOHNSON: That sounds great, but I still don't get it. We need a definition of empowerment. We need a definition of identity. I want a definition of how something is appropriated by something else and what that means.

First of all, as a writer, I don't believe that art imitates. There is a mimetic element, but I really think that what a writer does is create an experience on the pages of the book for the reader. You're creating experience. You're not transcribing experience. If you talk about the African American past in your work, you're obviously interpreting an experience. Language will distort and transform, as William Gass points out. It's all filtered through a consciousness, and the consciousness obviously of the author.

I think that these claims about black writing are simplistic. I kind of understand the intention behind them, but I don't think they make a great deal of sense. How does *Jazz* counteract oppression and historical conditions? How does any literature do that? There are certain instances and times when books have a huge impact, as with *Uncle Tom's Cabin* during the abolitionist movement. There are direct connections—this led to that in the public sphere—but claims are being made here for literature that have not been demonstrated at all. Is *The Great Gatsby* about empowering white people, is that what that's doing?

LITTLE: *Is that necessary? The privileged whites are already being represented. I think Morrison and Alice Walker, for example, are talking about people who have been left out of the tradition, left out of the representation. As writers they are celebrating an identity that had previously been silenced.*

JOHNSON: I think that's what they say they are doing. I think to put it that way, however, is really coded. People who were left out, silenced, marginalized. Yes, I buy that. You can write about people and publish works about individuals who have never had a story told about them before, or who have never been allowed to tell their own story. Of course, it's still Morrison telling the story, it's not that person. It's her imagining that person. Or Clarence Major can do that in his book *Such Was the Season,* where the protagonist is a black woman matriarch in an Atlanta political family. That does bring something new to our literature. It brings a new angle, a new perception, a new character's perspective to our literature. It may bring a different voice to our literature as well.

I'm not sure that American literature hasn't always done that. Bill Gass has an unusual and interesting analysis of character in fiction. He says that what we are dealing with on the page are concepts. And from Gass I have to go to Sartre. Characters are constructs, mental beings, who have more in common with mathematical entities than real people. They are not real people, but nevertheless, it is the act of consciousness that brings them to life during the reading experience, that creates a "fictional dream in the mind," to use a phrase from John Gardner.

These are created objects. We draw and apprehend from the world in the creation of any particular artwork, and that means you draw things you've heard from other people, their behavior and so forth. But when someone makes the claim that what we've done is empowered a certain class of people by giving a representation to them on the page, I'm not sure what that means. I sort of say, yeah, that seems to be a little bit of what's going on. Ten percent of what you're saying sounds right, but I'm not sure that claim can be made as strongly as some people would like to make it.

*Beloved* is about a woman who kills her kids. How representative is that of women during the period of slavery? I have no idea. Morrison says that it's based on a real woman. I would have to say that woman is probably, if not psychotic, then someone who needs a lot of help. If black people had done that en masse, we would not be here today. People killing their kids to save them from slavery? Come on, we're still talking the 1960s here, and certain very clever, cute ideas that I just don't think were the case. I don't think that the historical record confirms that.

LITTLE: *So you don't feel that African American literature has a social obligation or function?*

JOHNSON: I do, but not that one necessarily. I do think that art should be socially responsible. I do halfway believe most of the time in John Gardner's notion of moral fiction. Where social responsibility comes into play is in the simple fact that whatever the work is, whatever the book is, whatever the product is, it's something that we interject into the public space. It's a public act. It's our human expression, and we are responsible for all our forms of human expression, all our deeds and actions, of which art is one. The artist has a tremendous degree of responsibility. Whether it's the responsibility of promoting or supporting certain political ideas, I really don't know about that. I don't know if that's what art should be about. Somebody can write a book that is a political indictment, but should he or she write every book like that?

I would like for people to look at my books and feel that they are socially responsible. I say that because I try my very best to be fair to every character on one level. I remember when I used to pass drafts of things by John Gardner. I was still young, and I would set a certain character up to say and do things I didn't like, just so I could slap him around, and thereby slap around some people I knew who behaved like that. He would write in the margins of the manuscripts, "Shame on you. Why are you doing this? Why are you presenting this straw man to me? What am I supposed to do with this character, dislike him?" I really had to think about that aspect of John's criticism. I find that the most reprehensible characters, like a Captain Falcon, have to be characters I find enormously interesting, somebody I would like to poke at and get under the skin of and see as many sides of as I possibly can during the course of this fiction. That character must be subjected to the same kinds of things that everybody else is. Every major character for me is a character of evolution and change. They are not the same at the end of the book as when we first saw them. The ideal novel would be one in which there are no minor characters, where there are no flat characters. Everybody is in this situation of process and change. Everybody is being forced and pressured, as the main characters are, to move forward in their lives, to have their perceptions changed, to react differently in different situations. That would be the ideal novel. What I want is the process novel where everybody mentioned is a main character in the process of evolution. That would be the ultimate moral fiction.

LITTLE: *Couldn't you also say that you and Morrison have different political visions?*

JOHNSON: What is her political vision? Can it be stated? We know that Baraka at various times said he was a nationalist, and later he was a scientific socialist, and he explained what that meant. What's Morrison's political vision?

LITTLE: *I guess I was speaking more aesthetically, with her ties to the black arts movement.*

JOHNSON: The black arts movement, if you look at it as an ensemble of ideas, is contradictory. What was the black arts movement? You've got to look at Larry Neal, you've got to look at Baraka, you've got to look at John Oliver Killens. Was there a systematic body of beliefs? No, there wasn't. Look at Malcolm X, who had a big impact on my generation. At the end of Malcolm's life, someone asked him what his philosophy was, and he said, "I don't know." He was very honest. This was after his trip to Mecca. No, this was not systematic thought. Not in terms of having empirical evidence for what you're talking about. Not in terms of ethics hooking up in a systematic, intelligible way with epistemology and with ontology. No, it wasn't that. It was a passionate literary movement, in many ways, with a couple of ideas which took different form among different writers. If you talk about the black arts movement, you need to look at just what that was for different sorts of people. Let's take Ishmael Reed. He says he first began to write in cultural nationalist workshops. When I read Reed's work, I see a particular spin on cultural nationalism. He's said things that are quite different from Baraka and from Larry Neal. You have to ask the question, if he comes out of cultural nationalism, and has some belief in the black aesthetic, what is the relationship of that to what Morrison is talking about? Where are the points of similarity and where are the points of difference? I'm sure people are doing extensive work on both of those authors to see the variations. I don't think the black arts movement, as a body of thought, is coherent, consistent, or complete. By complete, I mean taking in as much as possible, taking in all the available profiles of phenomena. It's not philosophy, it's ideology.

I try in *Being and Race* to distinguish between philosophy and ideology. A philosopher is somebody who is perpetually asking questions. One who always goes back to his initial premise and presuppositions and is willing, if necessary, in the face of contrary evidence, to abandon them if he has to and start all over again from scratch. Ideological positions can't do that. They can't afford to do that. That's the problem I have with them. No philosopher can be comfortable with ideology. And I don't think everything is ideology. I don't think that every idea that we have, every ensemble of beliefs, must necessarily be ideology, whether in the scientific sphere or the philosophical sphere. Phenomenology, if I'm not mistaken, does not build up an architecture of propositions but rather goes back to try to eke out an understanding of what we think we already know. You're always standing in an interrogative mode toward the world.

I would like to believe that I could write book after book after book and someone could believe that they had been written by different people. In this book over here, *Faith and the Good Thing*, black folklore has this particular function. But over there, there's none of that in *Middle Passage*. The sea has this particular meaning there, but in the next book the sea might have an entirely different meaning, given the fictive universe that has evolved out of its unique set of characters. Things could absolutely change in terms of the overall experiential effect, from book to book. That's the kind of freedom I would like to see from novel to novel, from story to story.

LITTLE: *Let's say you are writing a novel on King and you are showing the inherent benefits of his position. Isn't that an ideological stance?*

JOHNSON: Why?

LITTLE: *Because it's imbued with a political application.*

JOHNSON: A political application? You mean I'm promoting King?

LITTLE: *You could be.*

JOHNSON: I'm interested in King. I think he's a very complex figure. I actually think we don't know enough about King. What I'm really interested in is the man, the evolution of the individual. I'm interested in a number of other things too, of a political-philosophical nature about the man. The vision of the civil rights movement—specifically integration—as it applies to King is there because that's part of the man. But I have to say of this man, that, when he first encountered racism, he wanted to hate white people. That's part of who he was. I have to have characters in there who represent the black nationalist position, because they're part of his world. All of the stuff that was there, as much as possible, I have to have it. I'm not sure that's an ideological position.

Someone will say, "Well, why did you write about this guy rather than Malcolm X?" I think we have a whole lot of popular material about Malcolm X, and very little on Martin. People don't really understand King, other than a couple of clichéd ideas about him, phrases, and sound bites. But I want to understand what his life was like after he led the Montgomery bus boycott at age twenty-six. I want to know that evolution, that history, up to his assassination. I want to know what a human being has to do to rise to that level of public service. He received fifty death threats. That's what interests me.

Why not Malcolm X? Other people have taken from Malcolm a number of things that they find interesting about him that aren't even true of the man. Even his daughter says that they don't take the whole man, and they've used him for political purposes that even Malcolm probably wouldn't agree with. Malcolm's just too much with us, and King not enough these days. I want people to see King in all his particularity and texture. I want to know how he shaved when he got up in the morning. He used a depilatory powder because he had very sensitive skin. The stuff stinks, I know exactly what it is. I want to know how much sugar he put in his coffee. That's what interests me.

If I did Malcolm, I'd do one different from the cliché. It would be about this unusual individual who goes from being a hustler to prison to the Nation of Islam to a break with the Nation of Islam, and a bloody public break at that. Nobody talks about the animosity between him and Elijah Muhammad's people. People forget that. And it almost spelled the end of the Nation of Islam. Things got very shaky. I'd go after what Malcolm's broader vision of Islam was about. It wouldn't be a couple of phrases or statements from Malcolm X. It would be his life in evolution, with all kinds of ideas and contradictions. As when he first joins the Nation of Islam, and he says, since he has a Jewish friend, "Do I have to hate Himey too?" This is a life in process. It isn't just one thing. That is the way I would do Malcolm X.

LITTLE: *In* Being and Race, *while you recognize the achievement of contemporary African American women writers, you also qualify this by saying that their writing is "more at the stage of criticism of social crimes." In* Possessing the Secret of Joy, *Alice Walker dwells on the physical and mental mutilation of black women and its result—insanity. Would Gardner call this vision "responsible" and "moral"? Would you?*

JOHNSON: Alice is talking about clitoridectomy. There's a social crime for you. I shouldn't speak for John here. Some of the portraits of black men in those books are so limited and so one-profiled, as opposed to thirty or forty images of black men, that they don't seem moral to me. It's not just Walker. You could also talk about Morrison. You do not see black men like Colin

Powell or W. E. B. Du Bois or astronaut Ron McNair or Frederick Douglass. It's an extremely narrow range of human beings. You basically see black men who are fuck-ups. And there's a lot that can be said about black men who are fuck-ups. But how does that tap into the general negative images we have of black males in the 1980s, coming from the Reagan administration, with Willy Horton and Bush, and these comic images of black men in film and on television? Where, finally, are the images of human beings who are black and male and lead responsible lives? You don't see anybody like the mayor of Seattle, Norman Rice, who's a remarkable human being. Those are not characters in our books. Stanley Crouch is of the opinion that that is going to be the next wave.

If we're going to talk about politics and black writing, then we've really got to talk about politics. You can talk about Jesse, who won't run for office because it's a lot easier to get in front of the cameras. Or you can talk about Ron Brown, or Norm Rice, who will indeed go through what the political process is. You present yourself to people, you have a list of proposals, you get elected, and you go in day after day to confront all manner of problems to serve the greatest number of people at any given moment. That's politics. The other stuff, with the rhetoric, that's not politics. Even if that gets someone elected, that human being, like Norm Rice and the other black mayors, is going to have to go in every day and deal with all kinds of interest groups. Politics is the art of compromise. That's real politics. It's not rhetoric. It's not about ideology. It's about solving problems on a daily basis.

Stanley is right. Someday we're going to have to get those kinds of black people into our fiction. All those workers in the NAACP, all those people, year in, year out, going to every one of the civil rights hearings in Washington. The work is boring, it's dull, it's everyday, it's pedestrian. But that's how you get the passage of civil rights legislation. Somebody can get in front of a crowd and microphones and scream at the top of his voice, but I have to say, for all my feeling for that, it's not politics. We need portraits of lives like that of Norm Rice in our literature to really understand politics. The problem is those lives aren't flashy. They lack dramatic, sensational drama. King used to say that, even with all the attention focused on him. He was certainly charismatic, and so was Malcolm—but what about the thousands of people who made King possible? That's what's also interesting. The people in the background, in the shadows.

LITTLE: *In a recent paper you gave at a conference for the National Council of Teacher Educators you cited Allan Bloom and Dinesh D'Souza and others who warn against the Balkanization of American society through multiculturalism. How do you feel about their ideas?*

JOHNSON: I first gave that paper as a way of providing an overview to foreign audiences of what the debate is in America, and I wanted to make it pro and con. I started out talking about the '60s, especially in historical terms, including Malcolm X and Martin Luther King, and the ideals of integration, and how we shifted to the black power movement. It's about literature for the most part, the emergence of different authors of color during the last twenty or thirty years. And I quote D'Souza and Bloom to indicate that there is a counter-argument, that there is opposition to what is called multiculturalism. I even quote President Bush, who gave that talk at Michigan a year ago. It came right out of Roger Kimball, *Tenured Radicals*. He used the phraseology of that book and D'Souza's book. My paper was descriptive, not promotional. I ended with a quote from Julius Lester, who is a writer I deeply admire. He speaks about his education at Fisk. It involved the canon. He didn't have any problem with it. To be honest, I don't have any problem with it either. I have no problem with reading the pre-Socratics any more than I do with reading the Vedas. We should read all those things.

One of the things we have to emphasize is that no student can hold the elementary school, high school, and university he attends responsible for his intellectual life. The only person responsible for someone's intellectual life is that person. The only thing we can do in the schools is create an atmosphere of curiosity so that people, after they get out of school, continue to be students to the very end of their days, and that's going to involve cross-cultural understanding.

I'm not sure I like the way the whole multiculturalism question is formulated. As I've said, I've been a student of Eastern philosophy since I was nineteen, when I got involved in the martial arts. All black students obviously are students of Western culture, if they are in America, right? So they're already multicultural. If you begin to look at the history of an idea, because all ideas have a history or biography, you find it threading back through time and all groups of people. For example, if you are going to study Aristotle, you've got to be able to look at what happened to Aristotle when he wasn't available in the Middle Ages but was very present in Arab countries. I think globally in that sense. I don't like some of the ways the arguments about multiculturalism have been formulated, although I think at heart they're absolutely right.

We should read as much as we possibly can from all cultures. It's that simple. For me, it never has been something I had to be noisy about. In the classes I taught, the texts were already from all sorts of different people and places. D'Souza's book pisses off a lot of people. But in a sense, he does say one or two things in there that are not all that bad. He's all for having study groups look at the work of W. E. B. Du Bois. I think we should all be looking at *The Souls of Black Folks,* and all that Du Bois did that was groundbreaking in the area of sociology. Even look at his fiction. Du Bois is a major thinker of the twentieth century. But I'm not sure D'Souza would be happy if we have to look at Iceberg Slim. I don't know if you know Iceberg Slim. There are works within black literature and black culture that are definitive and important and should be looked at, but

D'Souza is griping about mediocrity, about books that are not worth our attention. I can't help but agree with that.

LITTLE: *Wouldn't you draw a distinction between D'Souza and Bloom? Bloom has his traditional great books canon.*

JOHNSON: He does. The thing that's interesting about Bloom is that he was a philosopher. A whole lot of that book is about Plato. I have philosopher friends who like what he does with philosophy in there, but his claims are pretty extreme about women and blacks, about black studies and women's studies. It's a book that feels threatened. It's amazing that it sold as many copies as it did. But he has one line in there that really made a lot of sense to me. He says our task is to understand how Plato saw the world. That was always my sense of philosophy. I wanted to understand how Schopenhauer saw the world. I wanted to understand how Nagarjuna, among the Buddhists, saw the world. The issue is not my going to school to get images of myself, because I don't need that. I don't need a feel-good education. As Julius Lester says, you go to school to learn everything that you are not. Of course, that's ironic, because finally we are all those things, but we are not aware that we're all those things.

I'm not talking about multiculturalism so much as I am about Afrocentricism—the idea that a black student will say something like, "I'm going to study myself." I'm not sure what that means. The whole question of selfhood is a very large one. If you go back fifty generations in the life of any human being, you will discover that they share an ancestor with everybody else on the planet. Race breaks down fifty generations back. Alex Haley could trace his roots back to Africa following one side of his family—I think it was his mother's side. But if he followed his father's side, he would have ended up probably back in Europe. As a matter of fact, the book he didn't get a chance to write and was talking about doing was about how genetically mongrelized all Americans are. That, he felt, would be an even more powerful book than *Roots*. It will never get written now. That, you see, is the issue, the fact that we are a tissue of cultures. We are a tissue of races already; the concept of race, as Kwame Appiah points out, is false. Certainly in modern America there is mongrelization. So if the multiculturalists are using an outmoded notion of race, then their categories are problematic for me. I'm not going to read a book simply because it's by an Asian writer. I'm not going to read a book just because it's by a Native American, or just because it's by a black American. I want to read finely articulated thought, by whoever it is, anywhere on the planet, any culture. But it has to be something that meets the standards I bring to all literature, which means it has to disclose, reveal, and it needs to be worked over a lot in terms of revision and polishing. But I'm not interested in any work because it's by somebody from a particular race. That doesn't mean anything, finally.

LITTLE: *I find your arguments about the fluid, intersubjective nature of education and knowledge fascinating. But you don't want to use those arguments to keep out nontraditional texts, or to construct an elitist canon.*

JOHNSON: What do you mean by "elitist canon"?

LITTLE: *I mean in terms of Bloom's Eurocentricism.*

JOHNSON: Oh, no. I don't believe that. You should have Confucius, Chuang Tzŭ [Zhuangzi], and Lao Tzŭ [Laozi], and you should have the *Ten Oxherding Pictures,* and you should have the great documents out of the Hindu tradition. But those works have been around for a long time. You could go over to the philosophy department and get some of them, or you could go over to the Far Eastern departments and get other ones. They've been translated for a long, long time. They just weren't in the English departments, which were basically white male in their curriculum. Those texts are there, and the scholars are there to tell you about them, people who have devoted their entire lives to translations and interpretations. I feel extraordinarily enriched by their efforts. I couldn't have gotten it otherwise, prior to the rise of multiculturalism. That movement didn't bring those books into existence.

Now, when you say an elitist canon, I'm not sure what you're saying exactly. Some people would throw the canon out entirely. Why do we need a canon? I don't know about using the term "canon," but I do think there are certain works that have been valuable to human beings for five hundred years. Some of those works still speak to us. I finally went back and looked at Thomas à Kempis's *The Imitation of Christ.* Believe me, it *does* speak to contemporary life. The elegance of his thought, the way he delves into the human situation—it is beautiful. There are certain texts that we need to know because of the vast influence they've had on other people. That's why I say we need to know the teachings of Confucius, because they have influenced so much that people have done. We need to know the principal texts of Buddhism. We need to know the great literary works of China, India, Japan, Africa.

I do think that art is elitist. It is an elitist activity. That may sound like a strange thing to say, but I will say it. When I sit down to write a book, I put in the best thought, the best feeling, the best technique and skill I can muster. I'll go over it twenty-five times over five or ten years, I don't care. Because this may be the last utterance I make to any human being, my last statement in language. I have to be able to stand behind it. I push the language so that it's far above pedestrian, laundromat speech, or language you would overhear in the supermarket, because I care about the language. When I'm talking I can't revise my words over and over and over until they are as precise as I can make them. Also, when I write I can rethink my feelings, so that if I might hurt somebody I can look at that feeling again and try to create something that won't be harmful to others. I do believe in the masterpieces. I believe that a great work of art is a special appearance in our lives. There are works that do not have that intention. They are written for popular or commercial reasons. Some journalism has to be written too quickly for it to develop those layers of thought and feeling you find in masterworks, to reach that level where no sentence can be pulled out without disturbing the sentence in front of it, the sentence behind it, thereby making the paragraph in front of it and behind it collapse. That's the kind of art I'm talking about.

I do think art is elitist. I don't think you can substitute, just because it's a "text," an African American comic book for Melville's *Benito Cereno*. I used to be a cartoonist; I know how comic books are done. I know how much work goes into one and how much work goes into great fiction. That doesn't mean socially that I am elitist, because I'm not. But the reason I left journalism was because I couldn't do this in that field. The reason I left behind being a cartoonist was because I was looking for the means that would allow me to express the most I could. When I say best thought, best feeling, best skill, I mean even more than that. I mean the book will pull me to a new level of skill. It will demand that of me. When I start it, I will have to learn new things in order to finish it. I'm going to have to develop techniques I've never dreamed of to complete it. A great work of fiction has the same importance to me as a great work of philosophy. That's why I say it's elitist.

# AN INTERVIEW
# WITH CHARLES JOHNSON

## MARIAN BLUE

Charles Johnson
has written four books of fiction: *Faith and the Good Thing*
(Viking, 1974; Plume, 1991); *The Sorcerer's Apprentice* (Atheneum, 1986); *Oxherding Tale* (Indiana University Press, 1982);
and *Middle Passage* (Atheneum, 1990), which won the 1990
National Book Award in fiction. He has also published two collections of drawings, *Black Humor* (Johnson Publishing, 1970)
and *Half-Past Nation Time* (Aware Press, 1972), and a critical
book, *Being and Race: Black Writing Since 1970* (Indiana University Press, 1988).

BLUE: *You've been teaching creative writing at the University of
Washington for sixteen years. You've written three novels and a*

Reprinted from the *Writer's Chronicle* 25.4 (1993), by permission of Marian
Blue.

*collection of short stories, but you started as a cartoonist and journalist, and your first book was a collection of political cartoons. A recent work is a critical book. Your doctorate degree is in philosophy. How and why did you change careers?*

JOHNSON: Well, I was a cartoonist in high school actually. That was my great passion. At the age of twelve, I declared that I was going to be a commercial artist—a visual artist, to my father's great horror.

BLUE: *Why did he object?*

JOHNSON: He didn't know any artists and he didn't think I would be able to make a living. Sometimes I think he was right. But I took a two-year cartooning course through the mail. My dad paid for it because he saw I was really determined to do this. I started publishing in my own hometown around 1965 and doing illustrations for a magic catalog out of Chicago. For my high school paper, I started writing short fiction.

I was geared up to go to art school in Illinois. My high school art teacher—a man I really admired—said, "An artist is going to have such a hard life—from hand to mouth is how you're going to live. You should go to a four-year school." This was in May. So I went to my advisor and she went through her book and said Southern Illinois University was still accepting students. I said okay—I'll go there then. I decided to major in journalism, which would give me a chance to write and draw.

As soon as I hit the campus, I took my samples of published work to the campus newspaper and spent my entire undergraduate life drawing. In the next seven years I published over a thousand individual drawings. I also published the two volumes of cartoons, one in '70 and one in '72. And I did an early PBS series, *Charlie's Pad,* on which I taught people how to draw. We did fifty-two of those, fifteen minutes each. It ran about ten years around the country, even Canada. And at that time I would write for fun—short stories on my own.

I wasn't really that serious about writing fiction until 1969. When I had this idea for a novel, it kept bothering me at night.

I'd think about the character and I couldn't go to sleep. So I wrote the novel the next summer.

BLUE: *You weren't taking writing courses at the time?*

JOHNSON: No. I had journalism and philosophy as a double major. Philosophy had been a seduction for me ever since I was eighteen. But still I wanted the journalism because—again—I wanted to give my parents a degree that was marketable. I got my degree in journalism and gave it to my dad. I said, "Here, this is yours. This proves I can make a living on newspapers if I have to, but I'm going back to graduate school in philosophy." That's really around the time I was shifting over to writing novels, which I did all through my senior year and the two years I was working on a master's degree in philosophy at Southern Illinois University. I wrote about six books in two years, one every academic ten-week quarter. They were all good books in the sense that I learned from them. I don't think they were really publishable.

When I came to my seventh book, it was my last year in my master's program. Across the street in English was John Gardner, the novelist. Friends had taken classes with Gardner, and they were very enthusiastic. I opened the paper one day, and there was this ad for Gardner's class—it was called professional writing, I think—so I called him and said, "I'm a writer. I'm in the philosophy department, and I'm also on this paper part-time, and I have a novel I would like to do—a seventh novel and I'd like to get in your class to work on it." He said to come by his house, so I went by that evening. It was raining, I remember. I had six books under my arm, then put them on his dining room table. There was a room full of people in there, beginning writers. I didn't really feel like I should be in there because none of them had written a novel before, so I talked to John about it and he agreed that we would just meet in his office. That was the beginning of the first book I published, *Faith and the Good Thing,* which came out in 1974. By the time the book came out, I was a PhD student at Stony Brook. I was going to be a philosophy teacher who wrote novels on the side, sort of like Bill Gass.

BLUE: *So you were thinking of teaching at that time?*

JOHNSON: I was thinking of teaching philosophy. That was what I was geared up to do from the time I entered the master's program—I was even planning to do that as an undergraduate probably. I spent three years at Stony Brook in the PhD program and did everything but my dissertation, which I later came back to as a critical book called *Being and Race: Black Writing Since 1970*. But in my third year there, we had our first kid and I needed a job. There were no jobs in philosophy in the country at that point, in 1975 and 1976. The glory days were gone. The big period was the 1960s, early 1970s. But because I had published *Faith and the Good Thing,* the University of Washington called and asked if I wanted to apply for an opening in creative writing. Since I needed to finish the degree and since I had another novel I was really becoming immersed in— that was *Oxherding Tale*—I took the job and that's what took us from Long Island to Seattle in 1976.

I knew nothing of the Northwest—seriously, before we left I had never been west of the Mississippi. Basically, I went west for one reason: I wanted to finish *Oxherding Tale*. I was thinking I would later apply for jobs in philosophy elsewhere. But I fell in love with the city. And it's a very supportive environment— a writing program that goes all the way back to Theodore Roethke when he arrived there after WWII. I wrote and published a lot when I first got there, and they gave me early tenure after three years and an early full professorship. So I was secure and I was sort of entrenched.

BLUE: *You have a lot of magic in your books, like the god in* Middle Passage *and the witch in* Faith and the Good Thing. *Do you see your writing as magical realism?*

JOHNSON: I don't know. A friend of mine once said *magical* realism is a new word for allegory. Maybe he's right. I always associate it with South American writers and certain American writers influenced by South American writers. I wasn't thinking in those terms when I wrote *Faith and the Good Thing*. I was thinking magic, and I was thinking of a fusion of magic and realism and naturalism. I think in certain ways you could talk about my work that way, but I don't do everything in that fashion. That's my other concern. If that is appropriate for one story, fine. But I don't always write that way, and I'm not sure I always have the same intentions of magical realism. I think it's a loosely appropriate, or a weakly appropriate, term to use.

BLUE: *Are any categories useful to you when you teach or write?*

JOHNSON: No, not really—I'll say why that isn't so. I think literary categories are wonderful in terms of helping us to understand the end results of artistic production, but I think it's always important to realize that they are always artificial categories imposed upon creative work. First, we get the creative work, that's the practice. Later we get theory imposed upon practice to make sense out of it. A lot of great literature in the past we can identify as having fused two traditions, or more, or two different genres. So the slave narrative elements in *Middle Passage*—yes, they do make it a slave narrative, but it's also a philosophical novel; it's also a kind of send up of the nineteenth-century novel. You could call it, and many people do call it, a historical novel, but it's also a sea story. One of my colleagues says it starts out as a picaresque and it goes into being an epic and then it becomes a romance, and that's fairly accurate. But the reason I say all that is to say this: I think that the aesthetic category is like a little box and the work fills it up and spills beyond it. It's always richer than any particular genre definition that we come up with. What do you do with Jean Toomer's *Cane*? Part of it is poetry, part of it is sketches, part of it is narrative. The reason is the way he wrote it—his editor asked him to keep adding to it, but what form is it? Is it a novel?

Some people call it that, but if so, it is a very unusual novel. Is it a collection of short stories and sketches? It really is unique as an object in the world.

When a new art form emerges with all these elements from different forms, we say, "Oh, my god, what's all this coming at us? Look at all this rap music!" But once you really listen to the performers, you discover everybody isn't doing the same thing. I have a tendency when I do criticism—I think this is part of my background in phenomenology—to always want to go to the individual work and experience it first before I bring to it any sort of category that will be a presupposition that might prevent me from seeing something in the work. I really think it's important to let the theory come out of the experience of the individual work rather than for it to rest above the work like some kind of Platonic form. Now I also happen to believe that works are similar enough in the world that we can talk about them generically, too. Just to be able to talk about them. To even call something a "novel," we have to do that. But the work is always far richer, I think, than any one particular analysis of it.

BLUE: *Certainly* Oxherding Tale *has a feeling of mixed form—recalling* Tom Jones, *as well as Oriental philosophy. Did you begin by wanting to mix genres?*

JOHNSON: I began by wanting to work with the slave narrative and wanting to open it up, make it a vehicle for the deepest kind of philosophical probing. So I looked at scores of slave narratives to understand the inherent structure of these kinds of documents. Slave literature, we have to say, is one of the indigenous forms of American literature; and yet if you trace it back, as I believe some people have, you see elements of the form in the Puritan narrative and also in popular narrative of the nineteenth century. From the Puritan narrative, you can trace its origins to St. Augustine's *Confessions,* right? So the form fascinated me.

I think I acquired this idea of working in forms from John

Gardner because everything he wrote explored a different form. He would do novels-in-novels like *October Light*. He would do a college-story-cum-ghost-story in *Micklesson's Ghosts*. So I always have a tendency to explore, or subvert, the formal dimensions and literary tradition I'm working with for any particular novel.

So for *Oxherding Tale*, it had to be the slave narrative, but I was fascinated, too, by the question of slavery in a bigger sense than just chains and manacles: not just physical slavery but psychological slavery, sexual slavery, spiritual slavery. I wanted to make a book that would hit those levels in the course of a young man's progress from slavery to freedom and also from ignorance to enlightenment—so it travels the path of a character who is a spiritual seeker as in Eastern philosophy as well as a black person who is a slave moving towards greater freedom. All that had to enter the mix of the novel, but then you mention these eighteenth-century English novels—that is another thing I wanted to use in the shaping of this fiction. So there is a *Tom Jones* kind of feel to it—or *Joseph Andrews*—because I think those books are very delightful and they are the beginning of the English novel, so to speak. I saw the possibility for a novel to be very synthetic in its use of forms that way, but that synthesis was very difficult. I threw away 2,400 pages to get the 250 of the final manuscript.

I was going to give up on that book around Christmas of 1979. I sat down and said, "Okay, the New Year is coming. What are my projects for this year and which ones didn't I finish last year? Oh, yeah, *Oxherding Tale*. Let's just get rid of this book. Let's just think of all the reasons it can't be done. Okay, I'm not going to do this book because the main character, Andrew Hawkins, is boring to me. He's just like every other character in every other slave story I've ever read." So then it hit me—what if he's *mulatto*? Suppose he is of the white world and the black world, on this dividing line where he would experience the stresses of the racial world in the greatest way? "So,"

I said, "okay, that's a possibility but no, no, no. Another reason I can't do this book is because one of his masters is just as boring to me as that character." He was a male and very oppressive, just like every other master. Then it hit me, now wait a minute, suppose I shift genders? Suppose this is a woman? I said, "Ah, well, now that would open up the story to interesting possibilities about sexuality as well, right?" So Flo Hatfield introduced herself. I kept rethinking all the reasons I was giving myself for why I couldn't write this book—so I started again on New Year's day of 1980 and it was finished the following summer.

BLUE: *You also gave Andrew Hawkins a very good education for the time. Was that to give you access or to keep him on the edge?*

JOHNSON: He has literally an education very much like John Stuart Mill. I wanted Andrew to be at the very end of Western knowledge so that he was poised for the kinds of revelations you would get from the East, from Buddhism, Taoism, Hinduism, and the rest. In so many words, he doesn't have to pass through in book learning what Westerners already know. So what's left then are the questions that might, I felt, be deeper, such as the mystery of the self and personal identity which I think are discussed very eloquently for two to three thousand years in the Eastern tradition.

And then *nobody* understood that book. My agent must have sent the book to twenty-five publishers. This was around 1980, and I do think the climate for black American literature was such that we had certain kinds of books in mind that we thought were appropriate—usually the protest novel or the up-from-slavery or up-from-the-ghetto novel. This was a *philosophical* novel that was doing all the things we're talking about. A lot of people just couldn't figure out what in the devil was going on, *but* John Gallman did at Indiana University Press. He published that book, *Oxherding Tale,* and Raymond Federman's *The Twofold Vibration* at the same time. *Oxherding Tale* received good reviews, and the best of all reviews was Stanley Crouch's in the *Village Voice*—two pages. That review led to the book being purchased by Grove Press for paperback, which kept it in print for many years so it could build an audience.

BLUE: *Education and environment play more of a role for both Andrew Hawkins and Rutherford Calhoun than race. You boil your characters down to humanness before establishing racial influences. Do you believe in genetic factors?*

JOHNSON: I certainly don't believe in any form of racial essentialism at all. I think environment is far more important. Nurture more than nature in the case of a character's development. I'm not going to say that biology doesn't factor in because I do think all these things are factors but, no, my characters do not have any inherent racial natures. The reason it was interesting for me to make Andrew a mulatto was because it raises the whole question of racial identity. I mean, he belongs to both the white world and the black world simultaneously, and he catches a lot of heat from either side. I think it's very important for us to realize, particularly right about now when there's so much racial polarization and tension—and I would like to quote Kwame Anthony Appiah, a philosopher in African American studies at Harvard—that we are already contaminated by each other. I do believe he is quite right, culturally as well as genetically. If you go back to about 700 AD, you will find that we all share a common ancestor because the world was not that populated and racial interbreeding has been a fact for thousands of years.

I think we sometimes have to go to genetics to clarify all the nonsense that's in the air that causes antagonism between the races. If you look at Appiah's book, a wonderful book called *In My Father's House,* you'll see that our theory of race has its history going back only a couple of hundred years. We're trying to scientifically categorize races and making lots of mistakes and having all these different races among Europeans that don't make very much sense to us at all today. Some of those erroneous ideas and categories were picked up by W. E. B. Du Bois in the nineteenth century when he began to think about racial nationalism for black people. So our racial notions have a history, but again they are imposed upon human experience, and I think they do violence to human experience. I mean I was horrified by the violence during the Los Angeles riots. We have not worked out in one hundred years the fundamental questions that brought Nat Turner to his rage of violence in the early nineteenth century. We haven't. They are still with us today, right?

BLUE: *Meanwhile ideas of race are creating limitations for writers. Some say whites can't write black; Native Americans can't write white; men can't write women.*

JOHNSON: I know it.

BLUE: *That would seem to limit all writers to writing monologues.*

JOHNSON: Actually, that would limit everyone to writing autobiography. I take a real strong position against that in *Being and Race: Black Writing Since 1970.* You cannot make that argument and convince me unless we have far stronger evidence than we have, because throughout time great writers have always been able to transpose themselves imaginatively into not just the racial other, but the sexual other and also into other historical periods.

What this argument says is that, in effect, you can't imagine what it's like to be in the nineteenth century. You close off all historical curiosity. Coming here I was just reading John Updike's new book, *Memories of the Ford Administration.* The author has to go back and imagine in minute detail everything he can in the terms of the senses for President Buchanan's world. On the basis of the argument that you can't write other than what you are, he could never do that. Or take a look at Joyce Carol Oates's *Because It Is Bitter and Because It Is My Heart.* She writes alternately from the two principal characters, one a white girl and one a black boy. These are people she *knows,* people that she has observed, that she has been close to early in her life. She pulls it off in such a way that I am convinced that she knows what she is talking about. Writers have always done that, and always will do that, regardless of people who, for one political reason or another, feel that their territory is being appropriated. I think that we learn in terms of our own knowledge of other people through literature, and transposing ourselves imaginatively—with all the information we can muster through research—is one of the ways we do that. Now it's not a complete transposition. You can't live another person's life. But you can through empathy and sympathy try to transpose yourself over there behind another's eyes. If that argument is true—that we are bound by our race or origins—then all the years I was planning to teach philosophy—and I still do teach one class at Washington that is highly philosophical in terms of aesthetics and criticism for our graduate students—it means I could not teach Martin Heidegger because I have no real connection to the Black Forest and the language spoken there. It means finally no black person is going to be able to teach anything other than that which is supposedly black American. Now how are you going to slice *that* pie because you've got black Americans that grew up in the South and black Americans who grew up in the West. You are going to have to ultimately say that because Charlie Smith, a black slave in Texas, did not grow up in Alabama, he had better not try to talk about the experiences of people there. Ultimately that argument forces us not only to autobiography, it forces us to solipsism, the self only knowing its own operations. Finally, all possibility of knowledge, intersubjectivity, shared knowledge among people, breaks down; and if that breaks down, science breaks down. Communication breaks down. It's not even an argument. It's a very insidious statement for people to make.

BLUE: *Do you believe it's a kind of censorship?*

JOHNSON: Indeed, I think it's a form of censorship. I've seen it occur, for example, with women in women's studies who are very protective and don't want a man to teach that subject because it's hard enough to get women hired and why have a man be hired in women's studies? I understand the politics of the argument, but the whole thrust of women studies has to be ultimately for a man to be able to immerse himself deeply enough below—or, if you want, *beyond*—polarized notions of gender to understand and be able to articulate something about female experience. Everything we're talking about with integration in terms of America—certainly with black people—hinges on some ability to understand across racial lines. But that other argument means knowledge is racially bound. That's scary. Ultimately, that is racist. That's Nazism. That's fascism. Yes, it disturbs me greatly.

BLUE: *How about the modified version? It's okay to write about people not of your race, gender, etc., but it had better be favorable. A sighted person better not write about a nasty blind character. A man had better not write about a vicious woman.*

JOHNSON: I think that's censorship and really tying the writer to a lie. It might be one that is politically correct or something, but I just don't think it's allowing the writer to speak the truth of what he or she sees. You'll notice in *Oxherding Tale* and *Middle Passage*—I don't know what people think about this—but both the masters of Andrew Hawkins and Rutherford Calhoun are not evil masters. They aren't the kind you've seen stereotyped over and over again in every novel and every PBS drama, a few of which I even wrote. I have written more obligatory scenes of the slave running away and then the horses coming with the night riders and capturing this guy and beating him. You see the scars on his back—it's almost like a convention. But in those two novels we have masters—and there were masters like this—who didn't want to be masters, who didn't approve of the institution of slavery, who wanted to free their slaves at the first opportunity. But because of the world they were in, it was very difficult to do. I think we need a whole picture if we are really going to have any sense of what a remarkable period of history this was. Every human possibility was played through during the slave era. I read a review of a study of a black man who was freed by his master, who did rather well on his own, who bought slaves himself and then did not free them as he himself was freed, right? All these stories are wonderful and remarkable, but they're complex and they are ambiguous and they do not lead to easy cut-and-dried kinds of discussions. For example, most people really don't want to admit, and don't even want to think about, the fact that Europeans seldom went into the interior of Africa to get slaves. They waited on the west coast of Africa for Africans, or Arabs, to bring the slaves. It has been pointed out that the Ashanti grew fat on the slave trade. And to this very day, there are Africans who, when they hear African Americans talk about slavery, are contemptuous. They say, well, we sold you into slavery; we never were slaves, okay? The world is a very complex place.

BLUE: *All the Africans on the slave ship in* Middle Passage *are Allmuseri. Is that a real African tribe?*

JOHNSON: No. It's totally fictitious.

BLUE: *It has an interesting mix of philosophies.*

JOHNSON: Well, I first mention it in "The Education of Mingo," a story in *The Sorcerer's Apprentice.* He had to be from *some* tribe. And, again, since I was working on those stories and *Oxherding Tale* at the same time, I also made a character named Reb from the Allmuseri tribe. Well, all these people on the ship have to be Africans from somewhere, so what tribe? I could use a real tribe or I could invent a tribe. I wanted to create a tribe culturally that was counterpoised to the materialism of the West. I wanted this to be the most spiritual tribe imaginable. I wanted it to be a whole tribe of Mother Teresas and Gandhis.

I got the name, Allmuseri, when I was doing some research on *Faith and the Good Thing.* I read eighty books on magic; one of the books was on Africa and mentioned an African tribe that had a place like a hut that was called an *Al-museri.* It's an Arab term that means a spiritual gathering place or a mosque. That was in my notes, so what I did was drop out the hyphen and add another "l" and make Allmuseri. I have learned most recently that Al-museri means "Egyptian" as well. The Egyptian airline is called Al-museri. People joke about this airline, which they say doesn't have the best service, and they call it Air Misery.

For the character of the tribe, I went to every source I could think of. For example, Rutherford learns that if you are an explorer going to their tribe, which is hidden deep in Africa, the tribe members will spit at your feet. For a Westerner, that's an insult. For an Allmuseri, they figure you've traveled a long way and your feet are hot and tired and they are going to cool them with moisture. There is a tribe that does that. But then there are other things, like the Allmuseri priests who carry brooms and sweep in front of them so they don't step on innocent creatures too small for them to see because they cherish life—Hindu priests do that. It's mentioned that they have a holiday where they give up a selfish desire. That is actually a Hindu practice in a village in India. I made up very little. I just borrowed from different third world cultures to create a composite tribe that I wanted to be as non-Western in its values as possible. So this is the cargo brought on the ship by Captain Falcon, who is this kind of arch-character, the ultimate Ahab, sort of a super Wolf Larson. What we have is this conflict of values and conflict of vision that is played out painfully on the ship from the time they are brought on until the time the ship sinks. The consequence is that the values of the Westerners are changed.

BLUE: *The lead Allmuseri mentions that they are all also changed, no longer the same people.*

JOHNSON: Certainly they have been changed by the Westerners, as well. Because that's another question, a very important question. You are talking about transposition from one culture into another—from Africa to the New World. Well, when does that exactly happen? Does it happen with the learning of the language—because all language embodies a vision of the world? Does it happen in the so-called seasoning camps—these characters don't get that far because the ship sinks—which is the place where slaves were taken before they were sold? Or was it later, once they were in the New World? I suggest on this ship that these characters interpenetrate and change and transform each other. On the ship the people who survive— this is probably true of everything I write—are the ones who are capable of change. It's Squibb who is transformed by his exposure to the Allmuseri, to the extent that, even when he's working with Rutherford to save his life, his touch is almost like the Allmuseri. And it's Rutherford who learns their language and part of their vision, which he brings back to his encounter with Isadora. Those two survive and the little girl and some of the African kids. The characters who don't survive largely are those who cannot change. The nouns die in my books and the verbs go on. I think life is a process, more process than product. So even at the end of the book when you see Rutherford and Isadora, you know, well, that is the end of *that* story because the beginning, middle, and end are there— the action is completed—but that's not the end of their lives together. I would hope there would be a sort of telescoping beyond the book in terms of those characters and where they are going because they are still going somewhere.

BLUE: *Change has certainly been a part of the history of writing programs since you've been teaching. Weren't you once on the AWP Board early in your career?*

JOHNSON: I was director of the AWP short fiction contest for three years. Right after that I served on the board of directors. So all together, I worked for AWP for six years in the 1980s.

BLUE: *That's a long commitment.*

JOHNSON: I like the organization. I like the people. Any organization that's celebrating its twenty-fifth anniversary has become an institution in my opinion—a quarter of a century. It's part of the structural landscape of American arts and letters.

BLUE: *With the increase in writing programs, and general support of the writing community, do you think the general body of writing has been improving?*

JOHNSON: That's a good question. We must have I think over three hundred writing programs—AWP has the catalog. I think there is no poverty of writing instruction for those who want to learn. That's a very positive thing. Some of our best writers are at the moment teaching. Therefore, the benefit of what they just learned last night in their own work is given to their students the next morning or afternoon in the workshop.

It's a rare thing, but I've seen some unfortunate tendencies— I'm not the only person to point this out—the workshop situation tends to produce a kind of generic story. That is to say, you don't have stories on the far extreme of really terrible or really wonderful but rather in the middle of publishable. Because the workshop situation is almost like a committee situation, the story isn't offensive to a lot of people but rather hits this middle zone. Now, if that's what the writer wants, that's terrific—just to publish and to publish in certain contemporary markets—I think the workshop will help you do that. But one always wonders what would happen if a Kafka or a Dostoevski had fallen into a writers' workshop today and how the work would be received. Would somebody say, "*What* are you *doing* with this cockroach? What's going on here?" and "I don't understand this! *Make* me understand this!" I think Kafka and Dostoevski wouldn't last too long in a workshop. I think maybe they would benefit from learning the techniques that are presented by the teacher; but I think finally some writers have to go off alone and make their risky inventions, then show them after they are done.

We want originality of vision. We want fiction that breaks new ground. We want fiction that *advances* the form of the novel, the form of the short story. If you are talking about that, you are talking about something that will be maybe looked upon with shock in the workshop as well as in an editor's office. So it's always a risk, right, but that's always true of any creative art. When Picasso first began exhibiting, there were painters who swore up and down that they would devote themselves to ruining him because they felt he was destroying painting with what he was doing. Breakthroughs make people very nervous.

BLUE: *People talk about problems with limits imposed on what type of writing can be discussed in workshop; genre fiction is regarded as inferior. Do you see that as a problem?*

JOHNSON: One of my students was once told in a workshop, "I don't want anybody writing . . .", then the teacher just went down the list: science fiction, western, all the so-called pop categories. That, of course, is very deceptive. Look at the great works of science fiction; they simply happen to be fine works of literature that all use science in a particular way. And you can't reduce H. G. Wells that way. He happens to be one of the greatest English writers. Period.

There are certain basic storytelling things—I don't care what it is you're doing—that you are going to have to achieve for any reader whether it's a murder mystery or science fiction or any genre. I'm going to have to care about the people. I'm going to have to have language that in a funny kind of way is both accessible and at the same time a revelation if it is really going to be language that does all the things language should do— not just operate on the same level as supermarket speech or speech you hear in the laundromat. You might find something that is pure delight in genre fiction. Again, look at the individual work and try to make sense out of it; don't make judgments before you encounter the individual text. I like to keep a workshop open for all kinds of possibilities. My colleagues do the same thing. You have to be real careful about saying no to certain genres. They are artificial. What's real is the work. Division in writing programs is unfortunate.

BLUE: *How about division in your own life, in your own writing—do you schedule your writing time?*

JOHNSON: Not really. If I'm working on something, that's

all I work on at that time. This year I worked on screenplays. I did a screenplay for Columbia Pictures in January—first draft, on Tuskegee Airmen. I really enjoyed doing that—the Black Flyers who trained at Tuskegee Institute in 1942 who then later went on to the European theatre and had a remarkable record. I think it was 1,500 missions and they never lost a single bomber as bomber escorts. I started writing the first day of January, and I set myself a limit of ten pages a day. Some days I got five, some days I got seventeen, but by the end of the month it was done. I work on binges like that. On a day I've got nothing else to do, I get up and write all day—sometimes I won't eat, actually—and all night. I live it. It's at the dinner table with me; it's when I go to the bathroom. It's when I'm falling asleep. There's this real emotional connection that goes through the whole thing. I will go until I can't think of anything more to say or I just need to go to bed, but then my mind is still working on it and I may jump up in the middle of the night. Most of the stories in *Sorcerer's Apprentice* were written in anywhere from two to four days. The longest one was "Education of Mingo," which I started in New York and brought with me to Seattle; I finished it in about four days. But then I go over and over them after the first draft to polish and revise.

BLUE: *Your activities make you sound like a composite character. You're a partner in a martial arts studio. You teach. You write screenplays and you're making plans for your next novel on Martin Luther King, Jr. You have a family. How do you fit it all in?*

JOHNSON: A very simple way to focus and divide your life up is in terms of mind, body, and spirit. I needed something that would be pure physical exercise. I came to martial arts very early when I was nineteen. And I loved it. I had played soccer in high school and that was okay, but the martial arts were something I could study forever. I think everybody should get in an hour or hour and a half every day of some kind of physical exercise for their own overall benefit. And philosophy I loved because that was for the development of the mind. And in terms of development of the spirit, for me that was always art. Art has always been a large part of my spiritual life, and it is very much tied in with my long-term interest in Buddhism. The concentration that people bring to writing and art is very often compared by certain writers to the concentration involved in meditation, and the two really do fuse at certain points. Family life is of course an extension of that, I believe, because everything I do is for my wife and kids and, I hope, for their benefit. So it's all part of one life and one person. So when I'm not writing, I'm doing these other things that all are related to writing. It's just a question of the time and the day and how to fit everything in, but you can fit everything in because—well, I just think you can.

# CHARLES JOHNSON: INTERVIEW

## LINDA DAVIES

C HARLES JOHNSON IS
the author of the short-story collection *The Sorcerer's Apprentice* (1986 PEN/Faulkner Award nominee) and the highly
acclaimed novels *Faith and the Good Thing, Oxherding Tale,* and
*Middle Passage* (winner of the 1990 National Book Award). He
teaches creative writing, as he has for the past sixteen years, at
the University of Washington in Seattle, where he lives with his
wife of twenty years and their two children.

DAVIES: *One of the things I noticed in* Middle Passage *is that
each of your characters speaks some substantial truth. There
are no unnecessary characters. That struck me as sensible,
considering your background in philosophy. How did you*

Reprinted from *Glimmer Train Stories* 8 (Fall 1993), by permission of
Linda Davies.

come to be a person who seeks truth and works to put it out there?

JOHNSON: Well, I don't know if that's a reflex of my philosophy; it might be something I learned from John Gardner when I was a student, many years ago. He was a good friend of mine for about a decade. I hope you're right when you say that every character has a truth. Although I think that in most fiction there's one character who bears the author's message or burden necessarily, and all the others are foils or strawmen, my characters pass through a social world in which everybody they meet has a truth which they pick up on and learn from— sort of Hegelian in that respect—so that by the end of the story, there is a grand vision, a larger truth, that the main character experiences. So the truth is not static, but is something to be achieved. It's always a process and the more people you encounter the more your sense of understanding about the world deepens. I think that's one of the reasons the characters all speak something that's important to whoever the protagonist is.

DAVIES: *I really liked the lack of stereotypes in the characters. Captain Ebenezer Falcon is a hateable guy—but not totally.*

JOHNSON: Oh, yeah. He's a loathsome character, a monster of the ego, but he is, I hope, interesting. And he has reasons for being who he is and thinking as he does. John Gardner used to emphasize that with all of his writing students. It's John who put it in front of me in a very clear way when he was looking at chapters that I was writing for *Faith and the Good Thing*. There is one character—the husband of Faith—who was based on a good friend of mine, but I objected to many of his ideas, and so I used him as a strawman in the novel. John wrote in the margins: "Shame on you. Why present this character to us just for us to dislike this person, or to disagree with him? Why not dig as deeply as you can into his motivation, his background, his biography, his thought process, so we can understand how someone can inhabit this position?" And, you know, I think he was right. You have to see each and every character in their totality and from their own perspective. We can disagree with them, but they have integrity as human beings that has to come through at some point in the fiction.

DAVIES: *I believe that if we can get fully enough into another person's shoes, we'll be able to make sense of what goes on in their heads.*

JOHNSON: I do think so. I think writers have to do that with every character. You have to walk a mile in everybody else's shoes within that book, every major character's, at least.

DAVIES: *Occasionally,* Glimmer Train *will publish an author more than once and sometimes, as we see more of a person's work, we'll begin to see a theme taking shape that wouldn't have shown itself in just one story. I wonder if you feel something like that happening in your work?*

JOHNSON: I think it's clearly there—from the very first book I published to the new book I'm working on about Martin Luther King. The primary issue that I run into over and over and over again is the nature of the self, whatever that is, and the nature of human consciousness. I'm interested in that because of my background in philosophy. I'm interested in the nature of the self in our larger cultural discussions of identity, personal identity, racial identity, and so forth. I'm interested in where I end and you begin, for example, the difference between self and other. Those are deep mysteries, they really are. I think Eastern philosophy delivers a great many works that help us think about the question, which is why I always return to that. Also, phenomenology is a very useful way—in the history of Western philosophy—to angle in on the subject. You can see it over all my works. It's picked up with different characters and a different dramatic situation in one story and returned to in another, but all from different angles. Maybe all of our stories are ultimately about the nature of the self. I think that is finally the ultimate question: Who am I?

# Charles Johnson: Interview (1993)

DAVIES: *The Allmuseri tribe in* Middle Passage *embodies very non-Western values. The protagonist, Rutherford Calhoun, grows substantially through his association with those people. He also seems to develop a greater affection for America on that journey. Would you name what you consider to be some primary Western values and then tell me which of those is especially valuable to you?*

JOHNSON: Primary Western values? Okay, I can tell you what some of those are, but let me sort out one or two things because I have said that the Allmuseri are very non-Western. That was my intention, to create a very non-Western tribe, and I think they are in many ways, but they're human. They show something very deep about what human possibilities are. And Falcon to me does not represent all of Western or American existential possibilities. Rutherford's brother, Jackson, is very much a part of the novel, too, and Isadora, and they're both different from Rutherford and from Falcon. But, yes, there are certain American values that I do find extremely important. One is tolerance, at least as an ideal—sometimes we don't practice as well as we should. The appreciation of individuality is also extremely important in the Western world. We can trace that all the way back, if one wishes, to probably Greece. Also, the emphasis on reason or the rational faculties—again, that likely goes back to Aristotle. Those are three things I think that made possible the Enlightenment, that made possible the world that we live in.

DAVIES: *I read that you said, "Change and process, verbs rather than nouns, are the most important part" of your stories. How do you think we can tell what changes we need to make? Is this a constructive decision that we make, in your opinion, or is it simply an ability to flex in response to a need?*

JOHNSON: Well, I think it could be the latter. That is to say, adjusting flexibly to new situations as they arise, but I also think it could be, and ideally would be, a conscious thing. Maybe I could give you an example. Something I've done now for—how long now?—since 1980, is the practice of meditation, which is central to the practice of Buddhism. I find meditation to be a refuge and a source of renewal, but one of the things that we do in meditation is work on ourselves. There are meditations I do that I hope will lead to the opening up of, as they say in the literature, the heart—the so-called heart center. There was a point at which I was wondering if I was caring enough and loving enough and responding enough with the heart as opposed to with the head, and so I worked specifically on that. I would like to think that I made some constructive changes in that way. So I do think you can consciously work on those very things we would like to achieve, and direct where the process of one's life goes.

DAVIES: *So those decisions can be made without being pinched—without need?*

JOHNSON: I think you feel the need at some point—an internal pinch, perhaps it could be an external pinch, but it might be a combination of both of them—and you suddenly realize there's something more that you should be doing. And it is your potential to do it. It is something you can do, so the only question then becomes: How do I do it? I think we do it by, basically, trial and error, by repetition, and seeing if it works this way and works that way, and finally you get there. That's where the flexibility comes in—and you have to have patience.

DAVIES: *What changes, what kind of flexing do you think we need to do as a nation in the balance of this century so that we can live together more effectively and companionably in the next?*

JOHNSON: Boy, there's a big question—in the next century, which is fast approaching. That's a perpetual meditation for me. My way of answering the question is to immerse myself in the first twelve and a half years Martin Luther King was a public figure, was the nation's preacher, was our creative and ethical philosopher—to immerse myself in the evolution of his thought, and precisely what his position was at the time of his death, April 4, 1968, at the Lorraine Motel. If we, in fact, kept somewhere within our consciousness the idea of the beloved community, as King spoke about it, I think we would be more or less on the right track. It's a community that's, in King's case, based on social gospel Christianity. I don't think it would necessarily have to be that, but it would have to be based on an attitude in which we realize that, whatever it is we're dealing with, it is us. Maybe it's you, or it's me, but whoever it is I'm dealing with, that person is a part of me; I'm connected to that person. The world is a place of mutual relatedness and mutual connectedness and, as King said in one of his speeches, a beautiful speech, he said that when you get up in the morning, and do everything you have to do to go to work—you eat breakfast, you brush your teeth, you take a bath—you have relied upon the entire rest of the world. If you trace the physical evidence of where all the objects in this room came from—the coffee and tea from Colombia, that fabric over there may have been woven in a different country—we suddenly realize that the world really is a tissue that points to the presence of other people, their lives, their labors. That kind of consciousness might lead us away from the polarity, ethnic antagonism, and so forth. But it's a consciousness that has to be in the public arena. We have to be constantly reminded of it through the media, which bombards us with many other kinds of things that are alienating. I think literature has the obligation of doing that, to make us aware of how subtle and complex, and finally, how interwoven our lives all are. We need that consciousness and, again, this is why I'm saying that our most important questions are "Who am I?" and questions of the self. If we had that consciousness, I think we would approach each other differently.

DAVIES: *I'm sure that's true.*

JOHNSON: But that has been one of the tasks, I think, of humanity for as long as there has been humanity. You know, someone once said that if everybody acted like Gandhi and Mother Teresa, we wouldn't need governments. We have to try the best we can, I think, to communicate a vision that is all-inclusive, but all-inclusive from the inside, not from the outside. I think that could be a problem, by saying that all these people are different and you have to respect their differences and be together whether you want to or not. People revolt against that, but if they can see from the inside just how involved historically, genetically even, all our lives are, it could make a great difference. It's been pointed out by some geneticists that if we go back to the year AD 800, about fifty generations, we will find that every human being on the planet shares a common ancestor. I mean, it's there in the genes. It's there in our history, of people who have interacted since, my goodness, the ancient world. But somehow we lose sight of that. Our dramas need to emphasize that more, I think.

DAVIES: *You have a longtime involvement with the martial arts.*

JOHNSON: Pretty long, I guess—since I was nineteen.

DAVIES: *What drew you to it, initially, and what have you gotten from it that you didn't anticipate?*

JOHNSON: That I didn't anticipate? I started with a school in Chicago, and I had wanted to study martial arts because I had a friend in high school who, you know, left over the summer and came back practicing karate, which I thought was very interesting. I also tried judo when I first went to college—I went to one class, and I didn't like the idea of falling down all the time. I'll let the other guy fall down. So I was looking for a school, and in the summer of '67, I heard about one in Chicago. It was a kung fu school. At that time, I couldn't sort out kung fu from karate; I thought it didn't really matter. But this was a remarkable school for its time—a very dangerous school, and I've written about it now. This was before safety regulations, when instructors could have a little private stage, if they wanted one. It really was a demanding school. Our first test involved throwing forty-five punches in ten seconds to the front, back, and side—just physical kinds of things like that, right? But, also, there was instruction in philosophy. I remember the instructor

said that you don't have to be Buddhist to get good at this particular martial art, but it helps. Since I was never sure if I was
going to walk out of there alive, I thought maybe I should look
at anything I could to improve my chances. So I began, actually, looking at Buddhism and Eastern philosophy then. It
taught me some very interesting things—personal discipline and
humility—and I've seen this in every other martial-arts school
of quality. My son is a young martial artist. He's seventeen, and
this May he won a first and second place in kata and *kumite*
at a tournament in Seattle. I wanted him to learn these same
things, too—he started very early on, when he was about eight.
One goes out on the deck in front of another person that you're
going to spar with, with the intention, if it's a sparring situation, of helping each other learn. You bring nothing except your
*gi*, if it's karate, your pants and your shirt, and your belt that
shows how much work you've put in. That's all. You don't bring
anything other than your performance and your hard work and
sweat. "Kung fu" means "hard work," by the way. That's one
of the meanings of the word. Your father's history doesn't make
a difference, you know, your family background—none of that
makes a difference. What you do right then at that moment,
and what spirit you do it in, is the most important thing. It also
teaches you how to push your own limits. Things that you
*thought* might have been your limits, you suddenly discover are
not. I remember how I felt that the first time I broke wood, five
inches of wood, with my hand.

DAVIES: *People really do that?*

JOHNSON: People really do that. I had never done it, you
know, until—actually, it wasn't at my kung fu school—I was
at a karate school in Long Island, and it was part of our rank
test. I remember asking the instructor, "I've never done this.
How do I do this?"

He said, "Well, just think through the board."

And so I did. It was like it wasn't there. Your hand is a little
tender afterward, but you suddenly realize your own physical

capabilities after a while. And so you test yourself. It's always about testing yourself, improving. You can spend years learning one set—in karate, it's called kata; in kung fu, we call them sets—and it might have twenty moves or it might have a thousand moves. But you might spend ten years trying to master every move in that set to, as we say, honor the form. I find that intriguing.

Living simply is another virtue that usually is communicated through martial-arts practice. Most schools involve some meditation, too, at the end of class when you cool down. You train so that you're physically and mentally and psychologically and spiritually able to go out and be of greater service to those people who are closest to you, who need your help outside the school, that is to say, family and friends. And not just help in terms of self-defense, but to be there when they need something, regardless of what you might feel like at the moment. You're there for them. I think, basically, what martial arts do is train remarkably good citizens—for those who go in with the right attitude.

Some people just go into the martial arts because they want to get involved in a brawl or to learn self-defense. Usually, they'll come into the school because they fear something. I started in 1967, when there was a lot of racial violence and one of my friends, who was Jewish and had long hair, got beat up and hospitalized. So everybody usually comes into the school with that intention of "I want to defend myself," but later on, you realize that there's something far beyond just the physical aspect. There's something behind, beneath, and below this that is really much greater.

There are wonderful myths about a black belt. You know, everyone starts out with a white belt as a beginner. In principle, what it means is that the more you work and sweat, the darker the belt gets, until it's brown. Finally, it's so dark, it's black. Then, finally, after many, many years beyond black belt, you begin to see it fray and the white threads underneath begin to show. So it's almost like this passage from innocence to experience to a kind of innocence again on the other side. What one realizes, I think, after the black belt, is that you are now just ready to begin life. It's not the end. It is really the beginning. People in the martial arts always say this: "It's a way of life." I do feel that way. For me, there is an equivalent among all the martial arts, it doesn't matter which style you study. At one time, there were a thousand styles out there. It's okay. I think that if someone studies tai chi chuan, which I think is remarkably good for health and fitness and children can study it and so can people who are senior citizens, or if somebody takes a hard style like tae kwon do, that's fine, or a Chinese kung fu . . . it really doesn't matter as long as the spirit is there.

Our teacher over our system in San Francisco, grand master Doc Tai Wong, says that fighters are lovers. It takes a while before you really understand what that is. You do this, obviously, because you love it, because you're rewarded by it. It isn't out of fear or anger, but out of a real deep sense of love. You become very bonded with the other people in the school. You've known them for a decade or better and you've all worked out together and grown old together and helped each other. It's really kind of nice, and it's everybody—it doesn't matter— blacks, whites, males, females, younger people, teenagers, as well as older people. The idea of the school, the *kwoon*—and that's part of a story I published a couple of years ago in *Playboy:* that's its title, "Kwoon"—it's almost like a little society.

DAVIES: *It sounds very lovely. I didn't have that perspective on the martial arts.*

JOHNSON: Well, it's there. Most people see only one image of the martial arts, and that's the Hollywood version. But there's much more there. When I first started, at nineteen, I wasn't aware of that. It was only a little bit later that I began to look back and say, Now, wait a minute. There was a reason why the emphasis on practicing forms was always greater than just getting out and sparring. Sparring is what the young guys like to do, score points and all that, and your ego's in it. After a certain point, your ego is *not* in it. You realize that this form is very old, been practiced all over the world, in the West and in the East, for about 150 years and it's a cultural item. At the same time, it is a fighting set.

DAVIES: *I wonder if you were consciously seeking something like that to fill in an important place in your life?*

JOHNSON: I don't think I knew it was taking me to that place. But I know that during those times when I fell away from training for a while, maybe I got busy with something else for a year, I would miss it to such an extent that nothing would fill that void. You know, there was nothing that really compared, that did the same things for me, no other form of physical activity, because, somehow, the other dimensions, the cultural dimension, the philosophical dimensions, were not there. I didn't find anything that was really comparable. I think this is true of a lot of people I've talked to who had been out for a while—they *had* to come back. I think it's after the fact that you realized that this has been very good for you in a number of different ways.

I have seen things over the years in martial-arts classes that have astonished me. There was a club I was working out with in southern Illinois, which was different from the Chicago school, and there was a guy everybody could beat up on. I forget who this guy was now, but I remember everyone used to beat up on him and when it came time to spar with him, we'd say, "Oh no, not him! Good grief." Well, I watched him over a year—all the humiliation, all of the defeats—he never gave up! He really wanted this. He was not athletic or physically talented in any way. But he had overcome all of that, so that when he arrived at the place where so many other people in the class found easy to get to, you know, their first rank promotion, he had truly won. I think everybody recognized that and the respect factor for him, from where he had to come from to arrive at this place, was very high in the group. That's what impresses me more than anything else. You can be the tortoise or the hare, and he was not the hare. He was the tortoise, but he won the race. I'm convinced of that. There were a lot of flashy guys who were very athletic, the hares, who could just run circles around him, but they would fade away. They would lose interest. They would want to do something else, but he was very, very steady. Many martial artists, by the way, have started out with some physical handicap. Some of the greatest masters have started out with a physical handicap of one kind or another, and that's why they began martial-art training, to find a way to compensate for that. So I found it to be something that revives people's spirits.

DAVIES: *Sounds really marvelous. On a personal basis, I have been needing to find some physical form that is both strenuous and peacemaking, because that doesn't come to me very easily.*

JOHNSON: You know, tai chi chuan might be exactly right. It's very slow, but very controlled. You work a great deal on your breathing. Although it is a martial art, it takes a little bit longer to become street-effective with tai chi than with some others, maybe ten years, but you can do this until age seventy or eighty. It increases your balance and coordination and teaches you patience. It's a good thing. I have increasing admiration for tai chi.

DAVIES: *What do you hope your children will tell their children about you after you're gone?*

JOHNSON: I can't imagine my kids with kids. That's hard. Let me think about that for a minute. It's like writing what you'd like your epitaph to say. What would I want them to say about their grandfather? I already know what I want on my headstone.

DAVIES: *Oh, you do? What?*

JOHNSON: Actually, a friend of mine made it up for me and gave it to me as a present. We were both working on a master's degree in philosophy. I was pretty much immersed in Marxism at that time, and he in Eastern philosophy—we reversed those positions later on when he shifted to Marxism as he went further into the program at Northwestern and I began to move closer to Eastern philosophy when I was in the program at Stony Brook. A couple of years ago, he gave me a plaque with the symbol of the head of somebody on the path, pursuing the way, or the Tao. That I could very well have on my headstone. I guess I wouldn't mind my children and grandchildren having that sense of me as somebody who basically was a seeker after truth, as much as he could get into his lifetime. And maybe somebody who really believed in, maybe foolishly, those old virtues from the pre-Socratic era: the good, the true, and the beautiful. Those are very, very important to me—however we might interpret them, however we might try to seek them. I think John Gardner was very much about that too, and that's one of the reasons I was attracted to him as a mentor. That's what I would like them to see—that's what I was after. Whether I'll achieve it or not, I don't know.

DAVIES: *You have already told me a bit about what you value. May I ask from whom have you learned the most about that which matters the most to you?*

JOHNSON: The most? That's a hard one because you learn something from everyone, all the time. In one way or another, everybody is a teacher. I can't think of one person from whom I've learned more than anyone else, unless, quite possibly, it's my father. Quite possibly.

DAVIES: *May I ask what specific thing, what gift he gave you?*

JOHNSON: It wasn't so much a gift; it wasn't anything he was perfectly conscious of. My dad had me when he was twenty-five. He got through fifth grade and he was a farmboy who came north to work with his uncle, my great-uncle, who ran a construction company, to make a little money. He met my mother; they got married and had me, one kid. He didn't go back to the farm. My mom didn't like farms; she didn't want to leave the city to go back down to the farm. But, you know, we were his life. He was willing to make sacrifices for both of us, even though the fact was that living on the farm was very idyllic to him because they grew all their own food and were very self-sufficient. But even more than that, my father used to work two and three jobs. I remember this clearly. When I was young, he worked a day job in construction, sometimes an evening job as a night watchman, and then a kind of weekend job helping an elderly couple move things and paint and stuff they couldn't do. He always seems—you know, it's very odd—to me like the character Hoke, played by Morgan Freeman in *Driving Miss Daisy*. Even some speech patterns that he has are pretty much like my father's. I saw clearly that my father worked like that for my mother and me. I basically have this strong Protestant work ethic I got through osmosis, maybe, from my dad. He is never, even at seventy, not doing something. Even though semi-retired, he's got to be painting or repairing something. When he comes to visit, he looks around our house to see what's broken and goes out to the hardware store and, before he leaves, it's fixed. This is the kind of person he is. He's never just idle. He never let me be idle, either. My first summer home from college, I didn't have any job plans. I guess I was going to lie around all summer.

DAVIES: *He didn't guess so, huh?*

JOHNSON: No. He informed me that I was getting up at six the next morning because he had gotten me a job. He was a night watchman for the city of Evanston, and he had walked down the hallway where the garbagemen were and gotten me a job as a garbageman for the summer. So that's what I did. That was the same summer I started studying kung fu, so I hauled garbage in this great big tub on my back in the morning and went and practiced kung fu at night. I hated that job the first year. I hated that job, but he was right. I had that job the next summer, too. He was right about it. I didn't need to be lying around idle. Home from college, I should help pay for my own college education. My father had a big impact on me. If anybody ever taught me how to work, I think it was him, through his example more than anything else.

DAVIES: *That's probably the way we learn the best.*

JOHNSON: I do think so. Parents are the closest models that we have on a daily basis.

DAVIES: *And they're in our systems in so many ways.*

JOHNSON: That's right. It's not like listening to a teacher for a few hours. It's top to bottom, all day long, all week long, month after month, year after year.

DAVIES: *I don't know about other people, but I have these very personal recurring images or ideas that are always in the back of my head. I am wondering if you have any recurring images or ideas that hover with you? I'll give you an example of a couple of my own so that you know what I'm talking about. For instance, there's nothing that gives me more of a sense of deep peace and love and strength than the image of my daughter's face, sleeping on her little pillow. It just fills me, completely. On the other hand, I have another image of an old man's face smearing on my windshield; he just sort of falls in front of my car. One of those ugly, haunting things. Do you have any of those hovering things?*

JOHNSON: There are images in my head a lot, I think, because I used to be a cartoonist and I had to think visually anyway, so my head was always full of images. When I think, even if it's an idea, I might even concretize it in terms of image. For example, in terms of etymology, if you trace back a word, you often find a very concrete image behind it. So that something like the word "guru," which we all know, actually means "one who is too heavy to be moved," like a rock. Or the word "sin," if you trace it back, it means to miss the mark, as when an arrow does not hit its target. Words always go back to a concrete experience that someone had. Writers, of course, abstract from it so they can generalize, but there is usually something in the world, tangible, from which it comes. Although I sometimes think in terms of images that are very concrete, I'm not sure that I have *recurring* images.

DAVIES: *You may be a bit saner than I am.*

JOHNSON: No, no, people do what you're saying all the time—in dreams, for example. I don't know, maybe there is one that has recurred to me over and over again—there *is* one image. I've never written it, except maybe *Middle Passage* is closest to it. It's an image of a beach. There's a shipwreck and I'm the only survivor, and I wash up on this beach, which is a beautiful place. I've had that image ever since graduate school. I see the beach perfectly. I see the sand. I see the trees and the flora in the background. Basically, I'm sort of hanging onto a piece of driftwood, or something, and I wash up on this beach. I don't know how long I've been at sea, or anything like that, but I know that in the background something sank, otherwise I wouldn't be out there. That's the only one I've had over and over. Now, Rutherford never does get to land in this book because he's picked up by another boat.

Why did I have that image? It's because when I was in graduate school, living on Long Island, we rented a cabin just a few paces down from a beach. I remember one spring, sitting on the beach—it was very warm, and this image came to me. This was Long Island Sound. I've had that image over and over again. It's very potent for me. Also, there's a story by Hermann Hesse, I realize, "The Island Dream," published in 1899, where he's working with the story of Odysseus among the Phaeacians. I think there's something very archetypal about that particular image. Somehow, I always get it again and again.

DAVIES: *And it rests well with you?*

JOHNSON: Yeah. I don't know whether that's a positive or a negative. I reach the land—I notice that—I'm not going to drown. It's kind of a sad sweet thing, because I know there was a shipwreck. A ship had to go down and so there was something disastrous behind it, but, for me, I've arrived at the other shore. But, you see, all of this is shot through with Eastern philosophy, now that I look at the image. The Buddha was very often referred to as a ferryboat man, and so the Buddha helps you cross the sea of suffering. I mean, there's a lot of Buddhist imagery constructed around water. You can look at Hermann Hesse's *Siddhartha,* which is a book I have loved since my undergraduate days, and Siddhartha winds up as a ferryboat man, carrying people across this body of water. He meets, as it turns out, everybody he ever met earlier in the book, later in their lives, and carries them across this body of water.

You made me dredge that up. I've never talked to anybody about that before.

DAVIES: *I really appreciate your answering my questions. It's been a great pleasure.*

# INTERVIEWS WITH
# NORTHWEST WRITERS:
# CHARLES JOHNSON

## IRENE WANNER

## PART I

C HARLES JOHNSON'S
most recent novel, *Middle Passage,* won the National Book
Award in 1990. His earlier books are *Faith and the Good Thing*
(1974), *Oxherding Tale* (1982), *The Sorcerer's Apprentice*
(1986), *Being and Race: Black Writing Since 1970* (1988), and
two collections of drawings. He grew up in Evanston, Illinois,
studied with John Gardner at Southern Illinois University, and
completed doctoral coursework in philosophy at the State University of New York/Stonybrook. In 1976, he accepted a teaching position at the University of Washington, where he also
serves as the *Seattle Review*'s fiction editor.

This interview will appear in two parts, with the second half
scheduled for the special 1993 autumn issue focusing on the

Reprinted from the *Seattle Review* 16.1 (Spring/Summer 1993) and 16.2
(Fall 1993/Winter 1994), by permission of Charles Johnson.

topic of work. In anticipation of this upcoming theme and in keeping with *SR*'s "Writers and Their Craft Series," the following discussion has been edited to concentrate primarily on the art of fiction writing. The conversation with features editor, Irene Wanner, was taped on August 2, 1992, in Johnson's campus office, a small room filled with books, photographs, and the lingering scent of cigarette smoke.

WANNER: *You mentioned the first classes you were assigned to teach at the University of Washington were story classes. Did writing short pieces allow you to focus your ideas more than in novels?*

JOHNSON: Yes, it allowed me to treat them in a more compact way. Less characters, a tight framework in terms of the time that elapsed and location.

WANNER: *Fewer story lines?*

JOHNSON: Yes, fewer story lines. It wasn't the multiple kind of thing that a novel would have to involve like ten characters or something. You only use two or three.

WANNER: *You were fortunate that your short story classes taught you.*

JOHNSON: Well, I had to teach people about parables and things like that, and so I would have to go back and write a parable. That's how the stories in *The Sorcerer's Apprentice* got written over seven years. I'd do one or two a year. Because I was really working on *Oxherding Tale* . . . I finished it around 1980. And that book is still something that I can't understand. It went to twenty publishers. Seriously. Until it wound up at Indiana University Press because the editor there understood it.

I had been working since '83 on *Middle Passage,* right after *Oxherding Tale* came out. I did two chapters in the late summer of '83, showed them to my agent, and she got real excited. I said OK, I'll finish the book in a year. I spent the whole year until the next summer and rushed a number of things. The plot of that book was radically different in first draft.

WANNER: *What started you on* Middle Passage? *A character? The slave trade?*

JOHNSON: I wanted to work with the slave trade, that is to say, that voyage across the water, after *Oxherding Tale.* I had a few other things in mind. I wanted to work with a sea story as a form because I had never worked with a sea story as a form.

WANNER: *Have you been to sea?*

JOHNSON: No, I haven't.

WANNER: *I ask because I review so many books, say, that New Yorkers write about being New Yorkers. I think we may agree on this, that writers don't use their imaginations enough?*

JOHNSON: Oh, I agree. I agree absolutely.

WANNER: *One strong point in* Being and Race *was that you took writers to task and said you'd like us all to try to do more.*

JOHNSON: I do think that you have to stretch and push. You have to imaginatively project yourself into as many other human places as possible. The curiosity that human beings have is not limited by history or race or gender or any of that and you have to try to really understand . . . we wouldn't have historical novels if that were the case, if you only wrote out of what you've directly experienced. In *Being and Race,* one of the things I felt I had to do—and phenomenology provides the basis for this—is to look at what we *mean* by experience. Just what is that? How limited is it to a direct encounter with something? How much of imagination comes into that interpretation? What do we bring to a happening, right?

But that was an intention. It was a sea story. I also wanted to tell an adventure story at the same time. So even though I was writing a slave narrative, I wanted to get all the details of the slave trade that I could in there, all the stuff I'd accumulated since '71 . . . I have tons and I review books about history and slavery and so forth, so I wanted to bring all that into the story because people don't know about the middle passage. There's so very little written about it.

WANNER: *Now they know more.*

JOHNSON: Now they know more, yes. I can tell you the stuff that's out there. It's only a handful of books, maybe less than ten, and maybe you throw in one play in that ten.

WANNER: *Mostly academic work?*

JOHNSON: No. Some people put things in front of me I wasn't aware of until the book came out. A book called *Middle Passage,* a narrative poem published by the University of Chicago Press in the early 1960s. I wasn't aware of that. And then there's this book called *Slave Dancer* by Paula Fox, which is a Newberry Award–winner children's book about a young boy who plays the flute to dance the slaves on the ship. I taught that here in a children's lit class. I think it's a wonderful book, but it doesn't have the real horror of the slave trade . . . Let's see. Where was I going with this? I had all of the historical research at my fingertips. I have piles of the stuff, notebooks that sit like this [indicates stacks two and three feel high] on my desk, and then I got piles in the corners. I take notes on everything.

WANNER: *Can you keep track of everything? Have you found a system that works?*

JOHNSON: [laughs] No, basically what happens when I revise is I go through all of it. Tons of it. It takes six to twelve hours to go through all that stuff.

WANNER: *I'm glad to hear reviewing notes is chaos for others, too.*

JOHNSON: It's chaos, but it's fun. I mean, to go back to 1972 and see a note that I took or a thought that I had that's useful in 1992 for something I'm writing, it's recovery. It's basically a memory aid. So I had all the historical stuff at my fingertips in '82. What I didn't have was the sea stuff. So I spent six years, literally, reading every sea story that I could get my hands on. I went back and looked at Homer again. I looked at Apollonius of Rhodes.

WANNER: The Odyssey?

JOHNSON: Right, *The Odyssey. The Voyage of the Argo.* I looked at . . . oh my god.

WANNER: *Conrad?*

JOHNSON: Yes, Conrad. I looked at all of Melville. Literally, all of Melville. Believe me, I read everything. The Sinbad stories, slave narratives of black people who came over on ships . . . I looked at nautical dictionaries. I looked at ships' logs. I looked at one book on Cockney slang, a study of Cockney slang for the sake of getting the sailors' idiom right.

WANNER: *Did you give the nautical pieces to anyone to check?*

JOHNSON: I didn't feel the need to do that. The point is, it isn't about the tales of rigging sails. What you need is the *feel* of the ship. You need the texture, but this is background. All this is in the service of character and story. The story is basically the conflict of characters, the Western culture represented by the crew in a very degenerate form and this very non-Western culture for the Allmuseri, who I wanted to make the most spiritual people on the planet. A whole tribe of Mother Teresas and Gandhis, right? So I drew a lot of stuff from different cultures for them. Some African, some Chinese, some Hindu, some Japanese. They're supposed to be the ur-people, the original people on the planet.

WANNER: *You made them up?*

JOHNSON: They're invented. There are no Allmuseri in this world, although it'd be nice if there were.

WANNER: *I asked if you had anyone vet the manuscript because I'm curious about narrative authority. Writers must control a story's details for a sense of authority to emerge on the page. Some writers think, when they venture into fields that aren't theirs, they need someone to check whether there are errors.*

JOHNSON: Well, my agent reads it. My editor read it.

WANNER: *Anyone else?*

JOHNSON: Oh, Joan [Johnson] reads it. I used to have three people read my manuscripts at one point.

WANNER: *And now?*

JOHNSON: Now, one will be my wife because her reaction will be that of the average reader. She reads all kinds of things. One's my agent, and their specific purpose when they read it is to tell me if it works for them and if they can sell it. And the third one I had read it was John Gardner, before his death, because he could respond with so much of the theory and practice of Western literature . . . When someone finds a technical thing that can be corrected, fine. You know, a little detail. Every novel, I think, is constructed of details and decisions of that sort.

WANNER: *Well, every word is a decision.*

JOHNSON: Yes, every word's a decision. That's important. But what's *most* important to me is the story. The characters in action, in a situation, and what's going on. Everything else, if it isn't in the service of that, it's not important finally. So I didn't pass it by any old sailors or old salts, no. I didn't do that.

WANNER: *Do you pretty much work from front to back or can you work out of order?*

JOHNSON: Well, you know, if a scene occurs to me, I have to write it down—dialogue or something—I'll do that and put it aside.

WANNER: *Grab it while you have it?*

JOHNSON: Yeah, if it's unfolding. A lot of things happen that way. They usually have to be adjusted when you catch up to that moment. When you reach it, it's got to be incorporated into what came before and might be modified tremendously. But I write from front to back. Beginning, middle, end. Because I can't know . . . I don't write episodic novels or stories. I like stories that have this kind of *energeia,* as Gardner calls it, when one thing is cause and effect. One thing propels the next thing and I can't know that until I get to that point. It's like a cup you fill up with water. Say the cup is one chapter. I'll just keep filling it up and filling it up until it spills over into the next chapter and that's how I'll get there. Maybe there'll be a line of dialogue I'm thinking of for the next chapter, but it won't be very extensive.

WANNER: *Do you use outlines?*

JOHNSON: I use extensive outlines. I use them all the time. I outline a book usually after the first chapter. The first chapter just basically lets me get into the story, then I can look at it and try to figure out where it can possibly go. Actually there's a new issue of *Zyzzyva* [Fall 1992] that has working notes for the novel, and there's a page in there that has chapter breakdowns and it's a whole different plot than this book that exists because it's the earlier way I plotted it. That was the way I followed through on the story. But usually what happens to me is I have to abandon the outline after about a hundred pages or so because different things have happened. Then I re-plot it, you know, on the basis of what's come about that I did not expect earlier on.

WANNER: *Do your characters take the bit in their teeth and go their own way?*

JOHNSON: That's the ideal thing, but it takes a while to get to that. I have to keep thinking about biographical details for them that give them a certain density.

WANNER: *Their personalities emerge?*

JOHNSON: Exactly. I mean details right down to, say, how Captain Falcon eats his dinner, Captain Falcon's relationship to Meadows, his relationship to Cringle, his education . . . once I know all that, I know how he moves or jumps in a situation. But it's a layering effect of details that happens over several drafts. Then they move in all directions I would not necessarily have made them move. Character, I think, is primary. I think it's the most important thing, because action always comes out of that and from action comes plot. The real focus is always character.

WANNER: *Do characters develop as you go or do you write sketches?*

JOHNSON: You should see this issue of *Zyzzyva*. I wish I had brought it with me, because all the notes are basically character sketch notes. Details about somebody that I want to use later or think more deeply about—they're all character details. That's oddly enough the way that these things took form. There might be a couple of lines that are descriptive stuff in there, too, if I remember correctly. But they're all about these people, figuring out who, what, why, when, where about every one.

My feeling is that if you have a principal character, like a protagonist, the whole nature of that character's change and evolution has to move to a point that is different from where we first saw him or her at the beginning of the book. Otherwise, this character is flat or static. And if you have a novel—I usually have seven to eight, for some reason, principal characters—they all have to have that same propulsion of movement and it's predicated on their relationship and involvement with each other in a particular situation.

So you have to figure out the different lines of development based on every character's disequalibrium or desire from the very start, and that gives you the idea of where they're going to go by the end of the book and what their final fate might be. But you don't know that until the very third act, so to speak. The first act is usually the hardest, the second—we're talking screenplay terms—is getting easier, and the third act is usually very easy, because then all you're doing is playing through the implications of everything that was set up before. As some people have said, you give a character a nature and then what you want to do is let that nature perform.

At that point—in the beginning, say, the first act—there are any number of possibilities in the way you could define these characters. But once you do define them, in act two it's *probability* that rules their actions. We can begin to see why they act the way they do and make predictions, but then in the third act, all movement is in the realm of necessity. They do what has been determined *by themselves* in the first and second act. The end of the story is usually an inevitable thing that the writer can't really mess with unless you just redefine the characters utterly.

WANNER: *I'm curious if writing short stories is radically different.*

JOHNSON: For me it is.

WANNER: *I find that I start, I don't have a clue where it's going, I let the characters do what they want, and if they surprise me, that's best. But I don't know. Some people outline everything.*

JOHNSON: I'll sometimes do an outline, a sketchy one. Not the same length as for a novel, but I do think the same principle's involved for me. In every story I do, I try to change literary form. That's one of the things I think I learned from Gardner indirectly. Every story has a kind of meditation going on, so that something like "The Education of Mingo" is a parable and uses some of the conventions of the parables in the New Testament. And then you get something like a science fiction story like "Popper's Disease" or a fable like the third story, "Menagerie," or you get a tale, which is like the last story, "The Sorcerer's Apprentice." They're conventions I like to work with. The conventions actually shape the universe the characters are in and what their possibilities are and define also, in some ways, how you treat characters.

And so this is the same thing with the novel. *Middle Passage* is a sea story, the universe of a sea story that they're moving around in. Or in *Oxherding Tale,* it's the universe of the slave narrative. Or in *Faith and the Good Thing,* it's the universe of the folk tale. So for every story, I sort of come in the door with that as an aesthetic formal question, but I know I use very traditional means to construct the story.

For example, a short story happens over a relatively short period of time and, actually, the novels do that, too. A novel might go on for a year. *Middle Passage* is about four months. But the short stories may be a day, a twenty-four-hour period.

I use narrative to summarize, to get myself to the point of the critical action and that's dramatized. It's just like a scene in a play. We hear dialogue. People act. The characters come out of it with their reactions in pursuit of consequences. It all might happen within . . . I think the longest period of time that goes on in that collection is maybe in "China," which is the centerpiece story, it's six months. But in "Exchange Value," it's a couple of days. In the first story, "The Education of Mingo," I want to say the action, once we pick it up in the first scene, is almost a matter of hours.

Usually I also get a fixed location—I don't take the characters all over to different locations—so you have concentration of space. I try to shorten the time of action, so you have temporal concentration, because I think that, in fact, ups the ante on the drama. Very few stories do I write over the years because they get dramatically and emotionally diffuse. You're looking at a character, probably, at the most important moment emotionally and intellectually of his or her life.

WANNER: *The strong conflict is present at the story's opening?*

JOHNSON: There's a very strong conflict. It's right there and you come right in on that. Everything we needed to know about them before is usually narrated or summarized, but we're thrown into this moment when they're living for high stakes. If it goes on too long, it's not for high stakes. It's got to be really compressed in that sense.

WANNER: *In "Exchange Value," the opening is when we climb through an apartment window with the characters to rip off an old lady.*

JOHNSON: Yeah, exactly. We climb in the window with them; we make the discovery with them; there are consequences after that, right? And there's a little narrative that goes on to carry them over that evening and early the next day, but then bam! We're right into the next moment in the arc of the plot and then we're out. So it's just two or three days, I guess, the action of that story.

WANNER: *Just to bring the* Seattle Review *in, it was your idea to start the "Writers and Their Craft" series several years ago.*

JOHNSON: I love those essays.

WANNER: *What do you find the most challenging craft element of writing fiction?*

JOHNSON: Character. The hardest thing in the world is imaginatively getting yourself out of the way so these people can live. It's funny. I mean, you are those people, so you discover parts of yourself. But there's always, for me . . . and this isn't even a matter of craft, it's something else. We were talking earlier about teaching creative writing. We can teach technique all day long because we have so many works. We can analyze what strategies they use, and there are portable strategies for most fiction. But you can't teach the other thing, which is like imagination, which is also unteachable . . . and inspiration and talent. Those are unteachable things, but there's something else that goes on and I'm very aware of this now. It has to do with a very humbling experience that goes into fiction, where at least in terms of the kind of fiction that I want to write, it's not about me in a certain sense. It isn't an extension of my ego. It isn't about *my* life. It's not about me. People look at my picture and they wonder . . .

WANNER: . . . *who is this guy?*

JOHNSON: Yeah, where am I, right? The autobiographical detail from his life . . . it's not what fiction's about. No, it's not about us. It's about telling a story and trying to get behind the eyes of the individuals who interest me, whether Captain Falcon or Ngonyama or anybody.

WANNER: *You try to put yourself in their skin and think who are they? What do they feel?*

JOHNSON: Exactly. If I were in that person's skin, what would

I be thinking right now? It's kind of imagined transposition into another person's world. So I think that's a very humbling experience, and there's a lot of ego work that has to go on to get you to that. But that's not . . . I don't think that's really teachable.

WANNER: *Putting oneself aside seems to be a hard step, at least with students that I've known. We always tell them to start from what they know—themselves—but then we also say fiction must go beyond the self, must be* imagined *to become real. One of the first exercises I give is to write from the other gender's point of view.*

JOHNSON: That's a very good one.

WANNER: *A lot of them hate it, because they would never have thought of it. Then later they admit they had fun. The switch forces them to choose a point of view they might never have considered, but they still constantly ask how I come up with characters.*

JOHNSON: Actually, what they have to do is spend their entire life—and this is the hard part—observing other people and taking notes. It's the only way.

WANNER: *What sort of notes?*

JOHNSON: What you see them do, what's interesting, physical descriptions, idiosyncrasies, eccentricities, a little thing that might be illuminating . . . it's really a character, I think, who's illuminated by the small things.

WANNER: *Gestures?*

JOHNSON: Gestures, yes. Writers are always watching people. And then you're always watching yourself, always checking out your emotional states and saying, "Why do I think that? Where does that idea come from? Why do I feel that way? What's in the mix of that emotion I'm feeling?" You're always doing self-examination and looking at other people with a cruel eye, as one person once said. It's tough trying to understand, right? Why do people do what they do? And then once you begin to think in that way, you see an incredible eruption of human behavior that's a revelation of what's inside somebody's heart or their mind or their orientation toward the world. That's the hardest thing for students because, most of the time, most people are kind of self-absorbed. They're not thinking of anybody else.

WANNER: *You have to be generous? You have to put yourself in the background and put your character . . .*

JOHNSON: . . . in the foreground. I really think you do. And again, you'll get ironic, mysterious things. Of course, you *are* that person, finally. You have imbued all the details that you've taken from observation with a spirit that animates it and so you discover yourself in all these other people through the process of writing, which is I think what Gardner meant by moral fiction. Not slighting anybody, because you've got to try to immerse yourself as much as you can in everybody's head. It ultimately impinges upon a very interesting epistemological question such as, "What can I know? What is the nature of knowledge? You said to write about what you know." We say that to our students, but . . .

WANNER: . . . *but what does it mean?*

JOHNSON: Yeah, what does it mean? It should make them question, "How much *do* I know? And how much do I know about other people? And how much should I share with other people in terms of my experience and my vision of the world?" So it opens up all these marvelous questions that are just beneath the surface of technique. Technique, finally, is very much a doorway into vision when you think about it.

WANNER: *As an artist, you trained your eye to see. I tell students to go to plays, to the art museum, to symphonies. Sharpen your senses. The importance of sensory details in fiction is one of the hardest things to get across, giving a sensory reality to a world that's just made up of black type on white paper.*

JOHNSON: I think writers should hit all the senses, if possible, to make that world imaginatively full for the reader. And of course, I think what hits writers hits all artists—I really think so—is that you have to be observing everything around you in the world almost all the time. That's very taxing. I was talking to a friend the other night and realized that an awful lot of the way I talk about writing comes out of the way I used to talk about visual arts and painting. Keeping a sketchbook and sketching all the time.

WANNER: *Do you still draw?*

JOHNSON: No, I don't do that any more, but now it's the words. What I'm sketching with are the same details a painter might pick up, but they're about characters or it might be an image that hits me as the light comes through, say, the window at a certain time of day, early afternoon, and strikes a plant sitting there. It's so vivid. I have just the language for it, and it has to go down in my journal.

WANNER: *You keep a journal, a handwritten notebook?*

JOHNSON: I keep one current all the time. It gets filled up, and I go on to the next one. I go through all that stuff again when I revise. It's not unlike what a painter does or the artist's sketchbook, where you always carry it with you. What's in there can become later part of a composition that you're working on, a painting or something. I can't speak to the other arts like music, for example, or sculpture. I can usually do it with the visual arts, with drawing in particular.

WANNER: *When you see lazy writing like "he was ugly" or "she was beautiful," these descriptions are neither visual nor evocative. The writer still needs to do a lot of work on these images.*

JOHNSON: They do nothing. Even more, if someone says she was beautiful or ugly or whatever, that's a judgment. The ideal thing, finally, is to give full presentedness to the reader so you describe what it is that you think is ugly, then let the reader make the judgment if it's ugly or not rather than just put the judgment in front of the reader and try to control everything they see. If someone is beautiful, or is experienced that way, then the person looking at them in the story, the narrator, has got to give us all the concrete specific details.

WANNER: *Features that allow the reader to decide she's beautiful?*

JOHNSON: Exactly. Things that embody beauty and lead this person to that conclusion. If, in fact, the details are right, then the reader will make that judgment, and you won't even have to say it. That's always the difficulty. One of my students once said—he was in theater—something that I thought was useful. He was in a graduate class and was quoting someone. I don't know who. He said specificity of detail *is* generosity. Specificity is generosity. And I believe he's exactly right. That's a real struggle, I think, to invoke this fully rendered world. I think about it in much the same way as I think about the fully rendered world of certain canvases that I find striking, like the canvases of Diego Rivera. I love Rivera's murals. But many other artists as well, you know? I think you can always go deeper with detail because the world is so infinitely rich.

WANNER: *When you finished the first draft of* Middle Passage, *what sorts of craft items did you work on in revision?*

JOHNSON: I went back over the language and speeches of every character to see that everybody was individuated, because the ideal, finally, is that you should be able to hear the speech from a character without having the character identified by "Cringle said" or "Rutherford said." You know by the content, by the rhythm, the syntax, who this is. So everyone has to be differentiated. There are certain words Falcon would use that Meadows would not use.

And similarly, I care a lot about prose rhythm. I think a sentence has to be so worked over—twenty-five times, if necessary—that it cannot be pulled out. It'd be like pulling a finger off a human body. The entire work would be affected by it. The sentence in front of it rhythmically and musically and the one in back of it would be thrown off and you'd fall into this hole. And if that happened, the paragraph in front of that would fall into this hole. So you've got this musical composition that's going on that level of sound.

Similarly, I think sentence structure is very important. I tell my students this all the time. They'll begin, and six sentences in a row are simple sentences or they're compound sentences. The students don't know how to plastically use language for other kinds of compound-complex or periodic-loose formulations that make language sing from line to line.

Finally, if you begin to take out a sentence after doing all that, you affect everything else on the page, and that affects the pages prior to it. So that's a revision thing, over and over and over, until not a syllable can be changed.

Then what else do I look for? I begin to look at gaps. If there's a place where I can do one little thing that will turn something around the corner a bit more than I have . . . actually, if something's a bit more generous, that is to say, something unexpected, something that isn't even necessarily part of the story but will enhance it yet more, then I'll put that in if it'll work within the realm of the fiction.

WANNER: *There's a lot more room to do that in a novel than in a short story, isn't there?*

JOHNSON: Oh, yeah. A novel gives you a chance to reinvent the universe, quite literally, from the smallest atom right up to galactic complexes. Really, you can remake the universe in a novel, which is why it's such a great joy. You can even have a vision. It can be original, one hopes, and illuminating. Then you can support it with hundreds of thousands of details on every level.

WANNER: *It seems to me that's why books are more interesting than movies. In the movie, visual choices have been made for us, but on the page or even with radio plays, language lets you imagine.*

JOHNSON: I think that's right. Movies give everything to you in a particular way that closes off the imagination sometimes.

Not with really fine movies, but no movie is as rich and complex and multileveled as the book it was essentially based on. The greatest books, for example, are far greater as experiences to me than the greatest film; even if it's a three-hour film or a long six-hour film, still you can't do as much. One is using the image and one is using language, and language is . . . that's a whole other discussion, but it's this presence in our lives that is almost bottomless, in the sense that we live in language the way a fish lives in water. It surrounds us, it's highly diversified, and it defines our being in certain ways.

# PART II

WANNER: *How would you say your writing has grown and changed since you began teaching at the University of Washington in 1976?*

JOHNSON: Well, I taught really hard when I first got here. I had a moral commitment to it . . . I'd never turn students away. I learned a lot. Having to articulate and talk about aesthetics in the specific terms of literary practice was very illuminating for me, for my own work. I would articulate things and then see them in front of me as I spoke them and then I could go back and work with them on the page.

So there's always a very intimate relationship between what's called teaching and so-called research. If you go to the lab and you discover something—cutting edge—you go back to the classroom and your students benefit from that over in the sciences, right? Something that's not in the journals yet because it happened last night and hasn't even been written up.

I think the same thing is true for fiction. You're writing and you're making discoveries that actually force you to readjust your own teaching from the things you said a year ago. You've modified that in light of what you've just discovered. The students get the benefit of that before anybody sees the work or you can write about the work, which means, in effect, of course, that everybody teaching writing needs to be working at their own material and working in a way that is always covering new ground and not just doing formula fiction or something that doesn't challenge them.

WANNER: *Do you write poetry?*

JOHNSON: I wrote some in college, poetry, but it was not very good. I wrote it just for fun in my journals. About eighty poems or so. What I care about is poetic prose. I like prose to use the devices of poetry, but I don't write poetry . . . it's not what I reach for to express myself, although I admire deeply those people who can write both. You think the world differently to write a great poem than you do to write a great short story or a great novel.

WANNER: *I once heard a poet say she'd had a really good day. She'd written three poems.*

JOHNSON: Then maybe it was a gift from the gods, because I know poets who spend five years working on their poems. I've seen that confirmed in our poets here. It's not one poem they're working on five years—it's a lot—but they all come together to fruition, you know, over a four- or five-year germination period. Like a novel in many respects. Everything is essential. It's a style that goes into that, but it's not one that . . . I reach for when I want to express myself or write in my journal or a story, because I think more narratively than any other way. Or I'll even reach for criticism or nonfiction, because that's a way of getting quickly to the subject. You don't have to dramatize and come up with a half a million details for characters. You just make arguments and then conclusions. It's much, much easier. Much easier to do nonfiction than fiction.

WANNER: *Do you like to write dialogue?*

JOHNSON: I enjoy dialogue. I hear the voices in my head. When I'm really immersed in something, the responses back and forth between the characters will pop into my mind. It's never been difficult, dialogue, for me to do. What I really enjoy doing,

though, is individuating speech. I'm interested in speech patterns and linguistic idioms that people use depending on what
region of the country they're from or other countries. There are
certain ways people talk. I'd like, for example, to be able to do
an Indian, a Hindu, who's learned English. I'd love to be able
to capture certain voices. Some are so difficult. Having grown
up with certain voices, I think it's easier.

WANNER: *Some you hear?*

JOHNSON: Yeah, you grow up with them and you just *know*
them, but there are others, I think, that a writer can learn. It
all comes down to the same thing: hearing it, being attentive
to it, taking notes. That's fun.

WANNER: *You've been a fiction editor at the* Seattle Review
*for a long time. As an editor, what grabs you?*

JOHNSON: Something fresh. I want something original. I want
a lot when I read a story. I really hate to say it, but I find most
of contemporary fiction to be profoundly disappointing. Ninety
percent of it. We just finished—two other people and myself,
judging . . . this is the second year for me, and the last—the
*Los Angeles Times* book prize. So I got everything published
this last year, back to July of '91. One hundred and sixty-three
books we looked at. And there's a lot of interesting first fiction.
There's a lot of new writers out there, which is a pleasure to
see. We had two categories: fiction and first fiction. So we looked
at a lot. But one of the things that was so profoundly disappointing is the sameness. The sameness of vision, the sameness of understanding, the sameness of interpretation the writer
has brought to rendering a fictional world or a fictional universe. The problems are usually very small ones that the characters are dealing with, they're not really interesting people, and
there is nothing there in the way of plot, usually. Nothing really
happens.

WANNER: *Slices of life? In which the conflict is . . .*

JOHNSON: . . . very minimal, very vague. Even worse, the
language is hardly better than what, as we say, you hear in the

supermarket or laundromat. There's no effort to make language or urge language or *allow* language to perform in terms of its fullness. It's usually a very scaled down—if it's first-person or third-person narrative—diction, sentence structure . . . nothing. These are not writers who are prose stylists. I really like writers who are writers' writers. I learn something about technique and I also learn something about the world from the fiction. I want everything in fiction. I want character, I want suspense, I want plot, I want images that are like little windows through which I can look at the world in a different way, I want humor, I want to laugh, to cry, and to learn something, and I think a story or a novel can do all those things.

My feeling is that I don't think somebody should write unless they have something original to say, that they feel is not going to be said if they don't say it, or something to show us they feel nobody's seen yet, right? There's really a *reason* for the story, not just to be writing another story. That doesn't make a lot of sense to me. A lot of people want to be writers so they're always scrambling to come up with something more to write, another story to do, but that is not a service in the way that I think art really should be a service, which is to say, you're communicating or expressing something through the story or language and it quite literally is the best thought, the best feeling, the best technique and skill that you can muster in that communication to another person.

WANNER: *Sometimes I wonder why we tell stories. Is it how we identify ourselves? Or is it how we might say to each other this is the good life? Or maybe this is how we go about having an honorable life?*

JOHNSON: That could be a motivation. I think in a certain kind of cliché sense we talk about stories as being both entertaining and enlightening. But even more so, if there's a question that you have, and it really is a thorny question, if it's an issue and you're wondering about it, a situation, a problem, one of the things that you're going to do—this is what John

Gardner taught me, actually—is explore that in the course of a fiction in a way that you might not be so able to explore it in the real world. It might be dangerous to do so or you might endanger somebody else.

But in fiction . . . in many ways, I like his metaphor of fiction being a laboratory where you walk in the door and you have a hypothesis. You don't know what the conclusion will be. You suspect maybe it'll come out one way or another, right? But you have all your chemicals and tools, your Bunsen burner and all that sort of stuff.

Well, the writer's equivalent is a hypothesis or question about something. Your tools are character and plot and all those things. As with a laboratory experiment, what you discover may refute your hypothesis. It may confirm it or it may confirm it with qualifications. You don't know, but the whole point is to see what you can discover.

Now you must have a hypothesis. You can't just go and throw things together haphazardly. It might be a central question. Like in "The Education of Mingo," I remember what brought me to that. Actually, that story was written over a year because I started it in New York and finished when we moved out here. I'd just written something like the opening two pages and the question was about responsibility within the context of oppression. Who is responsible for the actions of a person who has been stripped of their culture and oppressed? Is it Moses Green or Mingo? And then the other question in there was, "What is education? To teach another person, what in the world does that mean? What are you teaching?"

Well, everything is a lens through an individual. I could go in and teach content, but something runs through my voice, my background, my personality, my values, and what I leave out of what I teach, what I add, and what spin I put on it, and I'm giving that to another individual. They, then, will absorb that and interpret it in their own way, perhaps, and act on it. And if their action is immoral, like going out as Mingo does and murdering somebody because he's misunderstood something, where's responsibility? How's it come back? Does it come back to Mingo or Moses?

So there's all these questions of education, cultural identity, all that stuff, the hypotheses I brought into the mix of the story. I didn't realize it's actually similar to *Frankenstein* until I got to after the murder. After the murder, I realized, oh, this is *Frankenstein*. Once I knew that, I knew he was going to kill again and I knew he would be playing out Moses's deepest fears that Moses had no capacity to express. And he would kill Harriet Bridgewater, whom Moses loved but had all these reservations about, and was going to marry but was hesitant about, and leave him, leave Moses with nobody in his world but Mingo, who is his creature, his shadow, his double, himself. So it really is a frightening, scary story.

*Frankenstein* does run through there, but I didn't walk in there knowing that. It suddenly hit me after he kills Isaiah Green that this is what's going on. And also it's a larger question, too, of what does it mean to teach another person. What kind of moral responsibility do you have if you do that? If my son goes out and murders somebody and he comes back and says, "Dad, you said . . ."

WANNER: *Whose fault is it?*

JOHNSON: Whose fault is that. I have to take some responsibility. Now you can't take it all, because maybe it was misinterpreted. But again, the purpose is not to have conclusions worked out when you start the story, but to go through it all and see as much as you can and get it out on the table and somehow make it an emotional, dramatic experience.

WANNER: *I like what you said earlier about discovery. Often writers who are starting, or even any of us at any stage, find that discovering where the story's trying to go is both the biggest joy and the biggest frustration.*

JOHNSON: Absolutely.

WANNER: *After all, most people go to work from Monday*

to Friday, expect a paycheck, and kind of know what they're doing in the meantime.

JOHNSON: [laughs]

WANNER: *Whereas we often sit down in the morning or evening or whenever we write and wonder what'll happen.*

JOHNSON: Yeah, because every time is different. Somebody can write for thirty years, I honestly believe, and they've figured out how to write a story, and if they're a commercial writer, they can do it over and over.

WANNER: *Fill in the formula?*

JOHNSON: Yeah, fill in the formula. And, actually, that's what their readers want. They don't want any variation from what they've come to enjoy.

WANNER: *So that's why there's Beattie-style and Carver-style?*

JOHNSON: Well, I'm thinking of *very* commercial writers. I'm thinking of Tom Clancy. Pulp, industrial fiction, as my friend Fred Pfeil calls it. It's a product. And you sell it. People want the same thing over and over again.

WANNER: *They see that label and know what to expect?*

JOHNSON: Exactly. Just like Harlequin Romances. But if it's literary fiction, I know you start all over again from scratch with the same kind of basic tools: You got people, you got them doing something, they talk to each other, they have a world.

WANNER: *But every story wants its own voice. So you have to start over.*

JOHNSON: Its own voice, its own form. You may be working with a voice that you've never used before, which you had to invent for that fiction. Finally, in looking at an entire body of work by a very inventive writer, and I've seen this to be the case, you might not know from book to book who wrote it if their name wasn't on it.

WANNER: *Wouldn't that be the best compliment? If anyone wrote that well?*

JOHNSON: I think that's the ideal compliment for an author.

Oddly enough, if you keep pushing at it, you'd see a thread running through it, something similar, because this is one life grappling with more or less the same issues over and over again.

WANNER: *We all have a few things that tug our chains.*

JOHNSON: For our whole lives. I really think so. We maybe give a different spin on it at age twenty or forty or sixty, but there're certain kinds of orientations that keep burning at us. Actually, changing that way—voice and form—is another way of opening up a similar question that you've been meditating on for forty years. So I think you're right. It's walking a tightrope with no net every time you write a work or do a painting.

WANNER: *And it requires such patience.*

JOHNSON: Great patience. Great patience over maybe a decade in the case of some books I can think of, like *Under the Volcano*. It's worth it.

WANNER: Invisible Man. *Wasn't that seven years for Ralph Ellison?*

JOHNSON: I believe that was seven years. I worked it out once when he said he started it until the time it was published. Such an exhaustive book in many, many ways. It's more of an exploratory book, I think, than most people give it credit for. They say, oh, it makes a racial statement. In fact, it does. But he had to be working through deep questions in there of consciousness and perception, what is seen and what is not, epistemological questions. It's remarkable . . .

Same thing with Richard Wright. That book [*Native Son*] is about consciousness all the way through, but when we talk about it, we talk about poor Bigger and his oppression. Well, Wright made a big effort so you wouldn't say "poor Bigger"— Bigger is self-created to a large extent—and he makes a point to show other black people in the book . . . You just can't play that book the easy way some people would like to play it, because Wright is working at trying to understand how human beings act in a certain situation given certain premises. But that happens all the time, I think, the way people interpret literature. They interpret it the way it's useful for them at a particular reading. They read a book again five years later, they may interpret it a different way. That's happened to me many times.

WANNER: *I've been troubled recently by the idea of writers having to be politically correct. An example came up in which a Latino said whites shouldn't write from that point of view. It's my feeling any writer should be able to try honestly to imagine how others live and attempt to do justice to them. Why should we be constrained by what we know? I'm troubled by that idea and wondered what you thought.*

JOHNSON: Well, I understand the argument. I think I understand both sides. I think a writer should be challenged. Human beings should be challenged to try to understand somebody else and, if you're an artist, to articulate that from that point of view, because it's illuminating for you—you learn—and if you can do it successfully, more power to you. It happens all the time.

On the other hand, there are people who assume they can do that and they make a lot of mistakes because they don't know enough about what it's like to live in the skin of a Latino person or a black person. And in our conversations about a work, sometimes we never get beyond: "You don't know, so you can't do this. Leave it alone." I don't buy that.

WANNER: *That's too simple, isn't it? Shouldn't you recognize you need to do research first and then take on the challenge?*

JOHNSON: Yeah, go do research and then you got to do all the emotional . . . you got to do a lot to be able to pull it off, there's no question. But I don't want to say it can't be done. See, if you flip that over to the other side, you have to say the same thing to black Americans. Black Americans can't write about white characters.

WANNER: *Why not?*

JOHNSON: Uh, 'cause they don't know. The argument would still pertain, wouldn't it?

WANNER: *See, I think you ought to be able to write a book*

*about a white woman and I ought to be able to write one about a black man. Why not?*

JOHNSON: Well, look at Joyce Carol Oates's *Because It Is Bitter and Because It Is My Heart*. Two characters, a teenage white girl and a teenage black boy. She handles that guy—his name is Jinx—as authentically as anybody could. She writes about him better than some black writers would. I'm serious about that. Because she knows people. She grew up with people who were like Jinx and other people in her novel.

WANNER: *She was a careful observer?*

JOHNSON: She's *very* careful, and she pulls it off. But I've seen other people who haven't, who just didn't know what they were doing, and make assumptions, attribute things that they think might be the case but aren't. But she really pulls it off in a successful way. Again, I think we have instances where this works quite well. So it's a dumb thing to say, finally. It's very limiting. It will not enrich our literature, certainly, if we cannot do that.

WANNER: *I knew a writer who only wrote about women because she said there were enough stories about men. I thought, well, you're leaving out half the people on earth. You're putting on a straitjacket. I don't see the point.*

JOHNSON: Nor do I. I have no problems writing stories sometimes—there was one in *Playboy* last December—in which there is no racial signature for some of the characters because it's not about race. It's about another kind of issue, which could apply to anybody. So I have no problem with the character. The protagonist *could* be black or could be white.

WANNER: *What's the focus of your work now?*

JOHNSON: When I write a novel now, it really is . . . I guess it's true, I think of the whole thing as being a sequence of scenes. Dramatic scenes. The bridges between those are narrative summary, which I try to make as sweet and poetic and lyric as possible. But really, they're all the particulars to get us to a dramatic scene. Because there the reader can see the action, can hear the voices, can make their own unmediated judgments. In narrative, you've got the reader . . .

WANNER: *They're told everything.*

JOHNSON: Yeah, you've got the narrator and then you've got the story. That is to say, it's coming through the narrator. But a scene, the principle is that it's like the fourth wall of a room's knocked out and you're sitting there looking at you and me talking, as opposed to having some guy standing over there saying, "And as Irene said that, she was feeling . . ." [laughs]

WANNER: *Yes. You cut the interpretation. Interplay of scene and narrative is one of the most interesting aspects of writing, I think. Everything comes alive in the scenes. The narrative gives the blocking and staging and background information for the scenes you've set up so the characters can act.*

JOHNSON: Yeah, I think narrative is really in the service of scene. But, again, you can do things with narrative that have all the full possibilities of prose writing. Period. You can do history, you can do biography, you can do philosophy in the narrative segment. You can do *all* that stuff, but, finally, we really do have to have, I do think, the dramatic scenes in a way that's compelling. It's called presentedness. It's what pulls the reader in. And fiction has often been called dramatic narrative. You know? Novels, dramatic narrative. You can put the emphasis on both sides.

I've only written one story that I can think of that was fundamentally all narrative. It's called "Moving Pictures" in *The Sorcerer's Apprentice*. It stands out differently from all the others because every one starts with narrative exposition to get us to the scene, then shuts up and lets it happen.

WANNER: *Lets the action start.*

JOHNSON: Right. That one is all about, in some ways, a reflective voice talking to you in second person. I could've had dramatic scenes. I chose to keep it just narrative and what's happening is language, language, language, sentence by sentence by sentence. I normally don't write that way. I normally ease into the scene and just let it play through. It's fun.

WANNER: *Do you ever revise narrative into scene as you rewrite a novel?*

JOHNSON: Not really. What I find is I'm writing narrative and then ultimately I'll get to the point where I'll say something and the next line is just a line of dialogue. That begins the scene. It's moving along and then I know I cannot narrate the next couple of lines. Suddenly a character's talking. They're moving around and doing something and somebody replies. And it goes back and forth like that until it ends and then there's no more of that scene to do as an action or whatever, then it goes back into narrative and picks up again. So it's basically *feeling* where it should happen for me more so than planning it out in a calculative manner.

WANNER: *Do you ever use narrative as a breather—if a scene is very intense—do you use narrative to give the reader a rest?*

JOHNSON: I almost never break up . . . I never try to break a scene with narrative because it destroys the rhythm of the movement. Every scene has, in a microcosmic kind of way, the same movement as plot. You come in . . . a friend of mine, in terms of Chinese theater, says a scene has four parts. I always tell my students a scene has four parts. There's the entrance, then there's what's called rhythm—because people come together and they start talking, but almost never get right to the issue that brings them in the room, so they talk about something and go back and forth—and they ease up to the third part called the hit. That's whatever has driven these two people together. It's finally on the table. And then after the hit, there's the exit. Those are the four fundamental parts of a scene. It actually does rise all the way up to the hit. They come out of that scene, one hopes, not the same people that they were when they went into it.

WANNER: *And it's like a small story?*

JOHNSON: It's like a small story. It's got that kind of traditional dramatic structure.

WANNER: *That pushes the progress of the play.*

JOHNSON: It pushes things forward and then you pick up the fallout of that scene in the narrative and you move us forward over time, a week or whatever, however much time until the next scene, which actually could be five, six pages later.

Usually I always seem to run three scenes per chapter. Or in a short story it's very often three scenes. I need a scene early so we see them—you get to see them, experience them, right?—and then we have another scene when the issue is at hand, whatever the plot is about, is right there vividly. You see the character reacting to it.

And somewhere, usually at the end, there's a scene because the consequence just can't be told to us at the end of the story. We need to see the character and feel it. So I usually can't get out without three scenes in a twenty-page story or a twenty- or twenty-five-page chapter. It's just kind of rough blocking out in my mind the way that falls together as a pattern.

I've never started a story or novel with dialogue. Some people do. They start with a scene, but then you've got to back up and say, well, who's talking and there they are and all this other stuff. To me it's easier just who, what, why, when, where in exposition, then, boom, into scene and you keep moving. Maybe you end with dialogue. Maybe with narrative. It all depends on where the story *feels* like it has the best sense of closure. Ending is usually not a problem.

WANNER: *The ending comes at the front sometimes. You start right near a story's end, then flash back and come through to find out why events happened that way.*

JOHNSON: That's true.

WANNER: *Do you ever change the entire structure of a story? Instead of a chronological and then, and then, and then?*

JOHNSON: In *Faith and the Good Thing*, I remember, it's full of flashbacks all over the place. I've started to use less and less of those. *Oxherding Tale* has a number of flashbacks.

WANNER: *They do stop the story. They add information, but every time you tell one . . .*

JOHNSON: . . . it stops the forward motion of the story. I'm not so much interested in that any more. It sets a whole different temporal rhythm to the story. *Middle Passage* has one flashback. There's only one scene that happens before the action actually begins, and I was very conscious of that one in there. I felt it was necessary. That's the only time you stop forward momentum.

WANNER: *When you went back to give the family history?*

JOHNSON: Yeah, when he goes back to talk about his brother and you see them in the scene with his master when he told them that they were free and all that. Then it gets back to the issue.

I have no problem at all, in principle, with an *A B C D E* to *Z* structure. You know, just linear. I have no problem with that at all. Not a bit. So the question always is, like Aristotle says— and I really do think he's right—a story is a sequence of action. That's the spine all the way through it. You start at the point before which there is no story to tell and you end at the point after which there is no story to tell. It's all controlled by this action that's running through, whether it's a twenty-page story or a four hundred-page novel. And the only question then is to find, really, where the story logically begins. That, to me, usually is the primary issue.

WANNER: *Do you sometimes read a story and finally on page six, say, your interest really gets hooked? So maybe pages one to five are just background the writer needed and should be cut?*

JOHNSON: That's very often the case. I heard David Wagoner talk about writers clearing their throats for a few pages before they actually speak. And that's true . . . for some reason, I never grope that way. One thing I learned from Gardner, something he always said—and I believe it—was that if the voice is right, you don't have to worry about anything else in the story. Usually before I start a story, I have this voice in mind. The voice—the character, diction, syntax, all that stuff so that the personality comes through the speaker in first person or third—is such that I can easily get into the story.

WANNER: *The voice arrives whole for you?*

JOHNSON: There's enough of it. I'm able to discover more later.

WANNER: *Something powerful gets you started?*

JOHNSON: Yes, and the voice is compelling. It's like listening to somebody talk. And then that person will tell me very soon what the issue is that has caused disequalibrium in his life or somebody else's or the conflict.

Someone once said you've got all these books in front of you, and it's very much like being at a party. You naturally gravitate toward the person at a party who's the most interesting speaker, who says the most interesting things, right? In the most interesting way.

It's the same thing with a book. I think if the narrative voice starts out like that, you're drawn in by the force of the character. And then after that, you're hooked. You'll stick with it. Some people push it a bit too long. I think John used to do that. He had a great voice but wouldn't really get down to the issue until six or seven pages later. The voice is just telling you about itself, biographical details, and while it's very interesting . . .

WANNER: *Let's go?*

JOHNSON: Sure. Then finally he'll get to it. His books were always very slow, he used to say. He's right. Particularly the longer books that you're supposed to read by the firelight, right. Like Dickens for a long winter night. But they were usually very slow. I like much faster pacing than that. I think there should be a certain economy, as in poetry, to fiction. No waste.

WANNER: *I agree. In stories especially. But you often hear people making excuses for novels because there's more room.*

*I still believe that the drive, the necessity to* get on *with the story should be there from the start.*

JOHNSON: I believe it. I believe it absolutely.

WANNER: *You know how—with short stories particularly— you better have a page one that gets an editor to page two? Even with a novel, I think writers ought to grab readers with their leads or characters or voice.*

JOHNSON: It has to be on the first page. I mentioned John Gallman at Indiana. When he reads a manuscript, fiction or non- or otherwise, he used to be in the habit when he was a smoker of smoking a cigarette, which took him seven minutes. If he wasn't hooked by the time he finished, forget it.

My editor, Lee Goerner at Atheneum, we talk about books and manuscripts and so forth. He'll tell me what he's reading. If it's a first page and it's not there, he says no. He's got too much other stuff to get to. It's got to be on the first page.

I mentioned Lawrence Lariar earlier and he was a writer and he mentioned to me—this is when I first started writing, I think—about a seminar he took in New York. This must've been in the 1930s or the 1940s. Some guy was talking about craft. It was an auditorium and the speaker came down in to the front of the room with a clock, and he put it down, wound it up, and it went tick tick tick tick for a minute. Then it went off. And the first thing out of his mouth was, "That's how long you have to interest me." One minute. That's about right. If it's not there within the first five or six pages, you can be generous, you can say great works of the past didn't kick in until the third chapter. [laughs]

WANNER: *But this isn't the past.*

JOHNSON: Right, this isn't. It's not that we're not being generous, but I do think that there's an obligation that you have to the reader. It's a contract. As long as I'm interesting, you keep reading, but as soon as I begin to get boring, I think the reader has a right to say, "I'm going to go walk my dog now."

WANNER: *In Nick O'Connell's interview [At the Field's*

End, *Madrona 1987] with Ursula Le Guin, she says she thinks consciously of writing as being a collaborative act with readers. As you were saying, she respects their time. We ought to get right in there and get on with the story.*

JOHNSON: It's only fair. I really think so. I mean, a writing teacher will be patient with a student's manuscript.

WANNER: *Not always. [laughs]*

JOHNSON: Well, you lose your patience after a while, but you've got to read it. You've got to comment on it and stick with it and say this is how you fix it. But editors—if they don't feel it's fixable—they won't do it. And readers, confronted with—what?—fifty thousand books a year? They're not going to bother. And there's no reason for them to unless you have given them *the best* that you possibly can.

# AN INTERVIEW WITH
# CHARLES JOHNSON

## MICHAEL BOCCIA

W<small>HEN APPROACHED</small>
to participate in this interview, Charles Johnson responded with
his usual enthusiasm: "Send me questions! I'll try to provide
everything on my end." So I sat down and produced questions
dealing with three general areas—artist, art, and audience. To
these questions, Johnson responded with insight and wit, providing information that illuminates his writing.

BOCCIA: *Is there any little-known or unknown autobiographical information that would help us better understand your
fiction?*

JOHNSON: As you probably know, my creative work did not

Reprinted from *African American Review* 30.3 (1996), by permission of
Michael Boccia.

begin when I started writing fiction. In 1967, when I was seventeen, I began publishing as a cartoonist (my first three short stories were published that same year, but in my teens the only thing I desired to be was a commercial artist). For seven years thereafter, I studied with cartoonist Lawrence Lariar; this career consumed me, leading to over one thousand published drawings in dozens of publications ranging from *Black World* to the *Chicago Tribune;* to scripting for Charlton comic books and working as a political cartoonist; to creating, hosting, and co-producing an early PBS how-to-draw series called *Charlie's Pad;* to publishing two early collections of comic art, *Black Humor* (1970) and *Half-Past Nation Time* (1972). My passion as a child was—and to a certain extent is still—for the visual arts. It occurs to me sometimes when I'm writing literary criticism, as in *Being and Race,* or discussing aesthetics, that I often cross genres in the language I use for analyzing fiction, borrowing certain terminology from the realm of drawing.

Thus, drawing was my first passion. My second, which I discovered when I was seventeen, was philosophy. Writing was something I did strictly for fun: ghost-authoring papers for other students in my college dormitory, collaborating on metaphysical plays with my best friend at the time (another philosophy major), religiously keeping a journal, composing about eighty bad poems during my undergraduate days, and writing news articles (my other major was journalism). I read fiction hungrily, but mainly the authors who would appeal to a lover of philosophy—Sartre and Camus, Mann and Hesse, Hawthorne and Melville, etc. In the late 1960s and early 1970s my friends and I were very cross-disciplinary in our interests, and we understood fiction and philosophy to be sister disciplines. But, no, I had no specific intention to become a writer of fiction. However, I did realize something, when my interests turned to black American fiction—namely, how few black authors were concerned with probing the perennial questions of Western and Eastern philosophy in their stories. Only three black writers qualified (for me) as philosophically engaging: Jean Toomer, Richard Wright, and Ralph Ellison.

I began writing novels in earnest in 1970 with one specific goal in mind, that of expanding the category we might call black philosophical fiction; i.e., opening up black literature to the same ethical, ontological, and epistemological questions—Western and Eastern—that I wrestled with as a student of philosophy. From the very beginning, I've had no other aim as a literary artist.

BOCCIA: *Can you tell us something about your life that we cannot find elsewhere, something which sheds light on your work?*

JOHNSON: Two things, I suppose, have importance: the martial arts and Buddhism. When I was nineteen, I trained at a Chicago martial arts kwoon called Chi Tao Chuan of the Monastery, a very rough school that I've written about (see the author's preface to the new Plume edition of *Oxherding Tale*). Over the years I've trained in three traditional karate and three kung fu systems, and for the last eight years have co-directed the Blue Phoenix Kung fu Club in Seattle. I started with this system in 1981 in San Francisco at the main studio of Grandmaster Doc Fai Wong, and many of my closest friends today are also practitioners of this style. For me, traditional martial arts was a doorway into the theory and practice of Buddhism, a philosophy (or religion) that attracted me since my teens. I've published two stories that thematize Buddhism in the martial arts, "Kwoon" and "China," and elements from Eastern thought— Taoism, Hinduism—can be found in virtually every story or novel I've published.

BOCCIA: *Is there a hidden uncle or maiden aunt, a childhood love or a hated enemy, your alter-ego or a shadow of yourself in one of your characters? For example, was there an innocent and beautiful Faith Cross in your life? (And if so, can I have her telephone number?)*

JOHNSON: All of the above appear in the stories and novels—people I've known or characters who are composites of people I've known, but I'd better not reveal any of them by name. (One of my relatives once contemplated litigation against me for my use of her brother's name in a story.) As for Faith Cross, her description parallels closely that of my wife Joan in 1972 when we were both twenty-four years old, and I started work on *Faith and the Good Thing*. You can have her (our) phone number anyway.

BOCCIA: *We are all members of various subcultures. My family is Sicilian and African and Hispanic, and I grew up on the streets of New York City, all of which have impacted my life. What do you identify as your subcultures, and how did they affect you?*

JOHNSON: This is a tough question for me. The only thing I can identify as a "subculture" is the black American experience, but that is—as we know—a cultural experience that has shaped American politics, economics, music, religion, entertainment, athletics, and the arts since 1619. Subculture, indeed! It's best to say that from my childhood forward I've always seen myself first and foremost as an American, because it is impossible to separate out black people from this nation's evolution.

BOCCIA: *How and where did you grow up? What was your family like? What was your socioeconomic situation?*

JOHNSON: On my mother's side of the family (all deceased now), I can trace back my ancestors to a New Orleans black coachman born in the 1820s. I think his name was Jeff Peters. My father's people come from rural South Carolina near Hodges and Abbeville. My dad was one of twelve kids—six boys, six girls—born to a man who was a farmer and a blacksmith. What brought my Dad north to Evanston, Illinois, where he met my mother, was a promise of work from his uncle, William Johnson, who'd moved to Illinois in the 1920s. There, he started his own milk company to serve the black community (whites didn't deliver to them), and I have under glass one of his milk bottles, one that was sealed up in a building in my home town sixty years ago and not unearthed until the mid-1970s when that building in the downtown area was torn apart for remodeling. Uncle Will's milk company went belly up during the Depression. He started another company, the Johnson Construction Co., and once it was going (it continued into the 1960s), he invited his brother's sons in the South to come to work for him. So Dad and his brothers traveled north to work for my great-uncle; my father was introduced to my mother by his brother, and all of this led to my being here.

As a kid I remember riding around Evanston and my father pointing out to me places Uncle Will had built—Springfield Baptist Church, apartment buildings, and residences. He erected architecture all over the North Shore area, so I always had a sense that my family members had created parts of the world in which we lived. Those structures remain today long after Uncle Will's death at age ninety-seven in 1989. He was something of a character, the family patriarch (a role my father later inherited), a man who surely was a student of Booker T. Washington in the 1920s, and who over and over counseled me when I was a kid to "get an education; that's the most important thing."

My mother and father were a complementary pair. Both were quietly pious, and Ebenezer A.M.E. Church in Evanston, where I was baptized and married (and my son Malik baptized) was a valued part of our lives. (My mother sometimes taught Sunday school there.) She, an only child (like me), had always wanted to be a school teacher, but health problems (asthma) prevented this. Still, her interests ran toward books—she belonged to numerous book clubs in the 1960s—which we often shared, and toward whatever was unusual, exotic, unique. She was a Democrat, a passionate woman with a wicked sense of humor who encouraged my childhood passion for drawing, and she was someone my father relied on completely. As for my father, there is simply this to say: He is the hardest working, most moral man I've ever known. In the South he went as far as the fifth grade before his parents needed him full time to help with farmwork during the Depression. After moving to Evanston, he often worked two jobs a week—in construction and as a night watchman—as well as odd jobs for an elderly white couple in the suburbs on the weekends. He was—and still is at age seventy-three—a proud, never-idle man who voted Republican in the 1950s before my mother got him to switch parties, and he demanded the same Protestant work ethic from me when I was growing up. We were, I suppose, looking back, lower middleclass, but my parents clearly had middle-class values.

Something else to say is that my hometown and high school were integrated long before I was born; in fact, my mother graduated from Evanston Township High. When I was there between 1962 and 1966, black students made up 15 percent of what was then the second best public high school in America—we were proud of this distinction. And proud, too, I believe, that integration was something we all took for granted. My friends from kindergarten through high school were white as well as black. Bigotry, as we understood it then, was simply "uncool."

BOCCIA: *Did your idea of your cultural identity change over the years? How would you say this has shaped you and your work?*

JOHNSON: Given my childhood, I think I can safely say that I was a child of integration. I never questioned its validity until I went away to college and met other black students more affected by black power than integration, by Malcolm X than Martin Luther King, Jr. The ideology of "blackness" was something I learned in the late 1960s and early 1970s on campus, not from the piously Christian black folks in my family or their friends. A part of me sympathizes with black nationalist concerns, such as economic self-sufficiency—remember, my Uncle Will was a black businessman devoted to helping his own. But I just never bought into black cultural nationalism. It always struck me as naïve (all cultures we know about are synthetic, a tissue of con-

# MICHAEL BOCCIA

tributions from others). The way its proponents portrayed other races—whites, for example—had nothing to do with the supportive people I knew when I was growing up. In the end, black cultural nationalism only served to remind me of how thoroughly American my family and I have always been.

BOCCIA: *What works of art do you consciously imitate? Clearly your works have parodied or imitated escaped slave narratives and visual art such as* Ten Oxherding Pictures. *What books would you suggest we read to better see the structure of your novels?*

JOHNSON: Parody may not be the right word here. My first (and only) writing mentor was novelist John Gardner. There was much we had in common—as teacher and apprentice—but one thing about Gardner stands out for me. In his work there is a formal virtuosity, a deep knowledge of literary forms from within, whether we are talking about the triple-decker *Sunlight Dialogues,* the pastoral *Nickel Mountain,* or the explosion of forms that inform his other works. In other words, something I deeply appreciated in Gardner—and have always tended to do myself—is to take form itself as a meditation when I'm writing. Each story in *The Sorcerer's Apprentice* should upon examination profile a different form—the tale, parable, animal fable, science fiction, etc. I suspect this way of approaching fiction is something we owe to the creators of the "New Fiction" that emerged in the late 1960s—including Gardner, John Barth, Robert Coover, Ron Sukenick, Ishmael Reed, and John Fowles, at least in terms of his magical novel *The French Lieutenant's Woman.*

BOCCIA: *What books did you read as a child or as you evolved as an artist? What films or paintings or cartoons did you see?*

JOHNSON: Although I spent a summer devouring James T. Farrell's *Studs Lonigan Trilogy* when I was in high school, my personal tastes don't incline much to "naturalism," which I see as being an interesting but limited theory and literary approach that began in the late nineteenth century. (For example, the life-world of naturalism falls short of adequately portraying the life of the spirit and, for that matter, anything we know about the sub-atomic realm of physics). Generally, I prefer the tale. In high school I made myself read at least one book a week, everything from science fiction (I joined a book club) to Plutarch's *Lives of the Noble Grecians.* As a young philosophy student I loved *Candide,* had fun with Jack London's *Martin Eden,* Shakespeare, Mary Shelley, Sartre's plays, all of D. H. Lawrence (including his letters), Dickens, Kafka, P. G. Wodehouse. This list could go on and on. When I discover an author, I tend to read everything I can by him or her until I'm saturated by their work.

As for films, I've loved since the 1950s Paddy Chayevsky's *Marty,* Disney's *Fantasia,* Capra's beautiful *Lost Horizon,* Sidney Poitier in *All the Young Men,* and Jane Fonda in *They Shoot Horses, Don't They?* I'll confess to admiring Peckinpah's *The Wild Bunch* and *Straw Dogs,* but right now a discovery I'm giddy about is Ang Lee's *Pushing Hands.*

As a kid, I regularly visited the Evanston Public Library and checked out *all* their books on art. I did the same as a student at Southern Illinois University, then at SUNY-Stony Brook. Diego Rivera is a favorite of mine. Also—and especially—Nicholas Roerich. Among cartoonists I deeply admired Jack Davis, caricaturist Mort Drucker, Charles Schultz, Gahan Wilson, Burne Hogarth, the prolific Jack Kirby, Wallace Wood, and the seminal Will Eisner. This, believe me, is only a partial list.

BOCCIA: *Who are the "dead" writers you most admire? I choose dead writers so that you will have no opportunity to offend by omission, but you need not limit yourself in any way.*

JOHNSON: Where to begin? Start with Homer and Plato. Move on to St. Augustine and Hegel. Throw in Voltaire, Melville, most of the phenomenologists—Husserl, Heidegger, Sartre, Scheler, Merleau-Ponty, Mikel Dufrenne—then ease on to Toomer, Wright, Ellison, Albert Murray (still going strong), and Gardner. Again, this list is woefully incomplete. I think my favorite "dead" writers are those who are involved in what has been called the "epic conversation"; that is, the writers dialoguing across centuries with each other about the nature of Being.

BOCCIA: *Your work has touched upon issues ranging from entropy to Asian philosophies. What are the central themes that run through all your work?*

JOHNSON: At last, an easy question! If the principal novels and stories in my body of work have a central theme it is the investigation of the nature of the self and personal identity. As a phenomenologist, I cannot help but believe that consciousness is primary for all "experience"—that the nature of the *I* is the deepest of mysteries, and that all other questions arise from this primordial one, *What am I?*

BOCCIA: *Do you feel that certain themes have been misunderstood?*

JOHNSON: Yes. One of the greatest mistakes that critics and readers make when approaching a novel by a black author is the tendency to read that work as sociology, anthropology, or as a political statement of some sort. By taking such a limited and narrowing approach, critics and readers miss time and again the remarkable passages on "history" and perception in Ellison's *Invisible Man,* the treatment of temporal experience in Wright's *Native Son,* the Buddhist-Hindu-Taoist meditations in *Oxherding Tale,* and the dramatization of Buddhist epistemology in my story "Moving Pictures." As educators, I feel we simply must help our students to become better readers—and to make clear the point that for many black writers "race" is not the only subject they can write about with authority.

BOCCIA: *You have told us that there's nothing worse than being haunted by a philosopher's ghost. What ghosts haunt you?*

JOHNSON: Gautama, the twenty-fifth Buddha. Lao Tzŭ [Laozi] and Chaung Tzŭ [Zhuanzi]. Gandhi when he speaks of *satyagraha.* Martin Luther King, Jr., when, as a philosopher, he speaks so beautifully of the "beloved community," of agapic love and the "network of mutuality" that binds all life as one.

## An Interview with Charles Johnson (1996)

BOCCIA: *You mention numerous world views and philosophies in your work. What was the path of your growth and personal philosophy?*

JOHNSON: I may have indirectly answered some of this already. Early in life, I found Buddhism deeply appealing and made the study of Eastern scholarship a lifelong avocation. But in college I encountered black cultural nationalism, which I felt the need to respond to, mainly as a cartoonist. Shortly thereafter I settled into Marxism, did my master's thesis on Wilhelm Reich and how he was influenced by Freud and Marx; then I taught Marxism as a PhD teaching assistant at Stony Brook—everything from the *1844 Manuscripts* to Mao—while immersing myself in the history, theory, and practice of phenomenology. I still believe the Marxist critique of capital, though I no longer much believe in Marxist solutions to social and economic problems. My philosophical method, the one I fall back on whenever in doubt, is phenomenology. And on the deeper spiritual levels, I fully embrace the so-called "three refuges" of the Buddha, the dharma, and the *sangha*. (Early Buddhism, by the way, has often been called a very rudimentary form of phenomenology—the two have much in common in respect to their forms of "radical empiricism.")

BOCCIA: *Assuming for the moment that there is an "American Culture," how do you think that this society affected your work?*

JOHNSON: The work I've done could only have been attempted and could only have found its audience in America. Why? I've visited many countries in Europe and the Far East as a lecturer, and something that struck me repeatedly was how closed many societies are. There is nothing in England that equals our First Amendment. In Indonesia, writers are routinely tossed in jail for criticizing the government. In Czechoslovakia in 1989 I met with PEN authors who'd only been released from jail three days earlier during the "Velvet Revolution," authors who explained to me how the former Czech government had its list of "approved" writers (none of them were on the list), most of whom they said were mediocre. There, I met with publishers who only after their Revolution felt they could translate certain American authors who previously had been banned (Gardner was one of them).

Whatever our faults as Americans, we have protected freedom of expression. Often I wonder if our cultural nationalists and Afrocentrists value this feature of American public life— this philosophical demand that we permit the airing of views contrary to our own—as much as I do. In a different, more closed society, or in another age (that of Copernicus or Socrates), I suspect my own work would be buried or banned as "ideologically unacceptable."

BOCCIA: *Do you feel that mainstream culture accepts your work?*

JOHNSON: It's hard to know what is meant by "mainstream culture." However, I do know that *Middle Passage,* the short stories, and even *Oxherding Tale* are taught nationwide in colleges, high schools (public and private), and even some middle schools. Courses have been designed around *Middle Passage;* dissertations have been—and are being—written; it's been taught at the U. S. Coast Guard Academy, is read by book clubs, and is in its tenth printing.

BOCCIA: *How has winning the National Book Award affected the popularity of your work?*

JOHNSON: Let's just say the NBA gave it a nice boost in 1990.

BOCCIA: *Are there plans for films of your fiction?*

JOHNSON: To date, I've written more than twenty screen- and teleplays. No need to list here those projects, but I have been working now for four years on the movie project for *Middle Passage,* first at Tri-Star, then at Interscope with the Hudlin brothers, Reggie and Warrington. I've written two screenplays for this project, and it's been optioned three times. We're about to option it again this June, and my hope is that we can be in production soon. I should say that this is an expensive movie—

between $40 and $70 million—which is quite a challenge for a studio, particularly since Hollywood has no track record yet with doing black epics. Nevertheless, we're confident it will get done.

BOCCIA: *Can you describe what you see as our historical era?*

JOHNSON: In twenty-five words or less? Okay, here goes: I think the best, most prosperous days for America came after World War II, when this country emerged unscatched from the battles that left much of Europe in smoldering ruins. Through the 1950s the baby boomers—and I am one—saw a decade and a half of unparalleled growth and opportunity. The civil rights movement only improved upon this. Then, with the escalation of the Vietnam War, a decade of political assassinations, and Watergate, American self-confidence was badly wounded. Next came the rise of Japan as a serious competitor (China will take that role in the twenty-first century), and the transformation of American capital—the loss of the kinds of jobs my father relied on in the 1950s and '60s, with the inner cities all but abandoned and corporations no longer restricted by national boundaries. This is the end, I believe, of an era. To be honest, I think we are at a crossroads as we approach the eleventh hour of the twentieth century. Though still a "super power"—in fact, the only super power left after the collapse of communism in Eastern Europe and the Soviet Union—the United States is facing, not its youth, but instead its middle age. A time of cutting back. Downsizing. Of letting some of its dreams go by the boards while other societies, at last free of colonialism, take their places as major players on the world stage.

BOCCIA: *In the battle between the ancients and moderns, how are we distinct?*

JOHNSON: As a Buddhist, I believe deeply that all things are impermanent, transitory. The Chinese have a lovely phrase, "A thousand years a city; a thousand years a forest." In other words, all things—nations included—go through the process of rising and passing away. Yet I think this country will be remembered, perhaps as a glorious oddity, for the way it struggled mightily to resolve the difference between its ideology of freedom and its treatment of blacks, minorities, women, and gays. No other nation has wrestled more with the ideals of "equality" and the commitment to individualism. The major domestic events in our history—the Civil War and the civil rights movement—attest to this. Whether or not we succeed in these social goals, it must be said of Americans in our time that we tried. We pushed the envelope of the question of social justice farther than any society in recorded history. *Are we being fair?* is our daily koan, and I think this defines the character of modern Americans.

BOCCIA: *What has happened to you as a human and as an artist that marks you as distinctly of our historical period?*

JOHNSON: Obviously, the civil rights movement was of central importance in shaping the lived-world (*Lebenswelt*) of my young manhood. I came of age at a time when America was still "the land of opportunity" but also fluid during the 1960s. As one of my friends during that time put it, "I'm a nigger, I can do anything!" That was the sense of life that I soaked up around me—there were no artistic or intellectual restrictions. If I wanted to be a cartoonist, a philosopher, a fiction writer, a college professor, an essayist, a screenwriter, a martial artist, all I needed to achieve any or all of these things was my own talent, disciplined labor, and the blessing of God. In other words, the self was a verb, not a noun—a process, not a product. You defined your life through action, deeds; or, as Sartre might put it, "Existence preceded essence." In the late 1960s, you did not see yourself or your essence—your life's meaning—as defined wholly by the past, or by race or class. As an artist, you were not confined to any single tradition; rather, you could creatively cross genres and in doing so bring something fresh in the way of meaning and form into existence. Whether we are talking about the arts, politics, or the art of living, the one word—the single driving idea—of this historical period is *freedom.*

BOCCIA: *What contemporary social, political, or cultural*

*issues are reflected in your writing that have been generally overlooked by your readers?*

JOHNSON: In his yet unpublished literary study of my work, critic Jonathan Little says, "Critics have surprisingly downplayed the spiritual in Johnson's fiction, tending to stress instead Western philosophy. As few critics have pointed out, Johnson's fiction and aesthetic have evolved into a pathway to the divine; they have come to show us the sacred already existent within the network of human interrelatedness and connections. His art and criticism now imply the preeminence of the intangible spiritual realm as a foundation for ethical, political, and social strategies in ways that are more liberal humanist than postmodern." I believe Little is absolutely right.

As I mentioned, I became a writer specifically to develop black (and thereby American) philosophical fiction. But over the last three decades, I found that intellectual integrity demanded that, along with the dramatization of Western philosophical concerns, I also had to acknowledge and explore the central questions in Eastern religions. In short, the life of the spirit has been something I could not—and did not want to—ignore. And sometimes, late at night when I think back over the products of thirty years, it seems to me that my fiction is at bottom a form of spiritual literature—that I want it on the shelf beside Somerset Maugham's *The Razor's Edge,* Hesse's *Siddhartha,* James Hilton's *Lost Horizon,* Thomas Mann's *The Transposed Heads,* Toomer's poem "Blue Meridian," beside St. Francis's famous prayer, beside *The Dhammapada,* the *Bhagavad-Gita,* and the work of Shankara. For in the pre-taxonomic space cleared by the phenomenological *epoché,* the little boxes and categories into which we sort "experience" do not exist. There is only Being, which holds within itself spirit, mind, and body without our limited, racial, parochial, and self-interested distinctions.

# A MAN OF
# HIS WORD

## BETH GRUBB

CHARLES JOHNSON, '71, MA '73, never gets writer's block. Not when facing a trainload of material for a novel that took seventeen years to research. Not when pumping out a dozen short stories in one month to meet a tight book deadline. And especially not when traipsing through the mountains of Thailand in search of spiritual experiences.

All of which might partially explain why Johnson is so prolific. Since 1970 he has published four novels; a book of short stories; scores of book reviews, introductions and literary criticism; twenty scripts for television and film; a volume of essays he co-edited; and a collection of short stories for a book on slavery—not to mention two volumes of cartoons and more than one thousand published drawings.

Reprinted from *Southern Alumni* 61 (Fall 1998), with permission.

Johnson's shelves are heavy with marks of his fame: a National Book Award (1990) for his third novel, *Middle Passage;* a Writer's Guild Award for his work on the PBS drama *Booker;* and a so-called genius grant worth $305,000 from the John D. and Catherine T. MacArthur Foundation (awarded earlier this year).

Want more evidence of Johnson's success? His answering machine identifies various agents to call for speaking engagements, literary matters, or screen writing. A collector might pay more than $200 for an unsigned first-edition copy of his debut novel, *Faith and the Good Thing.* Microsoft sent him on a ten-day adventure to anywhere he wanted (he chose Thailand), so he could write about his experience. His name pops up whenever the words "black" and "writer" are used in the same sentence.

At age fifty, Johnson is a major talent: popular in bookstores, respected in literary circles and successful at his craft. He is an ambidextrous wordsmith, deeply in love with words.

"The English language is so rich," Johnson says. "It has more words than any other language—more than two million. That is the writer's tool, our most basic, fundamental tool."

The man is a walking thesaurus. His writing is sprinkled with words such as *ensorcel* (which means "to hypnotize or mesmerize"), *orlop* (an archaic sailing term describing the lowest deck of a ship), and *samu* (a Japanese word meaning "monastic labor"). Readers of his work are advised to keep their dictionaries handy.

Johnson actually once read, and apparently absorbed, *Webster's New Twentieth Century Dictionary*—a notion he borrowed from former SIU professor John Gardner and from Malcolm X, who reportedly read the dictionary in prison.

"That's something every writer needs to do at some point in his or her life," Johnson says. "You discover that there is a word for every thing, every tangible object, every intangible object, every thought, every feeling. Oliver Wendell Holmes said, 'The word is the skin of a thought.'"

Students in Johnson's creative writing classes at the University of Washington, where he is the S. Wilson and Grace M. Pollock Professor of English, are asked to learn five new words every class day. When they bring especially evocative words to the class's attention, Johnson rewards them with a prize—an issue of the Writers' Guild magazine.

This love for the singular building blocks of language began early in Johnson's life. Always a copious reader, he remembers carefully choosing paperbacks from the neighborhood newsstand on Saturday afternoons and devouring two or three a week.

The small faculty office where Johnson conducts business on the University of Washington campus in Seattle holds little interest for visitors: just a university-issue desk, an extra chair, a funky lamp sporting a hand-painted figure of Martin Luther King, and hundreds of books stacked in descending order of circumstance, like sediment in a cross-section of earth.

One stratum contains first-edition novels he has judged for the Pulitzer Prize (twice) and the National Book Award, among other contests. Another tier reveals "important fiction" he refers to in his classes; philosophy tomes are squeezed in between layers for later reference. Recurring topics run in marbleized streaks: Martin Luther King, nineteenth-century sailing ships, slavery, Buddhism, martial arts, drawing.

"These are just the ones that don't fit in my house and garage," Johnson explains, with a self-amused chuckle.

On the desk is a letter informing him that his best-known novel, *Middle Passage,* will be read by all 1,600 Stanford freshmen this year.

"The book is kind of canonical by now," Johnson shrugs. "The publisher tells me they sell 1,100 copies a month."

But, at the moment, his mind is on more recent works, including last April's *Dreamer,* a fictionalized account of Martin Luther King, Jr.'s, 1966 campaign in Chicago. In September another book went on sale: *Africans in America: America's Journey through Slavery*, the companion book to a PBS series aired this fall.

The latest book became controversial last spring when Johnson's co-author, Patricia Smith, was forced to resign her position as a *Boston Globe* columnist after fabricating sources and information in several columns. Johnson was surprised by the incident, but still has high praise for Smith's writing.

"She's a splendid prose stylist," Johnson says, "I marvel at some of her imagery." He explains that his part in the book was to write twelve short stories (which he accomplished in one month), interspersed between chapters of historical text written by Smith. "It really is Patricia's book," he says humbly. "She had the harder job. I wrote sixty pages of stories, and she wrote three hundred pages of text to accompany the documentary."

In light of Smith's dismissal, the book's publisher, Harcourt Brace, went over the manuscript with the finest of combs—twice. "The book was thoroughly, microscopically checked," Johnson says. He adds that Smith is a talented woman who, he believes, will land on her feet. "She just got in over her head, and she cut corners."

Leaning into a subject he has obviously given some thought to, he continues: "What goes on in journalism now is a lot different than what we were taught. Objectivity was the ideal. Important facts were checked by three different sources. But now news has become entertainment, more like the supermarket tabloids. The pictures get bigger, the type gets bigger, and the stories are selected for their shock value. And some of the journalists feel pressured to get their stories out quickly. There's no time to be careful or your competitor will get the story first. So you go with what you've got and then there's a retraction because the story is false. That erodes public confidence in what they read."

This might be a good place to confess that the line about Johnson being a walking thesaurus is purloined from *Dreamer*. The novel's protagonist, Matthew Bishop, a shy, young black man who works for King, is told by another character that he "talks like a thesaurus." The similarity between the fictitious Bishop and the real-life Johnson was too tempting to resist.

Johnson was a senior in an Evanston high school when King unwillingly sparked the Chicago riots of 1966.

"I graduated that spring and then was preparing to go to college, so it didn't really touch me directly. My memories are very hazy. Researching that period was actually illuminating for me," he says.

Asked whether the character of Matthew Bishop is somewhat autobiographical, Johnson replies, "I imagine myself in all the characters of the book," especially, we may assume, the Reverend King, whose fictionalized thoughts we are privy to in alternating chapters of the novel.

"I have deep sympathetic feelings for King. That's always the case with a novel," Johnson says.

For four years, Johnson researched King's life in minute detail—his sermons and experiences, photos and films of him, commentary from his college professors, everything written about King and every word that King wrote from the time he was a teenager.

"What's interesting about King is how complex his life was, although he was only thirty-nine when he died. It's interesting how many aspects of the American and global experience his life touched upon, passed through, altered and altered him."

On his book tour for *Dreamer,* Johnson discovered that most people are not that knowledgeable about King. "They know so little about Dr. King's social vision, how it evolved and what were the central points in it." He explains that non-violence was not merely a strategy of the civil rights movement but a philosophy to which King was committed.

Johnson also wanted to write about King because no works of fiction had been written about him. "I get attracted to stories for which there are no precedents," he says. That desire has also led Johnson to merge two intellectual interests: writing and philosophy. "Philosophy is one of my passions," he explains.

"As I looked at black American literature, it occurred to me that there was a great void in respect to philosophical fiction. And for somebody with a background in philosophy, there were all kinds of basic philosophical questions—not terribly esoteric— that I knew could be addressed and dramatized but simply were not. That's the heart and soul and core of my body of work. I want my novels to be probing and I want them to unearth questions that are part of our human experience but sometimes never get talked about.

"There are stories that are not told, that are so important," Johnson suggests. "Why are there no stories about the late astronaut Ron McNair? Why no stories about Colin Powell? The expansion of our images and the stories we tell is important because there is so much of the human experience that is never told. There is so much that hasn't got anything to do with race. It's not about being black, it's about being American. It's about being human."

Johnson's journey to SIU was circuitous to say the least. His first love was drawing, and as a high school senior he was already publishing award-winning cartoons in the school paper. He planned to go to art school.

A warning from his art teacher about the realities of making a living as a professional artist caused a last-minute change of heart. "I thought about it and thought about it, and I said, 'Wait a minute. I'm the first member of my family to go to college—can I risk this?' So I ran back to my adviser and asked if there were any schools still accepting students. This was in May. She looked in her big book and the first one she came up with was Southern Illinois University, and I said, 'OK, I'll go there.' And I majored in journalism because I had worked on the paper and figured journalism would give me the opportunity to write *and* draw.

"That was a remarkable time in American history. I was one

of the first wave of black students pouring out of the north to go down to that school," Johnson says. "One of my friends who went to high school with me and also went to SIU said, 'It's wide open here!' And he was quite right. They were very flexible and open to creativity. A lot of things were changing, and the 1960s were an exciting time to be in college."

The roots of *Middle Passage,* Johnson's novel about a nineteenth-century slave trader, can be traced to an undergraduate course Johnson took at SIU. It began as a term paper, before he revised it several times into a novel. For many years Johnson was dissatisfied with the book's "voice." He originally wrote it from the point of view of the ship's captain, but later changed the perspective to that of Rutherford Calhoun, a stowaway freedman. Amid researching, thinking about, and rewriting *Middle Passage,* Johnson signed up for John Gardner's writing class. Gardner took Johnson under his wing, introduced him to the literary world, and served as his writing coach for many years.

Under Gardner's tutelage, Johnson published his first novel, *Faith and the Good Thing.* (Johnson set aside *Middle Passage,* returning to it again and again for seventeen years before finishing the novel in 1990.) Today, sixteen years after his mentor's death, Johnson frequently speaks of Gardner and uses his texts on writing in his classes.

Although focused on his writing, Johnson did not abandon drawing while in college. He drew cartoons for the student newspaper, the *Daily Egyptian,* as well as for *The Southern Illinoisan.* He even convinced the campus television station, WSIU, to produce a series of fifteen-minute shows teaching people how to draw. The station taped fifty-two segments of *Charlie's Pad,* which ran on PBS stations all over the country.

Johnson translated his fond memories into enthusiastic support for SIU, most notably through the Charles Johnson Award, given annually to talented young writers. Open to college students all over the country, the prize rewards minority writers or those who write about issues related to race, culture, or a minority subject. Johnson provided the award's initial funding, but SIU now includes the award in its budget.

"I feel good that I could give something back to the school," Johnson says. "I feel very indebted to the university and the professors I had there, particularly in the philosophy and communications departments.

"We had magnificent teachers, like John Gardner, prior to his becoming a best-selling author. Buckminster Fuller was there at the time. It was a most interesting group of people brought there by the president of the university." Johnson particularly remembers former English chair John Howell; Howard Long, who founded the Journalism School; and Louis Hahn and Elizabeth Eames in philosophy.

Back in present-day Seattle, after finishing three books and two book tours in the past year, Johnson is taking a breather, maybe for the first time in fifty years. He's catching up on reading, spending some time with his wife, Joan, and their two children, and thinking about his next book.

"Maybe by the end of the year I'll know what I'm going to do next," he says, relishing these rare days off. "Once I commit to a book, it's like a marriage. Everything I think about, read, hear, feel—it's got to relate to that book until it's done."

A promise of devotion from a man who is never at a loss for words.

# A CONVERSATION
# WITH CHARLES JOHNSON

## WILLIAM R. NASH

NASH: *I'D LIKE TO begin with your childhood—what can you tell us about your early life experience that is important to an understanding of your work? How did your home environment influence your development as an artist?*

JOHNSON: There's nothing unusual to report about my childhood, except perhaps that it was free of the stress that most sociologists seem to enjoy attributing to black life. I was an only child, the son of a mother who dreamed of being a school teacher (and was a Sunday school teacher) but for health reasons couldn't pursue that goal—she had severe asthma—so I became her only pupil. My father, as I relate in my essay in the anthology *Black Men Speaking,* is a very hardworking Christian who

Reprinted from *New England Review* 19 (Spring 1998), by permission of William Nash.

supported my early desire at age fourteen to become a professional cartoonist and illustrator. Added to which, I grew up in
Evanston, Illinois, which in the 1950s was a very attractive
community—integrated, with the number-one high school in
the nation in the 1960s, a community of black people—many
of them tradesmen—who came from the South determined to
make a better life for themselves and their children.

NASH: *I'm also interested to know what each of your parents gave you that has shaped your life experience and your
career.*

JOHNSON: My mother, who died in 1981, had a very artistic sensibility, an artist's eye for the beautiful, the exotic, the
unique. When I was a child she conjured things to beautify our
home from the humblest of materials, and had me help her. She
was in numerous book clubs, so our home was full of books,
and naturally I joined a book club on my own (for science fiction)
when I was a teenager. Most likely, this presence of literature
in our house led me to discipline myself to read one book a week
when I was in high school, everything from James Bond novels to westerns to Plutarch's *Lives of the Noble Grecians.* My
mother also introduced me to keeping a diary when I was twelve
years old, which later became a journal when I went away to
college, inexpensive books I filled up with poetry, reflections,
and later ideas for novels, etc. She recognized my drawing talent even before my teachers in school, of course, and she encouraged me in that direction. I suppose what I learned most from
my father was how to work. He held down three jobs in the
mid-1960s to support my mother and me, never complained
about doing so, and he is simply the most moral man I've ever
known. Doesn't swear. Goes to church. A generous, easy-to-
laugh gentleman who always measured himself by the quality
and quantity of his labor.

NASH: *Do you see your father and mother reappearing in
any ways in the fathers and mothers throughout your body of
work?*

JOHNSON: Elements of my father appear sometimes, though I've not yet drawn anything from my mother. As I look at my fiction, I see a recurrent pattern—the exploration of father/son relations, and perhaps this is so because my dad is the only man on earth I've ever felt I had to please or answer to unconditionally.

NASH: *You've noted that from early on your mother encouraged you to read and draw. Do you also remember being read to when young? What sorts of things did she read to you?*

JOHNSON: I just can't recall. Mom and I did go to movies together when I was little—she'd take me to see the great old sci-fi and horror flicks (one time I ran out in the lobby because I got so scared) and also musicals. Often, when I was older, we'd read the same books and discuss them.

NASH: *Can you recall the first book that you read that inspired you to consider being an author yourself?*

JOHNSON: In my teens my only interest really was in drawing, in becoming an illustrator and commercial artist. For example, I was planning on going to art school until the eleventh hour before my graduation when I withdrew from the art school in Illinois that accepted me and decided to major in journalism instead at a university. After reading my one book a week in high school, I'd stack them on my desk, and I do remember once looking at the spines of those books, at the titles, and thinking that, yes, someday I'd enjoy seeing my name on the spine of a book. But in the mid-1960s, it was a thought peripheral to my real passion, which was art.

NASH: *When you began writing in journals, again with your mother's encouragement, what sorts of things were you inspired to record?*

JOHNSON: Basically, I wrote down all the things I thought and felt that were impolite to say about my relatives and friends. Instead of carrying these things around in my head and heart, I found I could let them spill out on a blank page, where I could look at them—objectified, so to speak—and that was kind of miraculous to me, that the inner could become the outer, the intangible and subjective could crystallize before me in the world and be shaped and re-shaped through language or the drawn image.

NASH: *Was your drawing an integral part of keeping a journal then? Does it figure into your present journal writing in any way?*

JOHNSON: I drew in some of the journals—which I have boxes of by now, weighing down one of my filing cabinets. But, no, drawing wasn't integral. I will say, however, that sometimes when I'm working on a novel—*Faith* or *Oxherding Tale*—I did sketch some of the main characters for myself, just to visualize them.

NASH: *Did your journal writing change in any significant way when you shifted from the visual arts to fiction writing?*

JOHNSON: Yes, the journals became more literary and philosophical. Some entries are mini-essays on aesthetic problems, and often I gave them titles. During the late 1970s some of these entries ran for pages and pages because I was working through for myself issues relating to literature, race, and the highly politicized climate of the arts at that time and where I did (or did not) fit within it.

NASH: *What's the relationship between the material in the journal and your published work? Do your journals ever provide you with inspiration, ideas, etc., for your fiction?*

JOHNSON: The truth is that once I fill up a journal, I usually put it away and start a new one, seldom looking back. On the other hand, I did revisit my entries written at the time of John Gardner's death, edited them, and published them as an article called "Journal Entries on the Death of John Gardner," which appears in *New Myths* (1995), edited by Robert Mooney and Philip Brady, and published by the Binghampton University Foundation. Those entries proved invaluable for that project.

NASH: *Your careers as writer and cartoonist have over-lapped twice since you began publishing—first in the late 1960s and early 1970s and then more recently with your cartoons in the* Quarterly Black Review of Books. *What's the relationship between the comic art and the fiction you've produced in each of these periods? Has it changed?*

JOHNSON: One sense in which it hasn't changed is that I simply *have* to draw in order to feel self-fulfillment. It's a talent that I've had since I could pick up a pencil, and I feel it would be dreadful not to develop it—I feel that in a very biblical way (the story of the talents). Back in the 1960s, I worked full-time as an illustrator, political cartoonist, and teacher of cartooning (in *Charlie's Pad,* and a free course I taught on SIU-Carbondale's campus in 1968)—it was my life. Today I draw because I feel the artwork complements and completes my fiction, just as the stories and drawings of James Thurber complement each other. I see one's body of work as being like a big house with many rooms. There is a foundation for the house I'm building (*Oxherding Tale*); inside the house are rooms you can wander through or stay awhile in. One has novels. Another has short fiction. In a third you'll find screenplays. A fourth has philosophical essays. A sub-room of that has essays on many other subjects—Indonesia, how to draw political cartoons, etc. Yet another room is devoted to book reviews that (I hope) are position papers on art, as were the reviews of my teacher and friend John Gardner. Yet another room has comic art. On and on through this house, from the basement to the attic, you find art in numerous rooms. You find television dramas in one room. Fiction on the martial arts in a sub-room of the bigger room devoted to short stories. This is my conception of what a *total* body of work is about, one that is evolved over a lifetime, is generous, and offers a variety of different experiences.

NASH: *With regard to your earlier cartoons, those in* Half-Past Nation Time *and* Black Humor, *I know that in some ways they respond to the ideas of the black arts movement and the black power movement. What's your sense of the intentions—or phenomenologically speaking—the intentionality of the black arts movement?*

JOHNSON: That's an easy question. The intentionality is to replace white hegemony with black hegemony in all areas of human experience.

NASH: *What, in your view, are the benefits and limitations of those intentions?*

JOHNSON: The benefits are that a people (black) long disenfranchised, denied power, and marginalized culturally and politically, finally have a voice, self-determination, and a "place at the table," so it speak. The drawback is just what Martin Luther King, Jr., described in his famous sermon "The Drum Major Instinct," i.e., the danger is the tendency for blacks (or previously whites) to dominate others.

NASH: *Do you see the actual results of those intentions as successful or unsuccessful in the main?*

JOHNSON: The intention has proven to be successful when black Americans with integrity and talent have been given the opportunity to assume leadership positions in American politics, education, and the arts. It is unsuccessful, of course, when those blacks who simply wish to exploit America's racial problems for personal profit bully their way into leadership positions. Remember, King says in his sermon that we should not deny the "drum major instinct" to want to be first—rather we should redirect it toward the goals of being first in service to others, first in love, first in giving and generosity.

NASH: *How do you see the black arts movement affecting your development as a writer?*

JOHNSON: I've always striven to be the kind of writer for whom nothing of significance is lost or ignored. The black arts movement was in the air when I was a college student. It was, sad to say, unavoidable. It was something I had to deal with, whether I wanted to or not. And I did deal with it, mainly when I was working as a cartoonist. It's important to remember that one of its primary proponents, Amiri Baraka, left it behind in the early '70s—repudiated it, in other words—and embraced what he called "scientific socialism."

NASH: *At the heart of these questions is the assumption that you as a black writer will necessarily have commentary about "black issues," a position that you have resisted for years. There is, however, a great deal of pressure at present on black scholars and artists to become public figures who speak for the race, as it were. What do you see as the boundaries black critics and artists need to observe in the face of this pressure?*

JOHNSON: The best answer to that question is provided by Peter J. Harris in his essay "Testimony of a Good Nigger," which appears in *Black Men Speaking* (Indiana, 1997), an anthology of original works that I co-edited with John McCluskey, Jr. In his essay, Peter says, "I am not trying to be an expert or spokesman for black men. I see black men as experts on their own lives. I humbly ask them what's on their minds. I listen. I risk trust. . . ." In other words, no one can speak for 33 million black Americans. Our continuum of voices ranges from Thomas Sowell to Al Sharpton, Walter Williams and Ken Hamblin to Louis Farrakhan. Would anyone ask John Updike to speak for white Americans? The idea is absurd.

NASH: *What are the consequences attached to not acknowledging such boundaries?*

JOHNSON: The worst consequence is that we insult black people by denying their individuality and the variety of their visions. To counteract this foolishness, I tell my children time and time again that each of them is unique, like no one who has ever lived before or will ever live again, and if someone cannot approach them in terms of their individuality, then they should not let that person approach them at all.

NASH: *Building on that, let's set aside those assumptions for a moment and focus more specifically on your concerns as a writer. In what ways are racially related questions significant for you as an author? And in what ways is race not significant to your aesthetic project?*

JOHNSON: "Race" is significant to me simply—as I said earlier—because I wish to be a writer on whom nothing of importance is lost. But, as a Buddhist, I see "race" as an illusion, a product of the mind. I see it as *maya*. I certainly did not start writing in order to address only racial issues. That would, I'm afraid, bore me to death because this mysterious, wondrous universe we inhabit has so much *more* in it than the illusion of race. Sure, I'll write about it in order to clarify my feelings on, say, affirmative action (as I did in the story "Executive Decision"), but I'm just as happy exploring Mark Twain's novel *What Is Man?* or co-writing an article on the martial arts with a long-time friend I work out with, or doing a piece—as I soon have to—on the experience of "beauty" in Thailand. I write sometimes about race because I'm an American artist, first and foremost, and race is part of our discussion these days. But no, it's not central to my aesthetic position as a phenomenological Buddhist.

NASH: *You suggest that it is both possible and necessary to see you and other black writers as more than experts on one issue. What's your opinion of racial critics like bell hooks and Trey Ellis, among others, who call for an expansion of the possibilities inherent in black artistry beyond current limitations? Do you see connections between your work and their call for a new conception of African American art—what hooks calls an "aesthetics of blackness"?*

JOHNSON: I've read Trey's essay on a new black aesthetic, and I'm somewhat familiar with hooks's criticism. Yes, there are similarities when—as artists and critics—we speak to the need for black artists to create more expansively, but it's very important to sort out the differing landscapes of our critical positions, where we agree and disagree.

NASH: *Are there young writers publishing today whom you see benefiting from your resistance to racial essentialism?*

JOHNSON: That's a tough question. I don't want to take credit, you know, for any other artist's progress or evolution.

NASH: *That leads me to another large question again—you say in* Being and Race: Black Writing Since 1970 *that "our*

*most interesting writers . . . consciously formulate for them-*
*selves an aesthetic, a project." How do you see your body of*
*work as a whole in terms of a larger project? Are the published*
*works steps in a progression towards a definite end? If so, how*
*would you define that end, and where do you see yourself at*
*present in terms of your journey toward it?*

JOHNSON: Please look back to my metaphor of a body of
work as being like a many-roomed house (or mansion). That's
the goal: to create in great abundance, as a service, as an act of
giving. Specifically, I began writing to fill what I perceived as a
void in black philosophical fiction. To be perfectly honest, there
is more engagement with philosophy—Western and Eastern—
in my work than you will find anywhere in the history of black
American literature. At forty-nine, after working steadily as a
professional artist for thirty-two years, I see myself as just a little beyond the middle of my journey. I want another twenty
good years of creative production, in the arena of philosophical fiction, but also on the endless number of other subjects that
stimulate my imagination and intellect—"regional phenome-
nologies," as I believe Husserl once put it.

NASH: *In your first three novels, there are characters—*
*Richard Barrett in* Faith and the Good Thing, *Ezekiel Sykes-*
*Withers in* Oxherding Tale, *Ebenezer Falcon in* Middle
Passage—*whom you mock in some way for their devotion*
*to philosophy, which is, as you've made clear, one of your pas-*
*sions. What's the purpose of this mockery? How does it reflect*
*your understanding of yourself as a philosopher and a writer?*

JOHNSON: Well, I can laugh at myself. There are three things
in this world that mean more to me than anything else, things
I feel the world would be unbearable without—philosophy, art,
and religion. But the tradition of philosophers poking fun at
themselves goes back to Plato's dialogues. Take a look at Maurice Merleau-Ponty's wonderful inaugural lecture, *In Praise of*
*Philosophy,* which he delivered at the College de France on January 15, 1953 (The translation was published by Northwestern

University Press in 1963). There he writes, "it is useless to deny that philosophy limps. . . . [The philosopher] does not take sides like others, and in his assent something massive and carnal is lacking. He is not altogether a real being. . . . One must be able to withdraw and gain distance in order to become truly engaged, which is, also, always an engagement in the truth. . . . The limping of philosophy is its virtue . . . and the very detachment of the philosopher assigns to him a certain kind of action among men."

I think that statement says it all. Philosophers have long been persecuted by society, starting with Socrates, because they are the men and women who step back from the marketplace, reflect on experience, and when everyone else has made up their minds, the philosopher says, "Wait, let's look at this *another* way," or, "Excuse me, I believe you *missed* something here." Remember, for the Greeks the symbol of philosophy ("the love of wisdom") was the owl of Minerva. And it was said the owl of Minerva only flew at night, meaning that philosophy begins at the end of the day when men leave the self-interested realm of the marketplace, step back from the busy-ness of the world, and talk to each other in hopes of clarifying their experience and what it means.

NASH: *One interesting issue that arises in your frequent discussions of what you value is the notion of process as being important, that sense that people need to recognize that they are "verbs, not nouns," as you say. Can you say more about your own particular writing process and the way that you put your foundational ideas into practice as you write and as you teach?*

JOHNSON: More than anything else I value *discovery.* I'm certain what we *know* about this mysterious universe in which we find ourselves counts for less than one percent of what can be known. I distrust all explanatory models, whether they are sociological, political, or economic. That's why I settled into phenomenology, which is a *method,* not a metaphysics; and Buddhism, a religion that in its earliest forms some have described as being "rudimentally phenomenological." When I create—write or draw—I count on the creation to lead my thoughts and feelings to places they've never been. I expect to be surprised (and if the artist is not surprised during the process of creation, a reader will be bored). See the work of art as being like a laboratory. You enter into it, not with an answer, but instead a hypothesis you want to test. Instead of having test tubes and Bunsen burners, you have other tools—characters, plot, language's possibilities, the forms we inherit from the past—and you use those tools to test your hypothesis. By the end of the process, your initial hypothesis may be confirmed, denied, or significantly modified. Whatever the case, you will have *learned* something about the phenomenon you were investigating and about yourself. I think art must be seen this way—as a truth-seeking process. One that requires an open mind, an open heart, and the courage to face wherever the process of discovery will take you.

NASH: *As you've indicated, when you were a beginning writer, you had a close association with John Gardner. In what ways did that relationship influence you, both as a writing teacher and as a writer?*

JOHNSON: My best answer is to refer you to the essays I've written on precisely this matter—my introduction to Gardner's *On Writers and Writing* and my essay "John Gardner as Mentor" in the winter 1996 special issue of *African American Review* that's devoted to my work. To summarize, I can only say that John Gardner was one of the most important writers and theoreticians about writing in American literature in the twentieth century. He set a standard for himself and his students that was inspirational, total, and I'm pleased to report that fifteen years after his death there is now a Gardner revival—his discovery by an entire new generation of young writers, many of whom tell me they only wish they could have met him.

NASH: *You've said, "The heart of memorable, enduring fiction*

*is imaginative storytelling reinforced by massive technique."*
*What elements do you particularly value in a well-written*
*story? What counts in your eyes as "massive technique"?*

JOHNSON: I ask a lot from a story. I want it to be (like a
work of philosophy) coherent, consistent, and complete. I
want it to clarify some aspect of experience. I want suspense—
yes, *that.* I want original, vivid characters. I want to feel that
the author is someone I can intellectually trust, i.e., that he or
she knows intellectual history. I want to feel myself plunged into
a complete fictional *world,* one that is like a dream (as Gardner once put it). I want language that is rich and shows me the
possibilities of the English tongue. I want plot. I want a theme
or "conflict" that is explored in all its ambiguity and subtlety.
I want wit, irony, and humor. A sense of voice. Imagery that is
fresh and like a revelation. I want authorial "generosity," the
author giving as much as he (or she) can. In short, I want a masterpiece when I sit down to read—otherwise I could be meditating, doing kung fu, drawing, or doing something with my
wife and kids.

NASH: *Are there other contemporary authors you can name*
*who in your view achieved this level of skill? What elements of*
*technique do you admire in their work?*

JOHNSON: Different authors do things I admire, all specific
to them. No one can match Gardner for maddeningly microscopic detail in *Mickelsson's Ghosts.* We can always count on
Nicholas Delbanco for superb elegance on the level of the sentence. James Alan McPherson has a brutal, emotional honesty
I admire. Rebecca Goldstein risks intellectual fiction. David
Guterson, my friend and former student, labors hard at
verisimilitude. This list could go on and on, so I'll just mention those few.

NASH: *One of the striking and distinctive features of your*
*own fiction is your use of humor, which is often shocking or*
*surprising. What's the place of humor in your aesthetic?*

JOHNSON: I wonder why it's shocking. I did start off as a

*comic* artist, a cartoonist. And isn't humor part of the fabric of
human experience?

NASH: *It's my understanding that humor is an important
part of Zen teachings, and I know that as a Buddhist you are
profoundly influenced by Eastern philosophy and also by the
practice of the martial arts, which you have referred to as
"meditation in motion." There are several places where this
interest in the martial arts surfaces in your work—first of all,
some of your most powerful short fiction, stories like "China"
and "Kwoon," deal with the transformative power of life
in a martial arts school. Can you comment further on the
significance of the martial arts for you?*

JOHNSON: Well, I started training thirty years ago last summer at a kung fu kwoon in Chicago. For me it was a rite of passage. I teach martial arts at a club in Seattle. It's an integral part
of my life (and that of my son, who at twenty-two wins first-
place trophies in kata and sparring) because I've always believed
that we must develop ourselves along three lines—the mental,
the spiritual, and the physical. I chose philosophy for the first,
Buddhism for the second, and kung fu for the third. What's wonderful about a traditional, Shaolin-based system such as the one
I've practiced since 1981, Choy Li Fut, is that it doorways on
Buddhist practice, Chinese culture, Tai Chi Chuan and Taoism,
and the whole five-thousand-year-old wealth of the East.

NASH: *Is there a metaphorical and or an actual link between
the martial arts and your creative process?*

JOHNSON: Yes, all the fighting "sets" we do are (some are
over three hundred moves long) art, creations handed down over
a hundred years. Also, both writing and kung fu require discipline and *ekagratha* (one-pointedness of mind).

NASH: *Another place where Eastern thought appears in
your work is* Oxherding Tale, *which clearly draws on the*
Ten Oxherding Pictures. *One of the main characters in
the novel, Reb, is a coffin maker who has a rather unusual*

A Conversation with Charles Johnson (1998)

*approach to his craft. Can you talk a little bit about what Reb represents in the context of Eastern philosophy?*

JOHNSON: In that novel, Reb is the resident Taoist. His approach to creation is based on first getting himself out of the way, forgetting himself. As a Buddhist, I do believe that the self is an illusion, a fiction, something we must set aside if we hope to perform an action—art, a kung fu set, serving tea—well. By doing this, Reb transcends epistemological dualism, is able to act egolessly, and through his art serves others.

NASH: *Reb is also a member of the Allmuseri tribe, the mythic wizards you created who are one of your most interesting innovations. The tribe appears in some way in* Oxherding Tale, *in* Middle Passage, *and in the short stories "The Education of Mingo," "The Sorcerer's Apprentice," and "The Gift of the* Osua.*" You've suggested that the Swamp Woman, the werewitch in* Faith and the Good Thing, *might well be a proto-Allmuseri. Could you please explain the important features of the tribe and how it fits into the larger picture of your aesthetic project?*

JOHNSON: Put simply, I imagined the Allmuseri to be the most spiritually evolved people on earth. An entire tribe of Mother Teresas and Gandhis. The details of their culture, however, were not features I invented—I drew them from real cultures in Africa, India, and China. Imagine Shangri-la as a people. It's the tribe I want to belong to. They have transcended dualism, conquered that most ancient of objects—the self—and live lives of perfect peace, nonviolence, creativity, and *ahimsa* ("harmlessness to all sentient beings").

NASH: *Do you see yourself returning to the Allmuseri in future works? Do they have any role in your most recent work,* Dreamer?

Johnson: I just finished *Dreamer,* and I can report that, yes, I discovered the presence of the Allmuseri in that novel. I'm sure they'll appear in other works to come insofar as they give me a vehicle for exploring some of the ideas and experiences I find more intriguing.

NASH: *I've also noted that in each of the novels and stories where the Allmuseri appear there is a character who seems diametrically opposed to them—the clearest example I can think of is Flo Hatfield, the hedonistic plantation owner in* Oxherding Tale *who owns Reb and who makes Andrew Hawkins literally her "love slave." What do Flo and characters like her represent, and what do you intend in setting these forces in conflict?*

JOHNSON: As you've noticed, the structure of my novels tends to be Hegelian; I feel more comfortable (in the novel form) setting antimonies—visions of the world, each with their own truths—at war against each other, then tracing the process of this conflict as it plays itself out. Gary Storhoff nails what I'm doing in his essay "The Artist as Universal Mind: Berkeley's Influence on Charles Johnson" (which is included in that Winter 1996 issue of *African American Review*). In that piece, he says, "In general terms, the negative characters of Johnson's stories are all materialists. . . ." I despise crude materialism. As one of my Buddhist friends and I often joke, it's a vision of the world where you simply have, not people, but "meat moving around." It's soul-less. It's mechanical, reductionistic, and [it's] the *reason* Husserl and Albert Schweitzer wrote books in reaction to it early in this century. Flo Hatfield is a slave to Matter (which is only a concept, of course), and to me is a tragic creature lost—as a Buddhist would say—in samsara.

NASH: *What do you think the protagonists of your first three novels—Faith Cross* (Faith and the Good Thing), *Andrew Hawkins* (Oxherding Tale), *and Rutherford Calhoun* (Middle Passage)—*have in common?*

JOHNSON: All those characters are seekers, questers (and adventurers). Fredrick T. Griffiths, the critic, rightly calls them "phenomenological pilgrims." He's so right—my characters are adventurers of ideas, truth-seekers (and thus have the philosophical impulse, even when they're not trained philosophers), and hunger for wisdom.

NASH: *Is there a character in* Dreamer *who fits this profile?*

JOHNSON: Oh yes, the narrator. I can't conceive of ever writing about a character indifferent to truth or one dead to the wonder and mystery of Being.

NASH: *Your first novel,* Faith and the Good Thing, *is structured as a literary representation of an African American folktale, and I'm struck by your usage of some folkloric conventions—you use evocative expressions such as "The devil was beating his wife," which indicates that the sun is shining during a rainshower, for instance. Can you say something about how you came to be interested in using this form to tell a particular story?*

JOHNSON: Well, I love tales. And I love the astonishing authority and flexibility in the voice of the traditional narrator of tales (folk or fairy tales). Before writing *Faith,* I read Julius Lester's *Black Folktales* and enjoyed that immensely at the time. *Faith* gave me the opportunity to read eighty books on folklore and magic as I composed that novel. Furthermore, the tale has been a rather nice vehicle for philosophy and fun since at least Voltaire wrote *Candide.* It also gave me a chance to tell stories within a story, making *Faith* somewhat like a Chinese box. Believe me, I will return to the tale whenever I can as a break from naturalistic fiction as we inherit that approach from the late nineteenth century.

NASH: *In your second novel,* Oxherding Tale, *there's a character named Horace Bannon, or the Soulcatcher, who seems to be his own canvas, though the art he has perfected is killing, not painting.*

JOHNSON: In a way, perhaps all my fictions are about art. The Soulcatcher is a creation spun right from *The Bhagavad-Gita,* a work so devoted to transcending dualism that "slayer" and "slain" are depicted as unified, one, in God. Bannon is good at what he does: murder. Just as a snake produces poison and (in an old Buddhist tale) has nothing to offer Gautama but that as a gift (which he accepts), so too the Soulcatcher—the destroyers—have their place in the fabric of Being. What, in the end, is a martial art except a way to kill? Yes, it's an art form, but it's also *martial*. As practitioners, we hope we never have to use it, that we can keep it on the level of just health and self-defense, but if it doesn't work as a means to slay, it fails to fulfill its purpose. See all this in terms of yin and yang, or—even better—Bannon as a bit of an American Shiva.

NASH: *That language on "slayer" and "slain" reminds me of Emerson's poem "Brahma," and in* Oxherding Tale, *you poke fun, through the character of Ezekiel Sykes-Withers, at Transcendentalism. What's your sense of Transcendentalism as a Western attempt at understanding Eastern philosophy? In what ways are you linked to that effort, if at all? Do you see any connection between your own work and that of someone like Emerson?*

JOHNSON: I've always read Emerson as my spiritual brother, and I'm deeply thankful for the presence of Transcendentalism in nineteenth-century literature—as a first groping toward the vision of the dharma. In fact, I see myself (and certainly Jean Toomer) as writing in a latter-day version of that literary tradition. And, of course, just as I can embrace it, I can find a little healthy humor in it, too.

NASH: *You've also said that on some level this novel is a response to Herman Hesse's* Siddhartha. *In what ways do you feel you've responded to Hesse? What in his work demanded a response from you?*

JOHNSON: I first read *Siddhartha* when I was nineteen or twenty. What deeply impressed me was how Hesse, this German author, could express with such accuracy the progress of Gautama, the twenty-fifth Buddha, and at the novel's end deliver (if only in part) something of the experience of *moksha*. What he achieved should not have been possible through *language*, according to both Zen and Taoism. But he did it. He did it, where his friend Thomas Mann failed to do so in *The Transposed Heads.* I simply had to respond, to take up the challenge of confronting the religion that has meant so much to me since my teens, but in a black American context. Where Hesse confines himself to Buddhism, I chose to appropriate elements of that as well as Buddhism's source—Hinduism—and its Chinese complement, Taoism. Being an artist, I chose as my meditation the *Ten Oxherding Pictures,* the drawings (canonical in Buddhism) that fascinated me since my late teens.

In short, the only proper response to a work of art that deeply moves one is *another* work of art created as a reply.

NASH: *On the issue of response to predecessors, you mention Herman Melville directly or indirectly in both* Oxherding Tale *and* Middle Passage, *and you quote* The Confidence Man *in the epigraph to* The Sorcerer's Apprentice. *When did your interest in him develop? Why is his work interesting or useful to you as a writer?*

JOHNSON: Melville should be of interest to *anyone* who cares about and loves literature. For an American writer, he—a genius—is essential reading in what I call the "epic conversation" of writers tackling perennial philosophical questions across centuries. I just published a story in Susan Shreve's anthology *Outside the Law* (Beacon, 1997) that explores affirmative action, but that story, "Executive Decision," is informed by Melville's "Bartleby the Scrivener," which is one of the great tales in American literature. I discovered Melville in my early twenties, by which I mean *Moby-Dick,* and I found there a mind worth spending time with and trying to understand.

NASH: *You've described Captain Ebenezer Falcon, a character in* Middle Passage, *as a "Wolf Larsen" type, referring to Jack London's* The Sea Wolf. *What does London offer you as a writer and, more generally, how does your work respond to the larger aesthetic issues of naturalism that someone like London presents?*

JOHNSON: First, what London offers us all is spirited

storytelling—everything from *The Sea Wolf* to *Martin Eden,* from "To Build a Fire" to *Call of the Wild* and *The Iron Heel.* That alone is worth the price of admission: the gift for telling a great story. In addition to that, London's peculiar blend of Nietzsche and Marx gives his fiction—what shall I say?—a philosophical personality, which is more than can be said for 99 percent of the fiction published today. As for naturalism, it's a theory and a literary approach I can respect in our late nineteenth- and early twentieth-century authors, one I use myself when a story demands it, but you know, I think that I prefer the tale to stories that naively take the scientific method as understood at the turn of the century as a model for fiction, i.e., "social realism," that detotalizes the realms of experience and reduces everything to "meat moving around."

NASH: *Your remarks suggest that you're generally inclined to situate your work within the tradition of American philosophical fiction—certainly Bellow and Melville are of this tradition, and there are a number of other authors one would think of whom you seem to refer to in your fiction, including Jean Toomer, Ralph Ellison, Walker Percy, Nathaniel Hawthorne, and Edgar Allan Poe. What do you think you have in common with these authors, and how do you see your own work as differing from theirs?*

JOHNSON: My formal training is, as you know, in philosophy (to say nothing of it being my passion as well). The authors you've mentioned write what some have called "intellectual fiction," yet each in a different way, and with a different emphasis on primarily ethical questions. The questions I tend to explore, while they impact on the area of ethics (the bastard child of philosophy), fall within the areas of ontology and epistemology. Given my commitment to Buddhism, I return quite often to the question of the "self" and the nature of desire; as a phenomenologist, I take consciousness as the starting point of my fictional reflections. If I have anything in common with the authors you mention, it is simply (I believe) that all of the above and myself feel at home with ideas and regard fiction as traditionally a proper medium for exploring them.

NASH: *Your most recent novel,* Dreamer, *treats Dr. Martin Luther King, Jr.'s, 1966 Chicago campaign. What in particular do you think King has to offer us in this stage of the nation's history?*

JOHNSON: A social vision for an America that has fallen away from the ideals of integration and brotherhood. I've written about this in "The King We Left Behind" in *CommonQuest* (Fall 1996), and also in the article "Searching for the Hidden Martin Luther King."

NASH: Dreamer *will be the third in a series of novels for you dealing with historical subject matter—slavery, the middle passage, and now the civil rights movement. What draws you as a novelist to these historical subjects? Are there other historical subjects you'd like to address?*

JOHNSON: I hope no one ever mistakes me for an "historical writer." That's never been my intention. I would have set *Oxherding Tale* in the present, if I could have gotten away with doing so, but it had to be in the period of slavery. I suppose the truth is that I enjoy doing research when I write a novel—I come away from the experience knowing far, far more than when I started any of these projects. By working outside of the present I also find that I'm given a kind of *epoché,* or bracketing of the concerns of the moment, in 1997. If I'm writing a story set in 1830, I have the chance to reconstruct the entire world from scratch, right down to the clothing, the props, the language used by the characters (Johanna Russ once told me that is one of the delights enjoyed by science fiction writers, and I understand that pleasure fully). The problems of today—in 1997—can often be explored without the pressures of 1997, and with the required *distance* when we set them in either a different time frame or (if you like) an unusual setting, as in my short story, "Menagerie."

NASH: *For you as a novelist, what's the connection between the writing of history and the writing of fiction?*

JOHNSON: The similarities are striking. In a novel, one is in effect creating a slice of history for the protagonist. A good novelist must always relish the study of history (an interpretative art, like fiction) because the challenges are so close to novel writing—we're given a wealth of details all of which must be made to cohere through the connective tissue of the act of interpretation. In envisioning our fictive characters, we must do as the biographer does—inquiring into their birth, parents' lives, education, environmental circumstances, their psychology, etc., if we expect them to have a three-dimensional feel. The study of history provides excellent guidelines for precisely this kind of novelistic creation of characters.

NASH: *In addressing historical subject matter in the creation of fiction, what do you think are the author's responsibilities to the historical record?*

JOHNSON: I believe the historical record should be respected as much as possible, for delivering, say, aspects of the history of a marginalized people is in itself a form of service. But it's true, a creator must be given a degree of "poetic license" to omit or bend things a little in the service of the truth of the fiction. The "facts" are clearly important, but what concerns a novelist most, I believe, is the *truth* the "facts" can potentially deliver.

NASH: *This seems to me to connect with the larger issue of postmodernism, a category to which many critics want to assign* Oxherding Tale *because of the nineteenth- and twentieth-century interplay, the self-referential character of the text, and the challenge to the "actual" historical record that you include. Do you see yourself as a postmodern writer or this as a postmodern work?*

JOHNSON: Sorry, but I *don't* describe myself as postmodern. If some critics see *Oxherding Tale* that way, that's fair—some of the elements I've seen attributed to postmodernism do occur in some of my fictions (the ones that demanded self-referentiality and intertextuality, etc.) but certainly not in all my stories.

NASH: *Where do you see serious American fiction heading in the near future? And what's your sense of your own place in that progression?*

JOHNSON: Where I'd like to see serious American fiction heading is toward a greater appreciation of the life of the spirit. If my work contributes even a little to that development, then I'll feel I've done my job.

# THE HUMAN DIMENSION

*An Interview with Writer-Philosopher*
*Charles Johnson*

## CHARLES MUDEDE

CHARLES JOHNSON IS one of the most prominent writers living in America today. He has published three novels, twenty screenplays, and dozens of essays and reviews. In 1990 his novel *Middle Passage* earned him the National Book Award; last year he was named a MacArthur fellow by the John D. and Catherine T. MacArthur Foundation. His latest novel is *Dreamer,* a fictionalized account of the last year in the life of Martin Luther King, Jr. This month sees the publication of *I Call Myself an Artist: Writings by and about Charles Johnson* (from Indiana University Press, edited by Rudolph Byrd).

Charles Johnson, who is the Pollock Professor of English at the University of Washington, is a philosopher by training and, as in Sartre's fiction, this is reflected in his books, which med-

Reprinted from *Real Change* (1 June 1999), with permission.

itate on questions of being and race (which happens to be the title of one of his books). As a thinker, Johnson has clear and useful ideas about art and society. He is a humanist, meaning his point of reference, the area which absorbs him most, is that which involves the human condition, and how that condition can be improved and better understood.

I met this great writer in his office on the UW campus. He has a very warm personality, and this warmness permeates his office. Or was it, perhaps, the slanted late-winter sunlight streaming through the window behind him that made him and his room feel so warm? Whatever it was, I felt very comfortable in his presence; I didn't feel intimidated or uneasy, but just there, a warm being sitting in the sunlight.

MUDEDE: *I wanted to start off with a discussion of how you became a philosopher, considering that philosophers think about society and life and how the world works. How has philosophy brought you to becoming a writer?*

JOHNSON: You know, philosophers are writers. Traditionally, you look at Plato, who writes dialogues, which are both a philosophical form and also a dramatic form. The dialogues are dramatic settings, right? Some of my favorite writers among philosophers were also very literary people as well. George Santayana comes to mind; Sartre comes to mind; Camus has the equivalent of our master's degree in philosophy. In Germany and France there is an intellectual tradition that both of those countries have that we really don't have in America. Americans seem to be very anti-intellectual. There's always been interplay between philosophers and literature. Then there are some magnificent prose stylists in philosophy like Arthur Schopenhauer. *The World as Will and Representation,* I think, is gorgeous. It's gorgeous writing. Even in translation it comes across. Then you have some people who can't write at all, like Hegel. His is a really turgid and impossible style.

But I started out when I was a philosopher as a cartoonist,

for fun, on the side. Cartooning led me to journalism, because I'd publish my drawings and also write at the same time, which was again fun for me. I never seriously intended to become a writer until 1970, when a novel occurred to me that I really wanted to do. I looked at black American literature and I didn't see many philosophical writers. I saw three, principally: Wright, Ellison, and Toomer. So there was this void, not only in America in terms of the philosophical novel, but also in black American literature. With my background in philosophy, I thought that I could fill that void. So I wrote the first novel.

That's really why I showed up to be a writer, to write a specific kind of novel. Not a novel of ideas, so to speak, but really the philosophical novel. A novel that explores the dimension of thought and feeling that you just don't get in most American literary traditions. That's why I became a writer. Now, I did a lot of other things for reasons like they are fun to write and they make money, such as screenplays and literary journalism. I write everything and anything because it will all improve your skills, whatever it is. There is no assignment that I feel is too humble in terms of developing mastery. So actually I started out with those six first novels I did in two years. I couldn't quite get a handle on how one writes philosophical fiction until I met John Gardner. So I wrote *Faith and the Good Thing,* my first novel, under his direction in nine months. Then that came out and John told me, "That's what you did in nine months, I write a book in three months." Then I got even more serious as I wrote the philosophical novel *Oxherding Tale,* which I spent five years on. [*Oxherding Tale* won the 1983 Washington State Governor's Award for Literature.] Then *The Sorcerer's Apprentice,* short stories I wrote around the time I was writing *Oxherding Tale. Middle Passage* was one of the first six books I wrote in two years. It was number two. [*Middle Passage* was eventually published in 1990, to widespread acclaim.] In 1971, I was learning how to write; those were apprentice novels. So I came back to it during the six years from 1983 to 1989. The other novel after that is the King book, which is *Dreamer,* because I think King was probably the most important moral philosopher produced by America in the twentieth century.

We talk about the legacy of King, what's his vision, but we never talk specifically about what that was. He was a trained seminarian. He was a trained philosopher, in fact, and we never talk about him that way, only as a civil rights leader. His theology is the foundation, it seems to me, of his brilliance, as a man of action and as a man of the spirit. People don't know it and they just don't have enough interest. I was talking to a group of people, and I said, "Do you know what his favorite sermon of all of his sermons was?" It's not the "I Had a Dream" speech, it's really "The Drum Major Instinct." People don't know this man at all. He's canonized and we revere him, as one man in a bookstore wrote. He was talking about King and wrote, "We revere him, but we feel we don't need to know him."

MUDEDE: *That is an interesting point to make. Because he is a national figure, we just expect that we shouldn't look any further.*

JOHNSON: Yeah, I mean really look. What in his vision made him different from other civil rights leaders? What were the components of that? Ask the question philosophically, can you identify the principal concepts that animate this man's passion? I chose three that I thought were there. One was nonviolence as not just a strategy for civil rights demonstrations, but as a way of life, *a way of life,* as a constant meditation socially for all of us. Then another one, of course, is *agape,* or unconditional love. This was very important to him. The third one is integration, understood in the most profound sense of the interconnectedness of all life.

These are traditional, perennial questions in the history of philosophy that this man is grappling with. He's referencing Gandhi at the same time, attempting to do the Gandhian spiritual approach in materialistic North America. It is one of the most fascinating lives that I think we've had in twentieth century American history.

MUDEDE: *It is interesting because when I first heard of your book, I thought, "What a strange subject." That was the first thing that struck me.*

JOHNSON: Why?

MUDEDE: *I was caught off guard. I was surprised. I really was, because Martin Luther King, Jr., is, to me, similar to saying I'm going to write a book about the word "hospital." It is something so perfect in form that I forget that there is actually something behind it: a whole life, a whole philosophy, a whole discourse.*

JOHNSON: A life in process.

MUDEDE: *Exactly.*

JOHNSON: You have changing and evolving and internal contradiction, and that is the fascinating dimension. And of course nobody talks about the Chicago campaign in 1966. The guy at the bookstore told me that you'd think King died in 1963 because all anyone ever talks about is the "I Have a Dream" speech. But there were some dramatic years there, perhaps the most dramatic of his life from the Chicago campaign right down to the assassination in Memphis. That was the time frame that I took because it was manageable and because I'm from Chicago. Being from the Evanston/Chicago area, I know that area better than the South. I was an intern for the *Chicago Tribune* for a summer, and I was a stringer for them. I just know that area, so it was ideal for me. I was eighteen in Evanston, Illinois, a suburb of Chicago, when he came that year, mainly the summer of 1966, and attempted to open Chicago up, and didn't succeed quite the way the Southern Christian Leadership Conference wanted. And that is where Jesse Jackson emerges from. He was a theology student at that time and joined the movement and started Operation Breadbasket.

MUDEDE: *I've always thought the job of the artist has been*

*to break people of their habits. What the Russians call "defa-*
*miliarize." And to write a book on King, what an act of*
*defamiliarization.*

JOHNSON: In other words, we have such a canonized, cod-
ified image—we really need to disabuse the reader of that so
that he feels he doesn't know King and has to find out who this
man is. All I had to do was prove the historical record. Most
people just don't know what is there about him. His intellectual development, his childhood, they don't know the details
because they haven't read the books. And the books are all there
if they want to read them. They are all at the library. It's all
there with Claiborne Carson organizing all of King's papers and
the primary source material. So if you want to hear his voice,
it's right there. But nobody spends the time. Carson told me
that in the age of identity politics, King is an embarrassment.

MUDEDE: *Why is that?*

JOHNSON: Because King is not into identity politics. Unlike
Malcolm X, there is no Afrocentric dimension. He is a traditional humanist. He is basically a leader for all Americans.
Whether they are white . . . take, for instance, the Washington
campaign that he was preparing for, to address poverty among
whites who were in Appalachia, poor Hispanics, poor black
people, you know what I'm saying? He was a leader across the
board: as a peace advocate, against the Vietnam War, and an
advocate for the poor.

MUDEDE: *How does this impact or inform your fiction?*

JOHNSON: My fiction?

MUDEDE: *Yes. These concerns that Martin Luther King, Jr.,*
*presented. Especially humanist.*

JOHNSON: I am a humanist, and I actually grew up believing his vision. It seemed right to me. I went to integrated schools
since I was in kindergarten. But during the 1960s, after he was
dead, the black power movement kicked in and the black arts
movement and that was all around me; I worked in and around
that. But in the 1970s and '80s, I started to think about King

again, because he was beginning to recede from us more and more. Nobody talked about him. Then in the '80s I started to read these statistics about black men. Terrible statistics, to the effect that right now one out of three black men in California is being controlled by the criminal justice system: on probation, parole, or in prison. In Washington, D.C., 80 percent, at least, of black men can expect to be arrested in their lifetime. You have the gang violence in the '80s and early '90s. And I have a son who is now twenty-three, but at that time, in the '80s, was in the critical sixteen to thirty-four age group when black men were considered to be an endangered species.

I started thinking to myself, "I know King just didn't talk about segregation, I know he talked about other things." I remembered some of that. So I wanted to go back and recover, and see if he did in fact say some stuff that would have addressed some of the issues that arose with the terrible situations of black men and black families disintegrating in the '80s and the '90s.

My questions for King were of the moral and philosophical nature, primarily. The question is, how should we live? What is the moral life? Where do I end and you begin? What is our social connection as human beings, you know? So these were the old perennial questions in philosophy, and King addressed them. In various speeches he sort of put it all together to come up with a complete vision. If we had listened to what he had said, I don't think that we would have had the devastation in our communities that began in the '80s and early '90s. I think that you wouldn't have today the kind of inhumanity that everybody talks about.

A recent poll was done by a black columnist where people were saying that the primary problem today with America is moral failure of the parents and the blame because we're coming off of the Colorado killings. And how did that happen with these two boys? Well, the whole question of violence was raised by King before. We need to understand that nonviolence was never intended just to be a strategy for civil rights movements, but a way of life.

We would be in a different position as a people, and America would be in a different position if we had heeded this man. But America never really has. I have a phrase in *Dreamer* that's right out of the Bible, that a prophet is never accepted in his own country. . . . I don't know if that's an answer to your question, but in terms of my fiction, my thinking about America, King figures in there quite largely—and he did when I was a kid, but like everybody else I moved away, as America moved away, and black America moved away from what he represented.

MUDEDE: *What do you see now, in the late '90s, what do you see in America? I mean about the problem with poverty, the problem with guns, the whole gamut?*

JOHNSON: Half of the country is going into the twenty-first century with something of an identity crisis. It has to be an identity crisis because America is very much a pluralistic society. When you look at King, the dialogue was fundamentally between blacks and whites. Traditionally it was slaves, it was a black/white dialogue. Now it is not, it is a multivocal dialogue. Fifteen percent of the black population in America is foreign-born. So Ethiopia, Eritrea, the West Indies—that's a different cultural experience. Also you've got Asian Americans, Pacific Islanders. . . . In other words, America really is the point where so many cultures are crossing. And so the large questions that will be carried into the twenty-first century will be questions of who we are as Americans. And who we want to be as Americans. But it won't just be a black/white dialogue in that respect anymore.

And there are also things that are happening that are remarkable. Like I always think, this is 1999, and then think back to 1899 and the world of 1899 and how the world changed in the next twenty or thirty years. Everything that's in our world wasn't there in 1899. Telephones, light bulbs, cars, planes, you name it! In that first twenty years we had such a revolution, just technologically in the way people live. All this stuff happened—you get the new physics, subatomic physics, right, and then you get the changes in poetry. You get free verse and the rejection of that. Then you get changes in painting. They're going almost along with the same changes in science. You get changes in the novel, you get changes in everything! In that first twenty-something years of the new century. I'm just thinking we may have that for the first twenty of the next century. You think of what they're doing with cloning. They're cloning things left and right, whole herds of cattle, right? Bioengineering, probes to Mars, we have technology that is absolutely ridiculous. It is astonishing.

I happen to think in the next twenty years, in the lives of my kids, they are going to see changes in the next twenty to fifty years, the same kind of changes that overtook the world between the late nineteenth century and the early twentieth. It is a very exciting time to be alive. There are a lot of writers that are not keeping abreast with it in fiction. This stuff is breaking so fast that it is not happening with writers. We're still writing about stuff we remember from thirty years ago. This other stuff is so radical that I think fiction is going to change a lot.

MUDEDE: *It almost seems like a whole new consciousness is under construction.*

JOHNSON: I do think so.

MUDEDE: *We will have to re-evaluate all aspects of life. There is no language for what we might see yet to come.*

JOHNSON: Nothing comparable. I think it's just like the end of the nineteenth century. It's just an interesting time to be around, and to be a writer in particular.

MUDEDE: *It seems that history is very important to you.*

JOHNSON: It is! I think for every writer, history has got to be a passion because it's telling stories. And most stories are never told. One thing I love so much about Ellison is that he talks about falling out of history. Well, what does that mean? History, in a visible manner, is basically what is seen and what is recorded, but if you fall out of history you fall basically into life because most of life is not seen and recorded. It's like one percent of life is seen or recorded. So something like *Africans in America* [which Charles Johnson co-authored with Patricia Smith], and the research that Orlando Bagwell has done, is stuff that I had never seen before in American history texts. When I was going to school, there was hardly anything on black people in the history books. That has gotten better, but *Africans in America* has choice explorations of moments in American history that totally transform our understanding of the American experience. And that impacts, of course, on the fiction that we do and the ways we can think about writing fiction. It really is one of my passions, because we really just don't know enough about who we are if we don't know who we've been.

MUDEDE: *I wanted to ask . . . I learned that your wife works as a volunteer at the Broadview shelter. Do you share a commitment to those who are poor and homeless?*

JOHNSON: Yes, and my wife has a real talent for that. When we were first married, she was an elementary school teacher, but she really wanted to do social work. So she went back to school, and then came back here [University of Washington] and got her master's in social work, and then went to work at Broadview. She always wanted to be in social work. She's very good. When she was in training she worked with AIDS and cancer patients, some of whom died on her during the process. She's got a capacity to help, yet at the same time maintain emotional distance. Which I think you require when you work in a place like Broadview, because there's so much going on and if you get emotionally involved you might be ineffective in being helpful. I don't think I'm talented that way. I think my talents are basically in the area of art as life. That's how I address issues, by writing about them or creating something about them. I think everybody who is a compassionate, conscientious citizen should address the problems of our society in some way. It is appropriate to do.

# AN INTERVIEW WITH
# CHARLES JOHNSON

## JENNIFER LEVASSEUR
## AND KEVIN RABALAIS

T HOUGH PERHAPS BEST
known as the National Book Award-winning author of the novel
*Middle Passage,* Charles Johnson prefers to think of himself as
an artist. "I sometimes see myself mentioned as 'the novelist
Charles Johnson,' but I don't think of myself in that way," he
says. "I don't call myself a writer; I call myself an artist. I create things. Today it might be a cartoon. Next week I might write
an introduction to a book. Then it might be a short story."

Born in Evanston, Illinois, on April 23, 1948, Johnson's first
artistic inclinations were as a cartoonist, but his pursuits have
always been wide-ranging. In keeping with his earliest aspira-
tions, he has published two cartoon collections, *Black Humor*
and *Half-Past Nation Time.* Other early interests, including mar-

Reprinted from *Novel Voices* (Writer's Digest, 2003), by permission of Jennifer Levasseur and Kevin Rabalais. Originally published in *Brick* (2002).

tial arts and Eastern religion and philosophy, continue to enter his writing. Johnson has also worked as a journalist and contributes regularly to various magazines. In 1970, he forged what would become a longtime relationship with PBS when he became the host of *Charlie's Pad,* a fifty-two-part series on cartooning. He went on to write many scripts for PBS, including *Booker,* which won a Writers Guild Award. He recently contributed twelve original short stories to the PBS companion book *Africans in America.* Now, Johnson is studying Sanskrit.

As a student, Johnson wrote six of what he now calls "apprentice" novels over a two-year period before meeting novelist and teacher John Gardner at Southern Illinois University. Gardner served as Johnson's mentor and helped him through his first published novel, *Faith and the Good Thing,* which explores black folklore, humor, and magic. A story collection, *The Sorcerer's Apprentice,* and three novels followed. *Oxherding Tale,* which he calls "a metaphysical slave narrative," tells a humorous and philosophically charged story of a mulatto slave. With *Middle Passage,* the story of Rutherford Calhoun's attempt to flee debt and marriage by stowing away on a slave transport, Johnson became the first black male novelist since Ralph Ellison to win the National Book Award. Most recently, he published *Dreamer,* a novel about the life of Martin Luther King, Jr.

Charles Johnson lives with his wife in Seattle, where he is the Pollock Professor of English at the University of Washington.

LEVASSEUR & RABALAIS: *When you were twelve years old, your mother gave you a journal and told you to write. Did she have any idea what she started?*

JOHNSON: She started lots of things, most of which didn't succeed: clarinet lessons, piano lessons, dancing lessons. None of that stuck with me because I wanted to be a cartoonist. My mother was a woman with many artistic interests, and she shared those with me. I found the journal attractive because it gave me a place to write my thoughts. You're absolutely free, in a journal, to say whatever you want.

And that's why she gave it to me; she wanted to read it. But I couldn't get away from it after I began. It evolved into a kind of writer's journal. I have boxes of them. I put them aside once I'm done. By then, it has served its purpose of helping me clarify some of my thoughts. I think it's an extraordinarily good tool for beginning writers because it helps them get accustomed to thinking about experience in language.

I tell my students that it's difficult to write sometimes, just to get to the writing, to sit down and finish a story. But if you write each day, even just a paragraph in your journal, you're never outside the creative process. When I write fiction, I hardly touch my journal. I sometimes spend five or six years on a book, so there might be a big gap between journals, but that wasn't true in the beginning because I was writing a book every ten weeks.

LEVASSEUR & RABALAIS: *In your autobiographical essay in* I Call Myself an Artist, *you discuss the fact that you knew your mother read your journal. In a sense, she was your first reader. Did that help you realize that there could be an audience?*

JOHNSON: I never thought about it that way. I guess she was my first reader. But she wanted to read me more than she wanted to read a literary document. After I realized she read it, I hid my journal. I would never think of sharing that with anybody, though I think my wife took a peek when we were first married. The intention when you write for others is entirely different than when you keep a journal. Sometimes when I go back and look at my journals, I see whole essays I've written. With a little editing, they could be excerpted and published. But most of the time, I'm trying, basically, to take my own temperature.

When I first started teaching at the University of Washington, I had my students turn in a writer's notebook twice in a ten-week period. I told them, "I don't care what you use it for, but let me recommend that you write character sketches. Maybe you'll see an image when looking out the window that strikes you. Write that down. Clip a newspaper article. Just show me that you're observing the world." Some of the students got so hooked that they didn't want to leave their journals with me over the weekend because they needed them.

Every writer needs something like that. I clip articles all the time, things that I think I can use later. They can be about anything: woolly mammoths, statistics about social life in America. A pile of journals over one foot long sits on my bookshelf. When I revise my work, I set six to eight hours aside to go through all of my journals and clippings, just to see if there's one thought I might have had twenty years ago that's useful, and very often there is. More than anything, it's a memory aid. The heart of writing is rewriting, revision. So the writer's notebook is critical; it helps me recall what I thought and felt about certain things.

I think the purpose of a first draft of a novel or story should be written with the intention of seeing if you have something worth pursuing. You begin to clean up in the second draft. You take out what doesn't fit, and you fill the holes of the first draft. It's not until the third draft that you can really settle down and begin to revise. After that, you might go through twelve or twenty drafts to improve and refine. To me, that is not a lot to ask. Nothing is perfect. I'm not going to say certain things don't approach perfection, but the goal is to have something that is as consistent, coherent, and complete as you can make it in that moment. If you revise thoroughly, that moment might be a long moment. It might endure for decades as a work. Writing well is the same thing as thinking well.

**LEVASSEUR & RABALAIS:** *Can you remember any stories that came from searching through your old journals?*

**JOHNSON:** I'm on the Washington Commission for the Humanities, and last spring we held an event called "Bedtime Stories." I asked writers like Shawn Wong, who is chairman of

English at the University of Washington, and playwright August Wilson to write bedtime stories. I had to write a story, too. But I didn't have an idea for one until four days before the event. The only thing that bugged me at that time was taxes. I wracked my brain. I went through my notebooks and found one line: "What if the government decided to tax people's dreams?" In one night, I wrote a story called "Sweet Dreams," which is about a man who goes to have his dreams audited at the Department of Dream Revenue. I had fun with that story, and the audience went nuts—they just rolled. In that desperate situation, I went back to my notes and found a germ that could grow.

LEVASSEUR & RABALAIS: *You've talked a lot about what you refer to as your six "apprentice novels." Did you think of them in those terms when you wrote them?*

JOHNSON: Every time you do something, you try to do your best. I wrote those books over a rather quick time—two years. I never intended to become a writer. All of my orientation from childhood to college was as a cartoonist. But then, one idea for a novel occurred to me, and I had to write it because it wouldn't leave me alone.

Setting out to write a novel was something I was familiar with because I had friends who were writers. One very good friend, Charles A. Gilpin, to whom I dedicated *Faith and the Good Thing,* wrote six books by the age of twenty-six, then died of a rare form of cancer. I wrote my first novel, and it was rough. I realized that I needed to know more. I started another one immediately to see if I could improve things like character and plot description. Then I wrote a third novel to see if I could improve structure. By the time I got to the seventh, I had read every writing handbook I could find. I understood a lot, but there were certain things I realized that I still didn't know.

By good fortune, I happened to be at Southern Illinois University, where John Gardner taught English. According to editors who had looked at my work, I needed to learn two things:

voice and rhythm. Those were two things that John was quite good at. He was a narrative ventriloquist when it came to voice. John paid an extraordinary amount of attention to rhythm, meter, and cadence. And he was also familiar with philosophical fiction, which was what I focused on for those six books that I couldn't nail.

LEVASSEUR & RABALAIS: *So from the beginning, you have been motivated to write philosophical fiction?*

JOHNSON: I asked myself, what can American philosophical fiction achieve? My background is in philosophy, and in that first book I tried to achieve the American philosophical novel, of which we don't have many examples. At that time there were about five or six people who worked in that vein, including Gardner, William H. Gass, Walker Percy, and Saul Bellow. This was a natural way for me to develop because as a graduate student in philosophy I read philosophers who wrote fiction—Camus, Sartre, Santayana.

That is my little corner of the literary world. I've done other things because they interest me, but that is home base. That's why I was awarded a MacArthur, for exploring that place where fiction and philosophy meet. John Gardner represented what I've come to refer to as, stealing a phrase from Northrop Frye, "the educated imagination." The imagination is one thing, and that's fine, but if it isn't tempered with a base in the theory and practice of literature, then it's a wild imagination. That's not the kind of literature I'm most attracted to. I want literature to be intellectually vigorous. I want it to fit within the history, at least of the Western world, of the evolution of our literature. Why write? There's got to be a reason. Sartre writes about this in *What Is Literature?* It contains wonderful chapters: "What Is Writing?," "For Whom Does One Write?," "Why Write?" He says a writer writes because he has something to say that has not been said. That's why I write, and that's the kind of writing that I want to read. When I sit down to write, I think about what needs to be said.

Literature is like the sciences. There are objective problems in science that are handed down over generations, mistakes that were made, questions that were not resolved. It is the same with literature. There are books that need to be written. There are stories that need to be explored. There are subjects that never get treated. There may have been a book that treated a subject one hundred years ago but botched it, making that book obsolete. If this is the case, we need to revisit that subject again.

It's all about the evolution and the efflorescence of meaning and the exploration of possibilities. Most of our writers have not done that. This is an enormously complex world. They're eating cloned beef in Japan. We have technology that didn't exist twenty years ago. Some people compare the Internet to the Guttenberg Press. We are entering a period that will be as radically different as 1899 was to the 1920s, when we had a new science, a new poetry, a new evolving fiction, and all the trappings of our world today did not exist. I suspect that the next ten to fifteen years will be just like that. It's a remarkable time to be alive. Some people say that everything has been written. Not so. We have entirely new situations. These stories are dying to see print.

**LEVASSEUR & RABALAIS:** *Hasn't this always been a concern for you? Several of your novels deal with subjects that have received little or no attention in fiction.*

**JOHNSON:** Nobody had ever written a novel about Martin Luther King, Jr. This shocks me. There are libraries of nonfiction, and I looked at as much of that as I could. I spent two years reading and looking at documentaries and speeches before I wrote a word because I didn't know who King was. It astounded me that a figure of King's magnitude had not been in our imaginative literature. Now I understand why this was probably so. King is hard to write about.

And by the same token, there was no novel about the slave trade until *Middle Passage*. There was nothing that put people on the boat and took the reader through the daily routine of what happened on the ship with specificity and detail. *Middle Passage* was actually the second of the six books I wrote in two years. I wasn't ready to handle it properly, and I told it from the wrong viewpoint. But I had begun the research, and I kept it up. I continued to learn about the Middle Passage. When I returned to the book in '83, I didn't need to do any more research on the slave trade. What I didn't know was the sea. I had never been to sea. So I spent six years looking at all of Melville and Conrad. I looked at nautical dictionaries and films relating to the sea. I took copious notes about what was on board. As they say in theater, how do you dress the set of a slave ship? What are the props? Everything has to be as exact as you can possibly make it. These are stories that need to be written. Fiction writers need a little time to catch up on these matters. And they will.

I want the next thing I write to be that kind of book. My questions right now are: What is civilization? Where are we? What does it mean to be American these days? Do we have shared values, or are we all coming from very different balkanized places? Are there many Americas? And what does that bode for the future? These are pressing questions.

LEVASSEUR & RABALAIS: *How does writing historical fiction differ from writing about history? How related are these processes?*

JOHNSON: To write a novel, you have to know the history, and then you have to make up a story. I truly admire what historians do because fiction writers base what they do largely on that. But as a novelist, you have to know everything. When I tackled a figure as eminent as Martin Luther King, I had to learn many things about him. I didn't know, for instance, what his favorite sermon was, and it was important for me to learn that.

LEVASSEUR & RABALAIS: *I didn't know that he smoked.*

JOHNSON: Many people never knew that because he never let the camera take a picture of him while he smoked, except once or twice. There's one picture of him where he's leaning forward at a bus station, talking to Andrew Young, and there's a cigarette in his hand. When he died, there was a cigarette in his hand and somebody took it out. He had gone out on the balcony to smoke, and that's when he got shot.

As a writer, I need to know these things. One thing I couldn't discover was the brand of cigarettes he smoked. I needed to know the ordinary, everyday things. How did he shave? All of these things characterize an individual. Writers need to know all those details about a fictional character. For historical characters, it's great because the historians have already done all the work for you. But what you have to have is a story. History is made of stories. History and fiction are means of interpretation based upon narrative (beginning, middle, and end) which, of course, is an artificial structure. You choose a piece of time that you want to work with. In that respect, the historians and the novelists are like brothers and sisters in their efforts.

LEVASSEUR & RABALAIS: *Do you think fiction writers are able to enter history in a way that historians cannot?*

JOHNSON: One thing I like about *Africans in America*—which is the product of a ten-year project of historians working under the direction of Orlando Bagwell—is that it is the first history book I've ever seen that has short stories in it. It would be great to see more historical books like this because fiction writers can get into the moment and sink the reader into it in a way that historians can't.

I've talked to the historian Stephen Oates about this. I truly admire his *Let the Trumpet Sound,* which was one of my touchstone books for *Dreamer.* He said that he always wanted to go further with his book on King, but he felt that as a historian, one hand was tied behind his back. There were restraints he had that I didn't have. I could be speculative. I could connect things. One of the things I was delighted with about *Dreamer* was that I figured out what paper King was writing for a college course when he met Coretta. I could have her ask him what he's doing, what he's working on, and he could say, "Well, I'm working on this paper about. . . ." There are a couple of episodes in *Dreamer* like this.

King didn't have a religious conversion as a child. It was in Montgomery during a night when he couldn't sleep and was wondering if he should bail out of the movement that he heard God talking to him. King gives this event only three or four sentences in his writings, but I wanted to spend some time with it. There are possibilities grounded in the historical record, but a historian might not reference these events and put them in larger contexts. One of the things I want to do as a novelist is look at all the pieces, come to some decision and connect things. It's all there if you want to do the work.

LEVASSEUR & RABALAIS: *Each of the stories in* Africans in America *has a different tone and structure. Did you set out to accomplish this variety, or did the stories evolve in this manner as you wrote them?*

JOHNSON: I worked on *Dreamer* right up until the time that the stories were due. I wrote all twelve of the stories in *Africans in America* in one month, January 1998. It came down to about three stories a week. I hadn't done that in a long time. I quit living my life and wrote the stories because I had no choice: the deadline had arrived. Once I got into it, I discovered that I could make it very engaging for myself if I wrote each story in a different form. I use first person, second person, third person. There is an all-dialogue story, a story written in the form of a newspaper article. It was fun because I was able to shift forms aesthetically. Almost every one of John Gardner's exercises from *The Art of Fiction* shows up in those stories. There's one I had given my students for twenty years that I had never tried—a third-person monologue. I used that exercise in "Confession."

LEVASSEUR & RABALAIS: *Do you view* Africans in America *as your second story collection?*

JOHNSON: I always call it Patricia Smith's book because she had to do most of the work, a lot of work that I could not have taken on. She adapted the teleplays from the four-part series. The stories I wrote for that book make up a series, a cycle. I'd like to see those stories published separately someday. What I'd really like is to have a collection of stories I've written since *The Sorcerer's Apprentice* that also contains a section of the stories from *Africans in America,* rather than those stories by themselves.

LEVASSEUR & RABALAIS: *You wrote those first six apprentice novels over a two-year period. And then you met John Gardner. You've said that it was Gardner who taught you to slow down. How did he help change the way you wrote?*

JOHNSON: When I first started writing, I loved the work of Richard Wright, John A. Williams, and James Baldwin. They had distinctive visions. I hadn't gotten to my own vision yet, though I was trying to get there with a philosophical novel. One of the things that can seduce a young writer, unfortunately, is the publishing industry, which likes writers to turn over products very quickly. So a lot of writers produce rapidly, one book a year. One of the things I realized is how to deepen a work rather than just get it done.

It wasn't so much what John said. I'll talk about it this way: Gardner's idea was that you shouldn't go on with the next sentence until the last one is correct. You should not write below the best line you've ever written. He was a perfectionist in that way. He could sit and write for seventy-two-hour stretches. I've never seen anybody work that way. He was totally devoted to the craft of fiction. It was a religion for John. If you want to understand the craft, you must give total commitment. John would read my work and give me some comments, and I would say, "I'll go back and do that, but let me get to the end of the book first." He'd say, "You can't do that. You've got to get this part right now."

I realized that I could get deeper into something with each draft, that revising is like filling a cup. Basically, what happens is that you fill the cup and it spills over. You add more layers, and things pop up in the fifteenth draft that you had never dreamed of when you first began. These things lead you forward, and the book grows out of its own potential rather than following an outline regardless of the other possibilities. This process also results in having to throw lots of pages away.

For *Oxherding Tale,* I threw away 2,400 pages to get 250. It was three thousand for *Middle Passage* and easily three thousand for *Dreamer.* There are issues I pursued that were fascinating, but they didn't belong in the book. If I hadn't pursued those issues, I would not have gotten to other things that do belong in the book. I keep all those drafts. There might be a paragraph or a line that might be useful in something else. There is a section in *Dreamer* where Chaym Smith shoots heroin. I wrote that scene in another novel back in the early 1970s. When I was writing that scene for Chaym, I went back and found the passage so I wouldn't have to do the research again.

Sometimes there are nuggets of good writing that have to be cut when they don't fit, but some of it is publishable. There's a book called *Literary Outtakes* that includes poetry and passages from stories and novels that didn't make it into the final products. They are great, but they just didn't fit. The book contains a passage of *Oxherding Tale* in it.

If you want a really good example of what I'm talking about, look at *Juneteenth,* Ralph Ellison's second novel, which was edited by John Callahan. There is a two-volume edition of *Juneteenth* that will soon be published that contains all two thousand pages of the novel. It will be very instructive for us to look at the complete, uncut manuscript. Callahan edited that down to 350 pages of a story, more or less, so we could have something after Ellison's death. In the 350-page edited version, we read that the main character receives a letter from a woman. Well, Ellison actually wrote the letter, and it takes up a whole chapter (and is probably magnificent in itself) but Callahan decided it didn't fit. Ellison probably would have decided the same thing. But you have to be open to every possibility.

LEVASSEUR & RABALAIS: *How much does* Dreamer *differ from your original idea for the novel?*

JOHNSON: I worked on *Dreamer* for six years. The King stuff was easy. That was based on historical research. The hard part was writing about King's double. That was my original idea for the novel: suppose King had a double. It came from my notes. I tried it as a short story in the 1980s, and it didn't work. The double was tough. I tried him as an uneducated man who several of King's supporters had to bring up to speed, and that didn't work. Finally, through a series of coincidences, I discovered who this guy was, who he had to be. I went to a black writers' conference in California. As I was leaving, the man who brought us there for the conference, Ricardo Quinones, gave me a copy of his critical book *The Changes of Cain*. I thought it was very timely because I was about to participate in a program with Bill Moyers on the story of Genesis. Quinones's book contains two thousand years of the Cain figure, from Genesis through Byron, where he is a reprehensible, devil figure, to his birth as the new anti-hero.

If you want to know what I'm talking about, take a look at *Fight Club*. The film makes it clear that it is about Cain figures, men who have been rejected by their fathers and by God.

LEVASSEUR & RABALAIS: *When did you decide to use the Cain figure as the double in* Dreamer?

JOHNSON: I didn't connect the dots until my agent called me after she saw the program. She said, "What about Cain as the double?" As soon as she said that, I found the structure I had searched for, the scaffolding that I had tried to discover for six years. I rewrote the book in about six months from that angle. The material became new to me; it was energized in a completely different way. It took me to a place I had never been, and that was exciting. Things take time to grow and become richer. I had to give it time. Sometimes, it's just luck. When I work on a novel for five or six years, my senses are open; I look for anything that relates to the book.

When I was writing *Dreamer,* I asked myself, "How would Martin Luther King do this? What would he think about that?" That kind of dialogue was in my head all the time. It is an exhausting process, but I think it is the only way to create a truly rich work. Perhaps I picked that up from Gardner. I am sure I got that sense of devotion to the work as a gift from Gardner. There's something else I got from him that relates to this. He talked about moral fiction a lot. People sometimes misunderstood that. People often thought he meant moralistic fiction, and that's the opposite of what he wanted.

LEVASSEUR & RABALAIS: *What did he mean by "moral fiction"?*

JOHNSON: John saw fiction, novels, in particular, as being a process. A scientist goes into the lab with a hypothesis. He says, "What will be the result if we do this?" At the end of the experiment, the original hypothesis may be confirmed or denied, or a whole new question may appear. According to John, it's the same with fiction. He liked to use Dostoyevsky as an example. Dostoyevsky thought to himself, "What if God does not exist. What would that allow us to do? Does it allow us to commit murder?" Dostoyevsky couldn't go out on the street and commit murder, but in fiction we have mimesis. He could create Raskolnikov and explore these questions without going through the actions himself.

My question in *Dreamer* was, "What if King had a double?" I didn't want to close off any possibilities. And by the end of the book, my idea about King and the civil rights movement was completely different than when I began the process. I now have new perceptions. In *Dreamer,* as it turns out, Chaym never gets to be King's double. The long speech King gives in the church in Evanston, Illinois, was originally written for the double. Then I realized that he would not be able to do that. This is about Cain and Abel. This is about inequality on some basic level. So

Chaym doesn't get a chance to be, in the full sense, a stand-in. He and the narrator learn about King's life, and they are transformed by that.

As a writer, you may have a modification of your original idea, or the whole idea may go in a different direction. That is what Gardner meant by moral fiction. It's why you don't close off any ideas; and it's why you don't preach. Fiction is about discovery. It is trial and error, as in a scientific experiment. When you complete a project, you should be transformed.

Gardner said that when somebody writes a book and puts everything into it, including that person's best jokes and images, he is not ready to write another book for about two years. He needs to step back, live life, absorb the world. When I write a book, I write it as though it might be the last thing I ever do. I convince myself that this is it—my last will and testament in language. Gardner was big on the idea of emotional honesty. You need to go to those places that are emotionally difficult to visit, things that you don't want to confront, precisely because you don't want to confront them.

**LEVASSEUR & RABALAIS:** *Did John Gardner offer you any advice as your work began to be published?*

**JOHNSON:** He said the real danger for a well-known writer is that you don't get edited; nobody touches your stuff. This can be very serious. He said that when you submit your manuscript, it has to be perfect. You can't expect an editor to work through every line, as Maxwell Perkins did. You have to do it all yourself before you send it in. But you still need a good copyeditor and a good editor to ask questions like, "Don't we need a scene for that? Isn't this an idea you want to reinforce later in the book?" You need another eye, but you don't always get it. John taught me that I had to do much of that work myself.

**LEVASSEUR & RABALAIS:** *In what other ways did he instruct you in your writing?*

**JOHNSON:** I was working on my seventh book when I met

John. He was never my teacher in a classroom setting. I met with him in his office. He would give me suggestions about how to fix problems. I would usually go back and change the scene in a way that we hadn't talked about because I needed John, as an editor and friend, to identify the problem. That's the issue—the problem. I would find the solution. The solution has to come out of the writer's own sense of how this world works. John often told a story about a woman who approached him after a reading. She said, "I like your fiction, but I don't know if I like you." He said, "That's fine. That's the way it should be because I'm a better person when I write. I'm talking to you right now, and I can't revise what I say. But when I write, I can fix it." He believed he could fix language, even if it took twenty drafts, and make it more accurate so that it would not hurt anyone. And writing may be the only time in your life that you can be "right" because you can revise yourself.

LEVASSEUR & RABALAIS: *It seems like* Oxherding Tale *was the book you believed you had to write.*

JOHNSON: Yes, that's true. *Faith and the Good Thing,* my first novel that was published, was a fun book. I wanted to write a novel with black folklore, humor, and magic. The serious book I had in my soul was *Oxherding Tale.* No one understood what I was doing at the time. Alex Haley's *Roots* was popular then, and that book helped to form the way people thought about black American life and literature. *Oxherding Tale* is a slave narrative, and it's a philosophical novel. It deals with not just Western philosophy but Eastern philosophy as well.

If I hadn't written *Oxherding Tale,* I couldn't have written *Middle Passage.* I had to make a lot of the same decisions in both of those books about how to write in a historical context for a contemporary audience. For instance, the first-person narrator of *Oxherding Tale* is black and educated. I had to ask myself how to create a nineteenth-century black man with these qualities. I worked those issues out in *Oxherding Tale,* and the knowledge was there at my fingertips for *Middle Passage.* If I hadn't written *Oxherding Tale,* I wouldn't have written another novel. I wasn't interested in any other book.

*Levasseur & Rabalais: You've put a lot of pressure on yourself to be a spokesman and innovator of black fiction. In the introduction to the Plume edition of* Oxherding Tale, *you wrote that you believed your level of success with the book would have an impact on more than just your writing, that the entire field of black literature could be opened if you achieved success. "Black fiction—as I imagined its intellectual possibilities—hung in the balance," you wrote.*

JOHNSON: I did. I still do. I think that every black writer in America since the nineteenth century has been expected to write a certain way. Those expectations can smother the possibilities of creative expression. If you are writing only about racial oppression—and only about racial oppression in a particular way that, for example, white readers understand—you're missing something. Sartre said that if you're a black writer in America, you automatically know what your subject is: it has to be oppression. Maybe that was true in the period of segregation. But there was also Jean Toomer, who wrote *Cane* in 1923. He looked at everything, beginning with the nature of the self.

It is not true that if you are a black writer in America that you automatically know what you are going to focus on, but there has always been that trap that black writers can fall into. Why is it that nobody paid attention to Zora Neale Hurston until the 1960s and '70s? I'll tell you why. Richard Wright's *Native Son* and *Black Boy* are works of genius in the naturalistic tradition, and they defined black writing. He is the father of black literature. Hurston did not write about racial oppression. She wrote about relationships and culture. Her work was trapped in the background for a long time because of the conception of what black writing should be.

I knew when I began writing *Oxherding Tale* that this was going to be a danger. Some people couldn't conceive of black philosophical fiction, even though we have Toomer, Wright, and

Ellison as examples. I was determined to make the things that interested me the focus of the book. It is a slave narrative. I did not want to deny the history of slavery, but this book is not merely about legal or political slavery. It's about other kinds of bondage: sexual, emotional, psychological, and metaphysical. The main character, Andrew Hawkins, has to work his way through all these types of bondage, some of which are even more fundamental than chattel slavery. Eastern philosophy was very useful to me in that exploration, as it is in all my books.

Writers, especially black writers, have to fight against limitations. One of my buddies, a Hollywood screenwriter, told me that all the stories that he is asked to write are black stories. But he can write about anything. Why shouldn't he be able to write about anything? It's about other issues. That kind of freedom is not given to black writers. You have to fight for it. You have to claim it.

LEVASSEUR & RABALAIS: *In what ways do you feel that you have claimed your territory?*

JOHNSON: I'll tell you what I did with my editor when I was writing *Oxherding Tale*. He was a great editor, but he couldn't figure out the book. I gave him a ten-page, single-spaced outline. He wrestled with it. Midway though our conversation, I said, "I may not write this book. I think I might write a three-generation black family drama." His eyes lit up, and he said, "Yes. I can take that upstairs and sell it to the publisher right now."

I went home and wrote him a long letter stating that I never intended to write that book. I wanted to see what he would say. And I knew what he was going to say. He was going to jump on that idea because everyone was excited about *Roots,* but that was not the book I wanted to write. I didn't want to feed an audience something that just reconfirmed its own assumptions and prejudices. There are other things I'm interested in. That is what *Being and Race* is basically about. It is about shaking up those presuppositions, not just through black literature, but through black American life itself. I think Ellison did a marvelous job of this in *Invisible Man*. We are mostly invisible to each other. One of the things that literature ought to be about is liberation of perception and consciousness. Our voices need to be freed so that we don't fall into those traps that diminish or limit other human lives.

LEVASSEUR & RABALAIS: *It seems like you've actively tried to do this with each of your novels. Even when the character is a slave on a plantation, he's not the slave we've read about in other works of literature. He breaks that mold by having unexpected preoccupations.*

JOHNSON: Most people don't know anything about the history of slavery. They know a bit about Frederick Douglass, who was an incredible genius. And there are others like him, but Hollywood and literature give us images like the ones in *Gone with the Wind*. This is what *Africans in America* addresses. It clarifies the history of slavery.

When I was in junior high school, we read no black literature. It was not part of the curriculum. I remember when my teacher in junior high school talked about slavery. She botched it. Slavery comprised a paragraph in our history book, and she passed right over it. I don't blame my teachers; their educations were flawed. They did not know about Harriet Tubman and Sojourner Truth, so they couldn't deliver it to us. Black studies started around the time that I went to college. The people teaching the courses were black graduate students in history and philosophy. I was pulled in with about twenty others to be discussion group leaders. I cut most of my classes that quarter because the discussion group that I led was so important to me.

I got the idea for *Middle Passage* from one of the graduate students who was involved in the group. He showed us an image of a slave ship with little figures arranged spoon-fashion. That image burned itself into my mind. The next quarter, I wrote my research paper on the slave trade. That was the very beginning of *Middle Passage,* maybe about 1970. By 1971, I had written the first draft of the novel.

I don't fault my teachers for not knowing this history, but by now we should know it. I am shocked by how much general American history people don't know. For instance, the automatic stoplight was invented by Garrett Morgan, a black man. The phrase "the real McCoy" refers to a black man, Elijah McCoy, who invented the lubricating device for machinery. All this stuff is invisible, as Ellison would say. And then there are bigger things, as in all the black people who fought in the Revolutionary War for the crown and for the continental army. Most of that history is not known, and that's where we get assumptions, prejudices, and misinformation, which causes a lot of suffering. Literature can address some of that. It is entertainment, but all great literature also enlightens. All entertainment doesn't enlighten; it doesn't have to do that. Great literature does both, and that's difficult.

LEVASSEUR & RABALAIS: *Certain areas of study, such as black studies and women's studies, originated to try to correct this lack of education. What are your thoughts on this type of categorization of subjects like history and literature?*

JOHNSON: These programs have the wrong approach. Black studies came about because the information was available nowhere else. It had to start somewhere. But I think the ideal thing to do is that if you're teaching a course in American naturalism, you present Theodore Dreiser as well as Richard Wright. A course on the modern novel and surrealism should include Ellison. Everything doesn't have to be balkanized. That does disservice to the work itself. If black people are taken out of American history, nothing makes sense, not the Civil War, not the Southern economy, not Reconstruction. History must be taught in a much more sophisticated way. So, again, this is the difficulty. All of our knowledge is provisional; everything we know is partial. I believe that we know less than one percent of what is possible to know. Most of it is still a mystery.

Knowledge evolves in physics, in chemistry, just as it evolves in literature. Whatever we think we know right now is subject to change tomorrow when new revelations occur.

LEVASSEUR & RABALAIS: *What are some exercises you suggest to those who want to write?*

JOHNSON: John Gardner gave me the exercises that appeared later in his book *The Art of Fiction*. My students used to do all thirty of those exercises in ten weeks. I also have them write a plot outline every week. I want them to think constantly about how to come up with stories.

LEVASSEUR & RABALAIS: *You have juggled quite a lot —writing novels and short stories, studying and writing about Western and Eastern philosophy, writing for TV and film, cartooning, working as a journalist, learning and practicing martial arts, being a husband and father.*

JOHNSON: When I was in my twenties, it was all about skill acquisition. I still work in that way. I'm now in my second year of Sanskrit studies, and I love it. We have intensive seminars, two or three days in a row, six hours a day through the American Sanskrit Institute. I have always wanted to read Buddhist and Hindu texts in the original. I can begin to do that now.

Life is about learning and growing, and if you stop doing that—and I put these words in King's mouth in *Dreamer*—you might as well be dead. You sometimes have to fight to find those spaces that will allow you to grow and develop, but that's what life is about. It's like when a person learns a language. The second new language seems easier than the first. And the third is easier than the second. It's the same way with the arts. Many writers, like Ralph Ellison, begin as musicians, and then they suddenly realize the commonality between music and poetry or music and fiction. The arts become easier as you move from one to the other. If you write fiction, it seems to me you should be able to write nonfiction. If you write a novel, you should be able to write short stories. These are all part of the same universe, so to speak. It's about crossing boundaries, which isn't that difficult. There are certain things that I will never be able to do because they involve different concepts, like the hard sciences. But on the continent of art, there are similarities in the ways the creative imagination works. Most artists can cross boundaries quite easily. August Wilson began as a poet, and he still writes short fiction. When we put on "Bedtime Stories," he read a story he wrote twenty years ago called "The Oldest Man in the World."

LEVASSEUR & RABALAIS: *You started with cartoons and journalism, then you went on to philosophy and fiction. Do you think your education and experience with these fields aids you as a novelist?*

JOHNSON: The novel is one thing that I do. I don't rank the arts the way Hegel did, with philosophy at the top and music after that and then literature after that. The novel can be anything. It allows you to do things the short story cannot allow you to do. The short story is a very defined form, beginning with modern stories in the nineteenth century. We see its evolution from Edgar Allan Poe to O. Henry to people who reacted against the rigidity of the story, like Sherwood Anderson and Margaret Atwood. When you write a short story, you have to do a very specific thing. There is no waste, and there is always a structure, always a formula. The novel, on the other hand, can go in any direction. It can be a slave narrative, a folktale, anything. There can be unresolved matters. If it's original fiction and not formulaic, there is a world of possibilities to explore, and it can be any length. The novel is very flexible, but I don't privilege it as a form.

It bothers me when people put things in categories, boxes. All these boxes are arbitrary. Saying, "You belong in this box, and you belong in that box. And this is a better box than that box" is like segregation, apartheid. It's all creation, and the processes are so similar that it doesn't really matter. Whether it's journalism or a well-done drawing or a philosophical work, it's about clarity of thought and expression. I know when I write a short story that certain things must happen within the narrative. But I never tell myself I'm writing a short story. When I sat down to write the stories in *Africans in America,* I didn't say, "What's a short story?" I said, "What I have here is Phillis Wheatley, and she's working on a poem early in the morning and her mistress comes in and asks her what she is doing." I try to follow characters through a story. It's like Gardner said, you have to know the form from within. Students get hung up when they ask themselves, "How do I write a short story? How do I write an essay? How do I write a novel?" Don't worry about it. The engine of fiction is character. Everything comes out of the people. All you have to worry about is knowing who they are. This may involve research. You must know your characters and their situations. If you are faithful to how they would respond to things and you don't treat them as puppets to illustrate your own ideas, then you'll have revelations and you'll have a story or a novel. Readers want to know who these people are. Are these people I'm interested in? Do they relate to me? If they do, I must follow through with this because their stories may have implications for my own life. The hardest thing for writers is to get to the heart of a character, to create a character with more than one dimension, that is not just a prop that walks through the story.

LEVASSEUR & RABALAIS: *When you won the National Book Award, you gave tribute to Ralph Ellison. What did you learn from reading his work?*

JOHNSON: I've read *Invisible Man* many times. I was in my teens the first time, and I didn't really get everything. Every time I go back to Ellison, I find something new. It's sufficient to say that the most important thing Ellison ever said, and which is represented in all of his work, is that Americans have to learn over and over that we are individuals and we have the responsibility of individual vision. The other day, August Wilson asked me, "What do you think makes a great writer?" I said, "A major writer is someone who has a major vision." You usually can't explore that vision fully in one book. It's broad and specific at the same time. A major writer is someone who interprets the world for us, and it usually happens over a lifetime, a body of work, an oeuvre. You can walk through that work and see the entire universe rendered. That is difficult to do. I think Ellison achieved this in *Invisible Man.* We can go back to it and be enriched again and again, even as we grow older. We bring a richness to match the book through our experience as time goes on. That is what defines the image of a writer down through the ages.

LEVASSEUR & RABALAIS: *You lived a long time with Martin Luther King for* Dreamer. *Where will you go from here?*

JOHNSON: I'm not ready to write another novel that involves heavy research. Maybe I'll choose something close to home, a topic that I already know something about, and that would take about two years. I'm talking to an editor about writing a book that would be like a *Souls of Black Folk* for the twenty-first century, something that looks at black consciousness in a philosophical way, but for a broad audience. It would cover the post–civil rights period. I've already covered much of that material in some of my books, so I'm not sure that I want to write a race book. I'll spend about two years on the next novel, which is sufficient if a lot of research isn't necessary. This is my year off to think about it and do other things. The Buddhist review *Tricycle* printed an article I wrote on Buddhism in black America. I truly enjoyed writing that piece. I think I've waited my whole life to write that article. When I'm working on a novel, there is not a lot of time for these other things. Everything has to be focused on the book and the subject. But when I'm not writing a novel, I can learn and do other things.

August Wilson recently gave me the three volumes of Borges's works: the collected short fiction, poetry, and nonfiction. A body of work is like a house. In one room, there are novels. In another room, there are short stories. In the next room, screenplays. The next floor contains drawings and comic strips. It's a round, diverse body of work. When an artist creates a body of work like this, it is all about interpreting this world we live in. There is a unity that is brought to that—whatever the subject may be—by the personality and vision of the artist.

# AN INTERVIEW
# WITH CHARLES JOHNSON

## JIM McWILLIAMS

THIS INTERVIEW WAS
conducted by e-mail between August 2002 and January 2003.
Carla Kraehenbuehl, my research assistant for fall 2002, contributed the last two questions.

McWILLIAMS: *How has new technology (word-processing programs, e-mail, etc.) affected your composing process?*

JOHNSON: I've always loved technology and gadgets, so the
laborsaving devices made available to writers in the 1980s are
for me a blessing. Right now I'm learning how to use a voice-
recognition program to help me do a first draft hands-free.
Between 1970 and '73, I wrote my first seven novels (before
and including *Faith and the Good Thing*) on a typewriter. If I
made a mistake, I had to retype the entire page, which was time-

This interview is previously unpublished.

consuming and tedious, though authors were used to that since the era of Mark Twain.

And I do use the Web for research, or perhaps it's more accurate to say that it is now one more resource I turn to. But technology has not changed my "process" one iota. Yes, Microsoft Word allows me to make corrections faster, but after I write a few pages I have to print them off, spread them before me on my desk, then begin—with pencil in hand—to resculpt every syllable and sentence through at least three revisions and often as many as twenty or thirty. As the old chestnut goes, 90 percent of writing is rewriting. For me, that will never change.

McWILLIAMS: *My students often ask how they can tell when an essay is "finished." How do you respond to that question?*

JOHNSON: My ratio of throwaway pages to keep is about twenty to one for a novel. The finished manuscripts for *Oxherding Tale, Middle Passage,* and *Dreamer* were between 250 and 300 pages, but for *Ox* I threw away 2,400 pages (yes, I count these things and save old drafts in boxes, all crammed into my attic), and in the neighborhood of 3,000 for the other two novels. For *Faith and the Good Thing* I tossed out about 1,200, but I wrote that book in nine months while I devoted between five and seven years to the others. I know a novel or story is "finished" when I've revised it so thoroughly that I can't make any more changes without disrupting its meaning and music (rhythm) from one sentence to the next.

McWILLIAMS: *After you've decided that a piece is "finished," do you show it to anyone before sending it out?*

JOHNSON: When I believe I've finished all I can do on a particular piece of writing—a new story or essay—I share it with scores of people: my wife, children, my agent, the literary critics who have written—or are completing—articles and book-length studies on my fiction, with friends who are filmmakers, screenwriters, poets, book editors at the *New York Times Book Review,* colleagues at different colleges—with anyone who I think will find it interesting. And I always get back from them comments that are helpful for the next draft.

McWILLIAMS: *Unlike many contemporary writers, you don't write autobiographical fiction.*

JOHNSON: You're right, I don't write autobiographical fiction or memoir. I enjoy reading about other people's lives, of course, but I see my job as a writer to be that of simply telling a rousing good tale. Clearly, a writer's feelings, thoughts, pieces of his experience and that of people he knows—all that is grist for the mill of characterization. But if I draw on an incident from my (or my family's) life, it must be in the service of the story, something that amplifies its drama or meaning.

McWILLIAMS: *I wonder if there's a character that's more "you" than any other?*

JOHNSON: In terms of the novels, I would say that Andrew Hawkins in *Oxherding Tale* and Matthew Bishop in *Dreamer* are "more" me than, say, Rutherford Calhoun in *Middle Passage,* though in that sea story I feel a certain identification with his brother, Jackson. The truth, of course, is that I invest myself (emotional autobiography if not literal events from my life) in each and every principal character—Captain Falcon, Reb the Coffinmaker, and my fictitious Martin Luther King, Jr., especially, in *Dreamer.*

McWILLIAMS: *You said in* Being and Race *that "slave narratives . . . are the ancestral roots of black fiction," and it's clear from* Oxherding Tale, Middle Passage, *and* Soulcatcher *that you've read many of them. Which ones have influenced you the most? Are you able to read those narratives objectively, or do you feel strong emotional reactions as you read them?*

JOHNSON: The slave narratives that influenced me the most, because they were such powerful stories, were by Olaudah Equiano (Gustavus Vassa), Frederick Douglass, Nat Turner, and Solomon Northrup. There's no way for me to read them dispassionately. Sometimes the experience of living imaginatively in these texts is visceral and painful. These are stories about the suffering and heroism of my ancestors. But, yes, I can read them analytically in order to discern the structural features or essence (*eidos*) of the slave narrative as a form.

McWILLIAMS: *A few weeks ago I said something in my introduction to literature course that made sense to me at the time, but now I wonder if it's true. I was explaining how different points of view can change a story (first person versus third person, fully omniscient) when I said, "It's important to think about point of view because a writer makes a conscious decision about what point of view he will use to tell the story. He can choose whichever one he wants." I'm wondering now if a writer really does have a choice. In* Soulcatcher, *for example, could any of those stories be told from a different point of view? Or does a narrative force a particular point of view? Wouldn't the narrative of "Martha's Dilemma," for instance, lose its power if told in third person, fully omniscient, so that we know what the slaves are thinking? Perhaps narrative compels a particular point of view and, therefore, fiction takes a life of its own?*

JOHNSON: I'd like to think that form and content in the *Soulcatcher* stories fit together like a hand and glove. "A Soldier for the Crown" is in second person and has a surprise ending; it might have worked in first person, but probably not in third-person, limited or omniscient. Diary entries for "The Plague" provide, I think, a necessary reflective and philosophical feel to the musings of Reverend Richard Allen. Martha Washington's story works best in first person, because we need to hear the urgency in her voice and the immediacy of her grief and fear after her husband, George, dies. And, yes, we as readers need to have the same perceptual limitations she has, not knowing until midway through the story how eager their slaves are for her demise so they can be free. For me, one aesthetic question that always must be answered is, "What form is exactly right for the telling of a tale?"

McWILLIAMS: *The stories of* Soulcatcher *are quite different from your other fiction in that they lack the complexity and ambiguity so characteristic of your work. I'm not suggesting that they are inferior stories—it's certainly quite an achieve-ment for you to have captured so many different voices—but that they function more as mini-history lessons than as chal-lenging fiction. How do you see them fitting in with the rest of your work?*

JOHNSON: The twelve stories in *Soulcatcher* were originally commissioned in 1996 by Harcourt Brace to appear in a his-tory book, *Africans in America,* the companion volume for the 1998 PBS series of the same name. Producer Orlando Bagwell (whom I'd worked with on PBS shows in the 1980s) selected *Boston Globe* columnist Patricia Smith to adapt the series' scripts for the history book's text, and me to create twelve original sto-ries that dramatized slavery because he liked my use of history in *Middle Passage.*

I am, first and foremost, a writer of philosophical fiction. But for this assignment I felt it was best not to make the stories too intellectually complex—we did want them to be accessible to high school and even middle school students. So I stayed really close to the historical record and allowed my urge for aesthetic exploration to express itself primarily by letting each of the twelve stories assume a different form. For example, we have stories in first-, second-, and third-person viewpoint; stories told as diary entries, a newspaper article, a letter; we have stories in mixed prose and verse, all in dialogue without a line of description or narration, and tales expressed as a third-person monologue or as interconnected monologues. One radio inter-viewer I discussed the book with said she was startled to real-ize one person wrote all the stories—she told me she thought I'd collected them from different places, then edited all the sto-ries to create a unified book. That effect was exactly what I wanted readers to have when they experienced *Soulcatcher.*

There is a little philosophy to be found in that collection.

Plato's Myth of the Cave (from *The Republic*) appears in the story "Confession." And there should be a phenomenological feel to stories like "Martha's Dilemma" and "The Mayor's Tale," where the white protagonists undergo a change in their perceptions of the slaves around them, realizing just how deeply intertwined their own lives are with black people.

McWILLIAMS: *Speaking of point of view, men often write from a female point of view and women from a male point of view, but whites almost never write from a black point of view or blacks from a white point of view. In your own fiction, for instance, you've quite often written from a woman's point of view but almost never from a white point of view.*

JOHNSON: Well, my story "Executive Decision" (in Susan Shreve's anthology *Outside the Law*) has as its protagonist a white CEO who must decide between hiring a white woman or a black man (this is another second-person story, and with allusions to "Bartleby, the Scrivener"). The main character, Moses Green, in "The Education of Mingo" is a white, nineteenth-century farmer. And I've written lots of stories where the characters have no racial designation—"Kwoon," "Moving Pictures," "Sweet Dreams," "Better Than Counting Sheep"—because their race isn't important to the meaning of the story. As you point out, this is a thorny question. Growing up black in white America, I studied an all-white curriculum in elementary, middle school, and high school, and an overwhelmingly Eurocentric curriculum in college. I grew up watching whites on TV and in the movies (in the 1950s there were no black characters on television, except for *Amos 'n' Andy*); I've had many white friends from kindergarten through today. So—almost like an immigrant—I've been immersed in the "ways of white folk," and I feel I can write about them. If I wanted to pass my history and literature classes with a decent grade, I had to identify, as a student, with white historical figures and characters created by Shakespeare, Homer, Dickens, Orwell, Melville— you name it; emotionally identify with their dramatic conflicts and empathize with them, just like the white students in my class. The difference between them and me was that I also was immersed in black lives, history and culture, which I learned at home, in church, among black friends, and on my own. What I'm describing here is a classic example of W. E. B. Du Bois's "double consciousness," where from childhood a black American is forced to learn how to subtly "read" social and cultural phenomenon from two perspectives, one white, one black. If he or she doesn't learn how to do that, he or she won't survive. So, as controversial as it may be for me to say this, I think black Americans are better positioned, existentially, to write about white and black American characters than white authors are. Why? Because the white authors I've read never had to be immersed in the black world, or learn how to "read" it for the sake of their survival.

I suspect that is the reason why many white writers avoid writing about black characters. There are so many ways to get those portraits wrong if someone has not found it crucial during his lifetime to microscopically examine the racial other, as blacks in America have to do. But black writers generally tend to write about black characters precisely because the experience of black America remains largely "invisible," as Ralph Ellison once eloquently described it, forced to the margins of the mainstream and the media. For example, I think it's awfully amusing that so many white book reviewers said they were unaware of the existence of wealthy blacks—people who come from generations of wealth and vacation at Martha's Vineyard—until they read Stephen Carter's *The Emperor of Ocean Park*. Many white readers of *Soulcatcher* have also informed me that they were unaware that some antebellum African Americans were free since the Revolutionary War (and before), fought for the British in greater numbers than for the Continental Army, and that a few owned slaves.

MCWILLIAMS: *Do you remember the Daniel James/Danny Santiago controversy of 1984? A white writer named Daniel*

*James wrote a novel about life in the barrios and published it under the name "Danny Santiago." It won some awards, but then the fact came out that a non-Hispanic wrote it. The awards were rescinded, the publisher apologized, etc. Does a writer's race or sex have any bearing on the quality of his work? Did James' novel, for example, become an inferior novel after its creator's mask was pulled off?*

JOHNSON: I read about the Daniel James/Danny Santiago controversy at the time. I didn't read the book. And my remarks were wholly about black American literature, not Hispanic literature and culture, where I have no expertise.

Generally, though, I do not believe a writer's "race" has anything whatsoever to do with the "quality" of his (or her) work. Race is an illusion. But cultural experience is not. James' novel is as well-wrought technically, or as poorly composed, after its author's identity was revealed as when everyone thought "Danny Santiago" wrote it. I leave it to people in the barrio to decide if his understanding, interpretation, and vision of the life of the characters in that novel truly disclose their world. I know that the first *Shaft* novel (from which two bad movies were made), written by a white author, isn't worth talking about in terms of its understanding of African American history and culture. Nor is the work of Joel Chandler Harris.

McWILLIAMS: *What about Twain, most notably the character of Jim in* Huckleberry Finn? *Do you think Twain shows an understanding of nineteenth-century black America?*

JOHNSON: Generally, I'm a fan of Mark Twain because he is a spirited and imaginative storyteller. But, as a black American artist and philosopher, I am not a fan of *Adventures of Huckleberry Finn*. Nor am I a fan of Harriet Beecher Stowe's *Uncle Tom's Cabin,* or Harper Lee's *To Kill a Mockingbird.* I find all three books to be insulting.Why? Because while those texts contain "black" characters, they were written by white authors for a white audience, not for a black readership. All three are talented writers so they have the journalist's ability to observe others superficially from the outside, and to transcribe the speech of the racial Other—as much of that speech as they were privy to (what black people really say among themselves they could not know). They did not know, as W. E. B. Du Bois might say, "the souls of black folk." Their limited ideas and interpretations of these black characters render them as one-dimensional; they do not appear within the real context of black history, culture, and the complexity of African American lives and thought. Indeed, these characters—Jim and Uncle Tom, for example—are "relative beings" whose lives only have significance and meaning in relation to the white characters around them, at least as far as the drama is concerned. There is something downright creepy about supposedly full-grown black men like Tom and Jim having the important drama of their lives told through their relationships with white children—Little Eva and Huck. As a matter of fact, those men are portrayed as children or as childlike and, therefore, loveable (to white readers). No, Twain and Stowe did not do their homework, or enough of it, for those books.

I would refer readers interested in slavery to my stories in *Soulcatcher* for better portraits of black people in the nineteenth century. Or, if they want a more complex and less offensive depiction of black Americans by a white author, they might read Sinclair Lewis's *Kingsblood Royal*. That novel, technically, is a mess. A tract. But, as with all his novels, Lewis tried mightily to immerse himself in his subject before daring to write about it. (See my introduction for the Modern Library's 2001 edition of *Kingsblood Royal* for more information on the research he did; and also my introduction, coming out this September, for Oxford's new 150th anniversary edition of *Uncle Tom's Cabin*.)

McWILLIAMS: *I've never been a fan of* Uncle Tom's Cabin *(I'm not sure I've even read the whole thing), but I have to say that I've become increasingly more uncomfortable with* Huck Finn *and how it portrays Jim. I'm in agreement with you that the "black face" Twain shows through the character of Jim—*

*if indeed we accept it as authentic at all—is simply the facade
a slave shows whenever he's around a white, even if that white
seems friendly. Of course, there are a couple of scenes where
Jim is by himself (with Huck and Tom spying on him), but he
is still just a caricature there, too. I never get the sense that we
see the "real" Jim. Are you familiar with Twain's short story
called "A True Story"?*

*It only takes about five minutes to read. I'm curious if you
find it more authentic than the portrayal of Jim.* \*

JOHNSON: Just read "A True Story." I have to say I enjoyed
much more "Fenimore Cooper's Literary Offenses," which I
give to my grad and undergrad writing students each and every
school term as essential reading.

What can I say about "A True Story"? What the story is
about—the plot—is covered just as well by Charles Chesnutt
in "The Wife of His Youth." I always have trouble with so-
called "Negro dialect" in the late nineteenth and early twentieth century. Reading it is like walking through mud or a
swamp—one has to work hard to identify each step (or
butchered syllable and word). I believe my story "Confession"
in *Soulcatcher* delivers the black voice of an uneducated slave
in third-person monologue, but without the stylized and
choppy approach writers fell into one hundred years ago (and
that includes Dunbar, who wrote that way for white readers).
One thing I can't help but notice about Negro dialect is that
*all* the black characters talk the same—there is no individua-
tion based on their voices, diction, personality, or vision (as
expressed through language). In other words, I think it's a kind
of shorthand for the speech of the racial Other—the same thing
happened with portraits of the Chinese and the way they speak,
lasting well into the 1950s (rent old episodes of *Have Gun Will
Travel*. Paladin has a bus boy friend at the hotel where he stays

---

\* The text can be found at <http://www.pbs.org/marktwain/learnmore/
writings.html>

in San Francisco—his name is "Hey Boy," because that's what all the whites say when they want him to fetch their luggage; and one episode in the series is called, I think, "Hey Boy's Revenge."). All this is why I think Quentin Tarrantino, after his film *Jackie Brown* appeared, could say to Spike Lee during an interview, "I can write black." What he's learned, in my opinion, is stereotypical shorthand for "ghetto" speech—one heavy on profanity and sexual references.

To be perfectly honest, I think we need a fifty-year moratorium on certain stories. Have our students read Frederick Douglass and other writers of slave narratives. Anything that looks like it was even faintly influenced by the minstrel tradition or by the Plantation School writers shouldn't be the first thing we subject our students to because that may well be all they read on this subject, which means they won't have a feel for the complexity of black (and white) American lives a century and a half ago.

Twain says "A True Story" is "Repeated Word for Word as I Heard It." I don't believe him. Not unless he has a photographic memory or was transcribing every sentence as "Aunt Rachel" said it. He's making this diction and syntax up after hearing her story, relying on standard dialect of his day. That's what I think.

Sorry to go on so long about this. Have you seen Spike Lee's very controversial movie *Bamboozled?* Flawed as it is, I recommend it simply for the sake of discussion.

McWILLIAMS: *Was it difficult to write from the point of view of Martin Luther King? One of my students asked me if* Dreamer *could have been published if a white author had dared to write so intimately from Dr. King's point of view. What do you think?*

JOHNSON: I felt very comfortable writing from Martin Luther King, Jr.'s, viewpoint. We're both trained in philosophy (and for him, theology) through the PhD; we both grew up in the black church. We both value the life of the spirit above all else. And King was born to my parents' generation, i.e., to black people I saw daily in my childhood. I doubt that a white writer would have felt as comfortable writing from as deep inside his psyche as I did.

McWILLIAMS: *Nabokov once compared himself to a puppet master. How would you characterize your relationship with your fictional characters?*

JOHNSON: One thing I hope and pray for is that my characters never feel like puppets the author is manipulating. Ideally, each should have his (or her) own unique vocabulary, vision of the world, and biography. The fictional "world" of Andrew Hawkins, who is able to pass for white, simply can never be the same as the lifeworld (*Lebenswelt*) of Rutherford Calhoun, who—I should note this—speaks with the language of sailors in a way that landlubber Andrew never could. And my fictitious King's theology-drenched language, images, and metaphors would never be used by either Rutherford or Andrew.

McWILLIAMS: *You always deal with challenging, serious issues in your novels (racism, the search for self, etc.), yet you always have humor. Why is humor so important?*

JOHNSON: Humor in its various forms—wit, irony, and so forth—is so essential to our humanness that it can't be avoided. Even slaves in the eighteenth and nineteenth century delighted in humor, as we see in the hilarious folklore and "Master and John" story cycle that come down to us. The ability to laugh, and especially laugh at the master, is a human quality that slave owners could not take away.

McWILLIAMS: *You're saying humor can be serious, correct? The jokes in your fiction, then, aren't necessarily "comic relief"?*

JOHNSON: Humor is an example of our humanness. And it can be a vehicle for powerfully expressing truth—as in satire, or the humor in Zen parables, or in the work of the world's editorial cartoonists (I have a special affection for the tribe of cartoonists since I belong to it) who, in a single comic image, capture the essence of an event or situation. Twain used humor that way, as did Lenny Bruce and Richard Pryor. The examples I could give are endless and global and span two millennia.

McWILLIAMS: *Speaking of humor, the recent movie* The Barbershop *is stirring up controversy. Is Martin Luther King, Jr., beyond jokes?*

JOHNSON: I haven't seen this movie, but one of my best friends, a black screenwriter, did see it and he says it made him sick.

From what is described in this article about how the jokes are presented (by a character everyone condemns), I don't see a problem. People *do* make these remarks about King and Rosa Parks; the filmmakers chose to inject those comments—widespread among black people—into the film through a character who apparently would make them. The question is whether the comments are even necessary. As a Buddhist, I believe that if we wish to engage in Right Speech (part of the Eightfold Path), we would do well to test what we say and present by stopping it at Three Gates: (1) Is what we are about to say true? (2) Is it necessary? And (3) Will it cause harm?

If our public utterances and art pass those Three Gates, then a problem like the one *The Barbershop* is having should not arise.

McWILLIAMS: *You're a teacher yourself. Do you intend for your fiction to teach as well? Do you write "moral fiction"?*

JOHNSON: Yes, I hope my stories do instruct. My goal is for readers of my fiction to laugh, to cry, and to learn something. And if I ever publish an "immoral" fiction, then I figure that's when I should stop writing once and for all.

McWILLIAMS: *I think most of the writing teachers that I've known would prefer not to be teachers (they teach only because they can't make enough money from writing), yet the impression I get from you is that you love teaching. What rewards does it give you?*

JOHNSON: Over the last twenty-seven years at the University of Washington (and as a visitor at other schools), I've taught hundreds and hundreds of students who are now published authors, people like David Guterson, Gary Hawkes, Sandi Son-nenfeld, and Johanna Stoberock, whose first novel, *City of Ghosts,* will appear soon from Norton (I just had the pleasure of endorsing it). Naturally, I'm deeply rewarded and feel proud when my former students go forth into the world and secure a place for themselves as creators.

As you say, many writing teachers would prefer to just write and leave teaching behind, if they could afford to do so. I've made a lot of money from writing, especially after *Middle Passage* was on the bestsellers' list in 1991. But I also make a lot from teaching and speaking engagements. This year I decided to take early retirement from the Producer-Writers Pension Fund in order to receive for the rest of my life (and my wife's) a monthly check—I've written twenty screen- and teleplays since 1977, enough to become "vested," and the nice thing about this arrangement is that I can still work in the industry after "retiring." There's no question that artists have to be very serious about financial matters, especially if they have a family to support.

I decided very early in my writing life, when I was in my twenties, that I did not want to subject my wife and children to the financial vagaries of the art world. I have friends who are strictly commercial writers. They do romance novels, or science fiction, or horror stories, or murder mysteries. In other words, they create basically the same product (what writer Fred Pfeil once called "industrial fiction") over and over, and they have so little time to revise and polish their work. Real literary art takes time. Labor-time, as Marx would say—the quality of a creative work can be measured by the labor-time invested in it and the skill of the worker. David Guterson, for example, spent ten years writing *Snow Falling on Cedars.* My non-teaching friends simply don't have the luxury of devoting five or ten years to a book. In order to put food on the table, they do their best to write and publish a book a year. Even then they tell me how difficult it is sometimes to pay their monthly bills, and so often they are dissatisfied with their creations, which have to be done with such haste.

In my case, I wanted my wife and two kids to not only have everything they needed but also everything they wanted. And I abhor debt. As a literary writer, my goal is for every book to be different, to be a new process of discovery for both my readers and me. If it takes five years for a book's gestation period, so be it. I'd never do the same story twice. That would bore me to tears. Each book, I believe, should be the finest gift one can offer to a reader—groundbreaking, beautifully crafted, original. But the audience for one book—*King: A Photobiography,* for example—might well not be the same as for *The Sorcerer's Apprentice.* Working this way, always striving for originality, an artist will surely have up and down financial years and, as I said, I refused to subject my loved ones to that.

Teaching at a university, teaching what you love, and having a regular paycheck solves the problem of bills, frees one to write whatever he wishes and for as long as a project requires. And, after tenure, a writer has what John Gardner once called the best job in the world. I always planned to teach when I was working on my doctorate in philosophy. The university is the proper home for a scholar. Unlike most creative-writing teachers, I teach creative writing as I would a course in applied aesthetics, challenging my students (especially MFA students) to become technicians of form and language, and to be good critics who can analyze a story as they might a logical proof. So, yeah, I do enjoy teaching a good class where the students are eager to learn technique and the theory behind it. We have a duty—a moral obligation—to give to others as our teachers gave to us. The university has always had that transmission of knowledge as its mission.

McWILLIAMS: *Do you teach only creative-writing courses, or do you teach courses in the philosophy department, too?*

JOHNSON: I taught philosophy for a year at SUNY-Stony Brook when I did my PhD there. At UW, I haven't taught philosophy, but just about everything else in English—novel, short story, and essay writing, African American literature, and a theory class for graduate writers in which I immerse them in phenomenological criticism. UW's Philosophy Department did ask me a few years ago if I wanted to teach a class there, but I decided against doing so for several reasons. First, because we always seem understaffed when it comes to teaching our courses in creative writing; second, because I only teach two classes a year now; and third, because I love philosophy too much to teach it.

McWILLIAMS: *How can you love something too much to teach it?*

JOHNSON: All my life I've taught my passions, beginning in my late teens when, as an undergraduate, I first taught a free class in cartooning in what was called "Free School," where students at Southern Illinois University in 1969 could conceive, then teach their own classes. I tutored and taught philosophy and literature for three years at SUNY-Stony Brook, then creative writing, literature and criticism at the University of Washington for twenty-seven years now, and I've taught Choy Li Fut kung fu at a studio I co-founded in Seattle with friends.

When students bring the same love and passion I have for a subject to class, then teaching is a great pleasure. When they don't, it is—let us say—less than a pleasure. Everyone doesn't love philosophy. For me, that subject isn't just another academic discipline. In the West, it is the *first* intellectual discipline from which all others (physics, psychology, etc.) later emerged. It is, in fact, deeply intertwined with my being-in-the-world, one of the ways I sing the world, so one of my great pleasures in life is sharing the philosophical enterprise with others who live and love it.

But if philosophy isn't important to a student, then trying to spark his (or her) interest can be like pulling teeth. If, for example, someone doesn't believe that "the unexamined life is not worth living," or is taking a philosophy course just to fulfill a requirement, if the love of intellectual (and spiritual) challenge isn't there—well, that is the reason why Buddhists seldom, if ever, proselytize: you sat outside traditional Zen monasteries for a day, sometimes in the snow, before they let you inside, and then only provisionally as a "visitor." In other words, you must demonstrate your commitment before you join and have the privilege—and it is a privilege—of studying with people who have devoted their lives to the Dharma. The same was true for my first martial arts school in Chicago in 1967—three friends and I sat through a formal interview with the school's master, who kicked out one of my buddies before the interview was over ("Get out," he said, "you can't train here") when he made a disrespectful remark he thought was funny. (My other friend lasted a week before that school's regimen wore him out.)

As Martin Luther King, Jr., once said, "I can't be what I need to be until you are what you need to be, and you can't be what you need to be until I am what I need to be." I think this applies especially to teachers and students, both of whom must bring love, respect, and selfless dedication to the classroom in order to maximize the educational experience. If those conditions are not present, I don't attempt anymore to "sell" the things I love most to those who are indifferent to them.

MCWILLIAMS: *In a number of interviews you have expressed your disappointment with a lot of contemporary fiction, saying that it often lacks intellectual depth and has a "sameness." Other authors have argued that MFA programs are to blame for this "sameness" that you've pointed out. What do you think?*

JOHNSON: I think the answer can be found if we ask ourselves this question: How would Melville, Poe, Dostoyevsky, Emerson, and Kafka have fared in any of our contemporary fiction-writing workshops? I don't believe they would have come back after the first day. Today's workshop method produces what I call the Workshop Story, which is neither awful nor great, publishable but drained by the workshop process of anything truly daring or groundbreaking.

McWILLIAMS: *Where's the dividing line, then, between a workshop being a help and it being a hindrance?*

JOHNSON: As with any "skill acquisition" course, the best workshops, in my view, help us understand and acquire the craft to solve any creative problem at least three ways. They are labor-intensive. Students should master a new technique each week. They should be able to dream up a new imaginative story every week. In their critiques of their peers, if they identify a problem in a manuscript, they should be able to suggest at least one and ideally two or three ways for the writer to fix that problem. Last quarter I assigned one of Gardner's exercises—write a three-page monologue within a third-person narrative—and two or three of my graduate students couldn't get that assignment right until they'd tried it several times. One woman, very talented, moaned in class, "I can't *do* monologues." But by the end of the term, after a few attempts, she turned in a very fine example of just that.

And I would not, of course, give my students a writing task that I have not performed myself. (See the FBI agent's long monologue in *Dreamer* or the Soulcatcher's speech about how he works to capture runaway slaves in *Oxherding Tale*.) Basically, I tell my students I don't care a fig *what* they write, only *how* they write it.

Consider how music and painting are taught, how apprentices are called upon to master the techniques and performances of the "masters" in their disciplines (and the theory behind those techniques). Once they have done that, they become journeymen with a high skill level who go out in the world able to execute any assignment they are given. (Capable journeymen are the backbone of any discipline or craft.) Finally, when the journeyman creates his own masterpiece or makes a technical (and/or theoretical) breakthrough, that becomes part of the repertoire that future apprentices must learn. This is how I envision (and explain to my students) the difference between apprentice, journeyman, and master—and how an artistic discipline evolves. (This same progression, by the way, has its parallel within a particular martial arts tradition.)

McWILLIAMS: *If I understand you correctly, all a workshop (even the best ones) can do is develop tools through study and exercises. It can't teach creativity or vision or imagination. In other words, it doesn't really make someone a "writer." Yes?*

JOHNSON: You're right—we can't teach creativity, vision, or imagination. The students have to show up with that. We can't create writers. All we can do, I believe, is help those with talent, discipline, and dedication. However, it is true that writing courses do help everyone become better, more sophisticated readers of fiction—readers able to recognize the craft choices an author has made (good or bad) at every stage, every paragraph, in a story or novel.

McWILLIAMS: *Music departments typically require a recital before admitting a student into a program, but creative-writing courses are often open to all. (I'm speaking only about undergraduate courses.) Should English departments start requiring students to show some definite talent before allowing them to enroll in a creative-writing program?*

JOHNSON: I'd say, no. The students in beginning and intermediate workshops are really there to see if they have the ability to write stories. And they're so young they haven't experienced enough of life yet to write fiction that is culturally probing.

Here at the University of Washington, our beginning and intermediate short story classes are open to all students. We once required a writing sample for entry into intermediate classes, but we received too few applicants because students after only one workshop felt insecure about submitting their work. But we do "screen" applicants for the advanced short story workshop. And the creative writing faculty only admits about ten MFA fiction-writers a year if they have talent and, most importantly, show promise. (Also we keep the acceptances low for MFA students because we'd like to give financial support to as many as we can.)

McWILLIAMS: *In a recent peer review of your fiction-writing course, David Shields said the course "skillfully mixes nuanced attention to the most minute aspects of craft with rigorous investigation of timeless philosophical questions." Is your emphasis on "timeless philosophical questions" what distinguishes your courses from creative-writing courses taught by others?*

JOHNSON: I do ask my students to consider the ontology of the sentence (as William Gass once phrased it), and what a moral fiction might be (as John Gardner suggested), and to see their stories as being a theatre where meaning is dramatized. To write anything, and especially to write fiction, is to engage in the interpretation of this world that envelops us, just as we do in the fields of philosophy and history. American fiction, in my view, cannot afford to be philosophically naïve, not after our literature has seen the achievements of authors like Melville, Emerson, Wright, Toomer, Bellow, Pynchon, and Gardner, to name but a few.

McWILLIAMS: *You assign three texts in your course: John Gardner's* The Art of Fiction, *Julie Checkoway's* Creating Fiction, *and Northrup Frye's* The Educated Imagination. *Would you please comment on why you chose these particular texts?*

JOHNSON: Since 1976 all my graduate and undergraduate students have completed the thirty exercises in Gardner's *The Art of Fiction*, exercises like (1) "Write three effective long sentences: each at least one full typed page (or 250 words), each involving a different emotion (for example, anger, pensiveness, sorrow, joy), the purpose being control of tone in a complex sentence" (I give my students two examples from Dylan Thomas and Samuel Delany for this one); (2) "Write a two-page (or longer) character sketch using objects, landscape, weather, etc., to intensify the reader's sense of what the character is like.

Use no similes"; and (3) "Describe a character in a brief passage (one or two pages) using mostly long vowels and soft consonants (*o* as in "moan," *e* as in "see"; *i, m, n, sh,* etc.); then describe the same character, using mostly short vowels and hard consonants (*i* as in "sit"; *k, t, p, gg,* etc.)." These exercises demand that an apprentice writer learn every dimension of prose technique, first the dramatic structure of stories that Aristotle talks about in *The Poetics,* then the architecture of the prose sentence and paragraph that Longinus discusses in *On Literary Excellence.* Even my students who did not go on to become fiction writers have told me, decades later, how the exercises sharpened their craft. For example, one former student is now a Seattle police detective who works on serial murder cases. A few years ago he told me that the exercises made him conscious of how each and every report he files as a policeman must be accurate, right down to diction or word choice, because if that report isn't, the perpetrator will go free.

I use Julie Checkoway's *Creating Fiction* partly because it contains my essay (originally a keynote speech for the Associated Writing Program's conference in Portland in 1998) on how apprentice writers should train themselves to be technicians of literary form and language, and partly because the book offers the views of many other authors—all accomplished—on the craft of writing. As for Frye's *The Educated Imagination,* the title says it all—an educated, trained imagination is what I want my students to have. To paraphrase Kant: education without imagination is empty; imagination without education is blind.

McWILLIAMS: *Have you ever thought about writing a textbook for fiction writing?*

JOHNSON: No. My book *Being and Race: Black Writing Since 1970* is full of writing instruction and commentary on the principles of craft. We don't need another handbook after Gardner's magnificent *The Art of Fiction,* which crystallizes thirty years of his experience and knowledge.

McWILLIAMS: *You're an accomplished artist, so I'm a bit*

*surprised that you've never done an illustrated novel, maybe*
*something like Art Spiegelman's* Maus. *Have you ever thought*
*about it? I would imagine the stories of* Soulcatcher, *for*
*instance, would work beautifully as an illustrated collection*
*of stories.*

JOHNSON: Spiegelman works, of course, primarily as a cartoonist, though he received a literary award for *Maus*—the *Los*
*Angeles Times* Fiction Prize (I was one of the judges that year
who voted for his getting it). When I began seriously writing
novels and literary works in 1970, I put my seven years as a
cartoonist behind me in order to establish myself as a fiction
writer, essayist, and critic, and didn't dust off my drawing
board until the 1990s. I'd love to illustrate one of my own
books some day. We'll just have to wait for the right opportunity to arise.

McWILLIAMS: *When I taught at Alabama State University*
*(a historically black university), one of my students started the*
*semester of freshman composition very articulate and studious.*
*By the end of the semester, he had lapsed into mediocrity. From*
*reading his essays, I learned that he was continually harassed in*
*the dorm for being "too white." What can we do to combat this*
*insidious stereotyping that keeps so many young black males*
*from striving to do their best academically?*

JOHNSON: The best thing to do is remind young people that,
historically, black Americans have always seen education as the
real road to freedom—this devotion to excellence and learning
dates back to right after the Civil War, and the century of intellectual giants from that time (Du Bois, Jean Toomer, Richard
Wright, Ralph Ellison), to the present and provides a wealth of
role models.

McWILLIAMS: *Do you see yourself as a role model?*

JOHNSON: Actually, I never think of myself in those terms.
I just do what I do.

McWILLIAMS: *Nearly every one of my black male students*
*at Alabama State said that he had been harassed by a police*

*officer at some point. Typically, it was an instance of "driving while black." Have you ever experienced such racial profiling?*

JOHNSON: Once or twice in the early 1970s when I was in my early twenties that happened to me (or so I believed at the time) in Chicago. But not since then.

McWILLIAMS: *Your father has moved back to South Carolina, correct? A few years back, I read an article about blacks who had moved north in the 1940s and 1950s now returning to the South. Any thoughts on this reverse migration? Do you have any desire to "return to your roots" and live in the South?*

JOHNSON: Members of my father's family (and my father) have all made that reverse migration to their original home in South Carolina. But I was born in Evanston, Illinois. How could the South be seen as my "roots"? I didn't grow up there. To be perfectly honest, my spiritual home is the Northwest, where I've lived now—and by choice—for half my life.

McWILLIAMS: *Do you feel any spiritual connection with the South? Or to Africa, for that matter?*

JOHNSON: I'm afraid I don't know the South well enough for a spiritual connection. Nor Africa, which I've never visited. When writing, the "spirit of place" (to use a D. H. Lawrence phrase) I tap into most easily is that found in the Chicago area of my childhood and young manhood, or southern Illinois where I lived for seven years, or lately and increasingly the Pacific Northwest. I need to live in a place for a few years to feel acquainted enough with it for it to become the landscape or backdrop for my fiction. Of course, as a writer who takes on many assignments, I do have to write about other regions and locales—for that I rely on research.

McWILLIAMS: *How does that "spirit of place"—your memories—affect your fiction? I'm guessing that in* Dreamer, *for example, some of what Matthew Bishop experiences in Chicago and in southern Illinois are what you experienced? If so, where is the boundary between fiction and nonfiction?*

JOHNSON: Yes, in *Dreamer* I draw heavily on my earlier life in Evanston, Chicago, and southern Illinois, and for that I relied on vivid memories, research (into southern Illinois plant life, for example), consulting friends in Evanston (to clarify who did some of the wiring in the Great Expectations Book Store, which recently closed, by the way), and my family's recorded and orally transmitted history. In other words, I always try to check the accuracy of my memory.

One reader of *Dreamer* told me he couldn't tell where history ended and fiction began. I also was told that last night about a new short story, "Dr. King's Refrigerator," that I read at a benefit for the Washington Commission for the Humanities. This is what I want to hear about my fiction—that the fusion of fiction and fact is experienced, phenomenologically, as seamless. I have met readers, for example, who think the Allmuseri tribe in *Middle Passage* is real. As Gardner would say, I want the novel's final draft to be a "vivid and continuous dream" in the mind of the reader, where real facts and the descriptions I draw—with specificity and as much detailed texture as I can muster—can't be distinguished.

But there are no real Allmuseri, of course. And Martin Luther King, Jr., never had a double: those people and that imaginative premise are the "fictions" in *Dreamer* and *Middle Passage*. But, even though a writer conjures such fictions, he must incarnate them with thousands of well-chosen "significant details" (as a critic once put it) so that they have the illusion of real life. I sweat over those details more than I can say. Each and every datum, real or imagined—a gesture, an article of clothing, a phrase in a character's speech, a prop in the background, a word choice—must be examined over and over again to determine if it helps make the novel or story coherent, consistent, and complete; and if it adds to the "suspension of disbelief."

McWILLIAMS: *You said you gave a benefit reading last night. I had never thought about it, but I guess part of being a famous author is a lot of traveling (readings, interviews, book signings, lectures, etc.).*

JOHNSON: I can't speak for other authors, but that's *all* my life has been for three and a half decades, especially since the 1980s and after the 1990 National Book Award, 24/7 readings, teaching, dovetailing writing assignments, books by friends and writers I've never met to blurb, interviews, keynote speeches and lectures, public appearances to support various worthy projects, mentoring young talent—students, new and ones I first taught decades ago, etc. (Tomorrow I've got another newspaper interview—to discuss the new introduction I wrote for Oxford's 150th anniversary edition of *Uncle Tom's Cabin.*) It's all-consuming . . .

McWILLIAMS: *Our country continues to be preoccupied by "race." Are you optimistic about the future?*

JOHNSON: No, I'm not all that optimistic about the future, especially after September 11. The world seems these days to be awash in tribalism; and the "race industry," as some have called it, is still going strong in America as we begin a new century. For me, "race" is the grandest of illusions, a perfect example of what Buddhists (and I am Buddhist) call samsara. Yet I do believe that, as in any age, a respectable percentage of the population will slough off thinking in terms of racial essences or "natures." Just abandon it as excess baggage they realize they no longer need. As a creator, I want to be on the side of those who help encourage that next step in human evolution, however small my contribution might be.

McWILLIAMS: *So you're a bit more optimistic that individuals might overcome the illusion of "race," but feel pessimistic about American society as a whole? It is therefore a question of individual responsibility?*

JOHNSON: I think the health of American society and culture—and its continuation—always depend on how well individual citizens rise to the challenge of being civilized. No one is born civilized. That's something we have to work at every day of our lives. When a generation comes along that doesn't work at it—by knowing their own history, literature, and cultural formations—then what we call civilization can be lost in a mere twenty years, which is what I believe has indeed happened in America since 1970. It saddens me profoundly when I talk to high school and college teachers who have no knowledge—or only sketchy knowledge—of the Western classics in literature and philosophy (to say nothing of the seminal works of the East or of black Americans), or to students who want to write but don't like to read. If we are to live in a civilized world, it is the responsibility of each and every one of us to realize that world first in our own lives by the seriousness by which we approach every aspect of life: as students, teachers, artists with the highest creative and intellectual standards, and men and women who do their best to live—as Martin Luther King, Jr., did—by a moral ideal.

McWILLIAMS: *You've said that you're Buddhist, but I read in another interview that you were raised in a Christian home. Were you a sincere Christian, or did you have doubts? I know that martial arts sparked your initial interest in Buddhism, but what particular text or teacher convinced you? Did you explore any other faiths along the way?*

JOHNSON: I've always been a sincere Christian *and* a Buddhist, just as Thich Nhat Hahn has a portrait of Jesus right beside his Theravada Buddhist shrine. (And just as Jan Willis describes herself as a Buddhist-Baptist.) There's no contradiction, at least not for the Buddhadharma, which emphasizes the interdependence of all things and avoids dualism.

The essays in *Turning the Wheel* discuss in depth the relationship between the Buddhist vision and Christianity, as well as the Buddhadharma's relationship to philosophers ranging from Marcus Aurelius through Descartes to Heidegger.

McWILLIAMS: *Could you say something about* Turning the Wheel?

JOHNSON: Yes, it's a collection of fifteen essays. Most are previously published, but for this book I wrote a new forty-five-page essay (with eighty-nine footnotes), entitled "Reading the

Eightfold Path," plus a preface. All together, they cover a lot of literary territory (on the evolution of American short fiction and novels, on lots of black authors and John Gardner, as well as on the Buddhist Toro Nagashi ceremony, etc.) and the first section is devoted to essays reflecting on the dharma and black America. I think I've waited my whole life to get this book done.

McWILLIAMS: *What do you mean by "Eightfold Path"? And the "Toro Nagashi" ceremony?*

JOHNSON: The Eightfold Path (*Arya Astanga Marga*) is an essential part of Buddhism—it is, in fact, the Fourth Noble Truth, and in my essay I explain why it is a complete ethical system. Toro Nagashi is the candle-floating ceremony performed every year around the world, during the summer, to honor those killed at Hiroshima and Nagasaki—in short, a celebration of nonviolence where people light candles (with the name of a deceased loved one who died from violence) and release them on the water. In Seattle, we do it at Green Lake. My essay is the talk I gave last year at that event.

McWILLIAMS: *I'm getting interested in Buddhism because of your novels and because of the selections from Buddhist texts in the* Norton Anthology of World Literature. *What texts would you recommend I read next?*

JOHNSON: Start with the *Dhammapada*, then add *The Diamond Sutra, The Lotus Sutra*, and *The Mahasatipanna Sutra*. Just now, I'm working through versions of the *Dhammapada* and *The Heart Sutra* in Sanskrit, doing my own translation for practice—and for the spiritual reward that comes from seeing how various translations differ from the original Sanskrit and Pali (which is a modified version of Sanskrit).

McWILLIAMS: *More particularly, if you were designing a syllabus of essential texts (not just Buddhist ones) to help someone understand your work, what would make that list?*

JOHNSON: I would do my best to represent Theravada, *Mahayana, Madhyamika, Ch'an* (Zen), and Tibetian Buddhist traditions on such a syllabus. I would also introduce the class to *vipassana* ("insight") meditation techniques and have them read Thich Nhat Hahn, probably his book *Being Peace* or *The Miracle of Mindfulness*. Also, if someone wanted a good list of texts for interpreting my work, I suggest they look at my annotated "Twenty List" on my home page, http://oxherdingtale.com; or pick up the new book, *The Book That Changed My Life: Interviews with National Book Award Winners and Finalists*, edited by Diane Osen (Modern Library, September, 2002), which contains a list by each author of works that were influential on their thinking.

McWILLIAMS: *In rereading McCullough's 1978 interview with you, I was struck by how consistent your aesthetics have been over the past twenty-five years. You said in that interview, "When you edit fiction what you want to achieve is a musical underpinning, for example, to the prose. . . ." Do you think you've changed much as a writer over the past twenty-five years?*

JOHNSON: By the time I published *Faith and the Good Thing* (1974) I had worked out my aesthetic position. Later, I refined it with phenomenological aesthetics, then Buddhist aesthetics, but the general theoretical outline was there thirty years ago.

McWILLIAMS: *In* Faith and the Good Thing, *Alpha Omega Holmes says, "a real artist is his own canvas," adding that "someday . . . there won't be a dime's worth of difference between what I'm creatin' and myself—you won't be able to separate me from my works by space, or by a difference in materials because—and I know it sounds crazy—my life'll be the finished work." As an artist yourself, do you agree with Alpha Omega?*

JOHNSON: At the time I wrote those lines in *Faith and the Good Thing*, probably in the spring of 1973, that was my ideal of the artist—someone who empties himself completely in expression, projecting everything he has in the way of ideas and feelings and images onto the page. Twenty-nine years later, I think I've achieved a whole lot of that externalization of the subjective into objective, public documents—novels, stories, essays, teleplays, drawings, etc. I guess I still feel that way, but now I don't have such a huge freight of feelings and ideas to unload as when I was twenty-five.

McWILLIAMS: *In some of your interviews you've talked at length about your journals, six "apprentice novels," and mounds of early drafts of published stories and novels. Are you planning to destroy it all or leave it for scholars to examine? How do you feel about a scholar sorting through your papers, perhaps even publishing some?*

JOHNSON: In a new will that my lawyer just worked out, a full page minutely describes "literary properties" that I want protected for my wife, our children, and then their offspring. (I'm referring to the rights for various work.) But I've asked my wife and kids to burn my journals for the last forty years (they were simply for my use, for me to take my own temperature daily) and abandoned drafts of novels, etc. A couple of schools have asked for my papers, but I'm not ready to part with them yet. In other words, I plan to determine what future scholars pick through.

McWILLIAMS: *Now that you've looked over your interviews from the past few years, is there anything that you wished you hadn't said?*

JOHNSON: Nope, I'm OK with everything.

KRAEHENBUEHL: *If you could meet any historical person, living or dead, who would you pick and why?*

JOHNSON: Shakyamuni Buddha would be the person I'd most like to meet. Jesus, too. After those two, I'd settle for meeting Socrates, Marcus Aurelius, and Gandhi.

*Kraehenbuehl: What is one life goal that you would like to accomplish that you haven't?*

JOHNSON: I have to say in all humility, and with the deepest gratitude, that I've accomplished my life's various goals.

# SHOULDER TO THE WHEEL

*An Interview with Charles Johnson*

## JOHN WHALEN-BRIDGE

T HIS INTERVIEW BY e-mail between February 2001 and July 2003 was conducted for this book to address Johnson's thoughts concerning Buddhism, with special attention to his newest publication, *Turning the Wheel: Essays on Buddhism and Writing*.

WHALEN-BRIDGE: *What has the response to* Turning the Wheel *been like?*

JOHNSON: Just the other day I did a two-and-a-half-hour reading and Q & A for 140 people who showed up at Elliott Bay Book Company here in Seattle (this, after I got back last Sunday from five days on the East Coast), and then I have to fly to Los Angeles to do two more bookstores. The turnout at these bookstores has been amazing—no literary types, just a capac-

This interview is previously unpublished.

ity crowd (even at an all-black bookstore in a black mall in Maryland last Saturday) that is a cross section of humankind: white, black, Asian, young, old, Zen and Christian priests, long-time and new meditators. It's been *sangha* time each time, so, though tired, I feel profoundly rewarded by the people I've met. They are *so* different from the people I've met on previous book tours.

WHALEN-BRIDGE: *I've lived in Asia for ten years and jaws drop whenever I tell people I'm a Buddhist. I find this tiresome and sometimes even a tad racist. Do you get this too?*

JOHNSON: I had an interesting experience recently. I did an interview for Evergreen Radio (taped) here in Seattle, and my interviewer was a wonderfully warm black man about my age. He just had to say, though, "People in the community are wondering how did a brother get over there with Buddhism?" And then he asked, "Why *this* book. And why *now?*" I've been musing on his question for a couple of days—why *Turning the Wheel* now—and I know the answer: in this phase of my life, what I call Act Three, I finally had to declare myself someone devoted to the dharma. Six years ago I made the decision to direct my creative writing energies to the dharma after my Microsoft-sponsored trip to Thailand (and my interview with the abbot in the town of Phrae)—no longer tucking the dharma into my fiction and keeping Buddhism tucked close to my vest, but addressing it directly in nonfiction prose. Truth to tell, *Turning the Wheel* may have cost me a few old friends in the book world. Since receiving their copies, other writers (I'll name no names), some black and some white academic and literary colleagues, haven't said as much as "boo" to me about it in two months. I think the book may be alienating to them; I think they are, in fact, as deeply afraid of Buddhism as my old teacher Gardner once was. I think as well that their perception, ideas, or beliefs about me—who I am, what I think, what I stand for—have been roughed up a little. Or more than a little. And I think that's good. It may lead, on their part, to a little more "epistemological humility," a hesitancy to judge too quickly, make assumptions—or it may just lead them to avoid me like the plague, which is OK, too. I'll still love 'em.

As one of my friends who *did* respond to the book said, with *Turning the Wheel* what I'm doing is just saying, "This is where I stand. Period. Deal with it." Some apparently have decided not to deal with it. And so that, I think, is the answer, in part, to the black gentleman's question.

WHALEN-BRIDGE: *In* Turning the Wheel *you pursue connections between Buddhism and phenomenology. Given the similarity between Merleau-Ponty's descriptions of phenomenological practice and Dogen's notion that we study the self to forget the self, one wonders what difference actually exists between the two systems of thought. Is it fair to say that phenomenology and Buddhism are but different pathways to the same place, for you?*

JOHNSON: Early Buddhism has, as so many have noted, a distinctly phenomenological "flavor." Phenomenology, as a Western attempt to achieve a "presuppositionless philosophy of experience," with its emphasis being on the *method* that arises from the *epoché* and the "phenomenological reduction" and its aim being an intuition of things before our explanatory models obscure them, has *much* in common with Buddhism, where the method is meditation and the goal is awakening. Husserl had one Japanese student, a man who returned to Japan, taught, then entered a Zen monastery for the remainder of his life.

Consider this quote from Bhikku Bodhi, which I use in the article I wrote for this summer's issue of *Turning Wheel* devoted to African Americans and Buddhism: "The task of Right Mindfulness is to clear up the cognitive field. Mindfulness brings to light experience in its pure immediacy. It reveals the object as it is before it has been plastered over with conceptual paint, overlaid with interpretations. To practice mindfulness is thus a matter not so much of doing but of undoing: not thinking, not judging, not associating, not planning, not imagining, not wishing."

"Planning, imagining, wishing" are for the phenomenologist the intentions with which consciousness aims at a thing (*noema*) and causes it to appear in a particular way; these intentions, arising from the noetic pole, are simply examined as they arise in the phenomenal field. How close *that* is to Vipassana "insight" meditation. There is waiting to be done, I believe, a major interdisciplinary study of the similar *thrust* that we find in Buddhism and phenomenology. Surely Heidegger suspected the importance of this. See his piece, "A Dialogue on Language between a Japanese and an Inquirer," that opens the essays in *On the Way to Language.*

So, in *Turning the Wheel,* I felt no hesitancy at all in occasionally "reading" the Buddhadharma phenomenologically as a "radical empiricism," as Husserl phrased it.

WHALEN-BRIDGE: *You're now working on another study of phenomenology, Buddhism, and race. The relationship between Buddhism and phenomenology is clear, but isn't there a contradiction between your espousal of Buddhist emptiness and your attachment to race as a category? In* Turning the Wheel *you complain about America's obsession with race and with the way African American intellectuals are limited by this concept, and yet you write quite a bit about race yourself.*

JOHNSON: But do I care about "race"? Nope, not a bit. I *do* care about people and how the samsaric illusion of race hurts them so. (I just blurbed yesterday a book by Tananarive Due, the horror writer, and her mother, a civil rights activist, called *Freedom in the Family.* Just reading the details in this was a chore—the senseless racism and bigotry they experienced, the nightmare that was the Freedom Rides, but in the end their joint-told story is ennobling, and precisely because they fought, however futilely or successfully, for a society where people might be judged, as King put it, by their character, not the color of their skin.)

Yet race-consciousness might well be called a "structure" of the *Lebenswelt* or world of "lived-experience." There's the tragedy, in my view. It's part of the way the world is put together—and, by golly, people *like* having it that way. We won't, I believe, ever have King's "color-blind" society (or world), and I'm doubtful that humankind can ever shake off the easy tendency to project generalizations onto racial "difference," i.e., it's fertile ground for the ego—the illusory self—to build its Them versus Us sense of self-importance (based on "race").

What should a Buddhist do? If the ideas are false . . . well, let them go. I remember how Shakyamuni resisted the idea of teaching after he experienced enlightenment, but some god told him that if only *one* person understood the dharma, that was worth the shitstorm that would come down on his head for turning the wheel. I'm damned glad he did. And at least he avoided the fate that awaited Socrates. On the other hand, as much as I love the bodhisattvas, I *am* drawn to the arhats. . . .

WHALEN-BRIDGE: *You've said that you had to stop being a cartoonist because the medium forced you into oversimplification, but some of your most popular writing, such as* Oxherding Tale, *draws inspiration from a ten-panel Zen cartoon, and the characters in the novel are (delightfully) cartoonish.*

JOHNSON: The problem some have with the idea of characters being "cartoonish" is (for me) a little off to one side of where the discussion should be. Dickens is clearly a caricaturist and was friends with cartoonists of his day. And how can *any* character be called "realistic" when, as Aristotle (and Gass) and others have pointed out for two thousand years in the West, words and things belong to separate ontological orders? Is there a correspondence between, say, a description of my daughter and, well, the living, breathing twenty-one-year-old who surprises me every day we talk? Whatever descriptions we make are, as Plato might put it, at best a "likely story." And for a Buddhist? Words and concepts *are* the problem that prevents one from experiencing the "suchness" of being (and suchness is just another word, another sound we make, too). So, no, I have a deep suspicion of what people too easily refer to as "realism" before they answer the question, "What is reality?," and especially with that late nineteenth-century ideology called naturalism, which Husserl (and others) went on record dismantling for its simplicity, though it sure was popular as an approach, by God, in the twentieth century in the West before postmodernism happily confused the world of the naturalists by talking about the sub-atomic realm and equally valid alternative worldviews from non-Western cultures. Cartoonish? Bah! If American pop films are any indication—all the fantasy movies, horror stuff, science fiction, and movies based on video games—Americans aren't really all that attached, I suspect, to "naturalism."

WHALEN-BRIDGE: *You've also commented on the representation of African Americans by white writers, especially in your introduction to the new edition of* Uncle Tom's Cabin. *We had some correspondence about the philosophical problem of ever getting a human identity "right," and you liked the phrase "right enough" for what an artist might shoot for.*

JOHNSON: Let me share something August Wilson sent me in a fax when I was working on that introduction. He said the "core of black-white relations" is contained in the first sentence of chapter fifteen in Stowe's novel. That sentence reads: "Since the thread of our humble hero's life has now become interwoven with that of higher ones, it is necessary to give some brief introduction to them." August says, "Therein lies the rub. Theirs [whites] is always a higher intelligence, grace, standing, place, meaning, calling, order, truth, morality, etc."

Regarding "getting it right," I want to slip back to *Being and Race,* where I think I wrote that I can describe my son and daughter at length to a reader—physically, psychologically, etc.—but I will never deliver them through language (and I suppose I might have added thought and concepts as well) to someone who has never met them. So, yes, the *really* deep epistemological question is whether we can "know" anyone: our wives, husbands, fathers, best friends, etc. And what does it mean to "know" another? For myself, I see the other as a great and grand mystery, one that is ultimately ineffable—even holy. Which demands (on my side) a humble listening to how the other speaks and appears, and always a sense (for me) that my knowing is provisional, incomplete, partial since the other is process, a becoming that is open-ended in its being, or meaning. That's how I was using the phrase "epistemological humility."

WHALEN-BRIDGE: *When Gary Snyder asked Joan Kyger if she wanted to come to Japan to meditate and lose her ego, she responded that she'd been trying for the last ten years just to get an ego. One might say that an absolute kind of humility is "selflessness," but isn't it important, especially if you're in the less powerful position in society, to try to* get *a self?*

JOHNSON: As long as we live I don't think we're ever free of some residual experience of the "self." If we were free of that, we couldn't distinguish between ourselves and the car bearing down on us—and we'd be killed. That little smidgen of illusion remains (for our survival, I suppose) and is captured in the Dance of Shiva, who has one foot lifted off the demon of ignorance but not both—one stills rests on the demon, which implies (for me) that *some* degree of samsara remains as long as we're breathing in this *rupam* (form).

But to return to the "getting it right" question: I didn't mean to commit a logical fallacy, that of the false choice. But this question, I think, transcends freshman logic. What is at stake, as August is trying to point out, is the quality of life—the suffering and happiness—of our children as they move through a predominantly white culture and society. That's why, I think, my daughter and her boyfriend spent two hours last night talking to me—not because race is entertaining (though it is), but because they are trying to negotiate every day their way through a racial minefield. *Uncle Tom's Cabin* is important because it gives a glimpse where some of the mines (minds?) were manufactured. I can tell them, of course, that it's all illusion, samsara. But it's a lived-illusion, one they're pulled into, whether they want to participate in it or not, the moment they walk out their door. The kids (and August) share with me *numerous* examples, too many to cite, but I know what they're talking about. They're talking about the white woman reporter who once asked me, "Oh, you had a father?" Or my friend Bob Adelman, who did the King photobiography with me, who said when we were on tour that black kids engaging in "the dozens" was a good thing because the insults hardened them for the insults they'd receive later from whites. (This was something he'd read, obviously.) A black person moving through a landscape riddled with the likes of that (only two small examples) either sighs, remains quiet, or takes a deep breath to address such ignorance—what I call "taking out the garbage." August has a great one; after reading a poem, an elderly white man walked up to him and said, "You didn't write that," meaning that he couldn't have written it.

On and on, the examples are too many to bother with, and, of course, someone will reply to each, "But that's not what he meant, or it doesn't prove your point." Whether they're good examples or not, I'm pretty sure the speaker in each case didn't "get it right," or even try very hard to.

WHALEN-BRIDGE: *You've written about martial arts and philosophical texts as alternative sources of your interest in Asian philosophy and Buddhism in particular, but I'm not clear exactly on which was a more important motivation—the dojo or the library.*

JOHNSON: As for meditation, well this: I first "sat" for half an hour when I was fourteen after reading a chapter on meditation in a book my mother had on yoga (now in my library). It was like no thirty minutes I'd ever known in my life—I emerged totally at peace, with a feeling of inner quiet, no awareness of myself, and the feeling that I could be patient with all the people I knew who annoyed me—which is a damned unusual thing, I think, for a fourteen-year-old. But the experience startled and scared me, too. I was afraid I'd be *too* peaceful, too detached, when, at fourteen, what I hungered for was experience of all kinds. So I left meditation alone for eighteen years. Instead, I read every Buddhist, Hindu, Taoist, meditation-related text I could find—in other words, I was content to just study and write about all this, right through *Oxherding Tale.*

From age nineteen on, some "practice" was involved in the three kung fu and three karate systems I passed through. But it wasn't until I was thirty-two, right after I finished *Ox,* right after early tenure, that I *had* to (1) re-immerse myself in martial arts (Choy Li Fut), and (2) take to meditation like the proverbial man "whose hair is on fire." I talked to meditation teachers in 1980–81, among them James DeMille, one of Bruce Lee's students in Seattle, who gave a seminar on meditation that a friend and I attended when I briefly studied Wing Chun Do from one of DeMille's students. I studied various methods, and got Grandmaster Doc Fai Wong to sign off on my practice when I studied at his kwoon in San Francisco in 1981, but in 1980 life's pressures—as an artist and academic—became so acute that I literally had to learn how to practice meditation in order to save my life and sanity. I am not exaggerating: I'm *sure* I wouldn't be here today if I hadn't eased into practice after studying Buddhism (Hinduism and Taoism), on my own and in philosophy classes, since the late '60s.

WHALEN-BRIDGE: *Are you a member of a particular meditation group right now?*

JOHNSON: Well, I suppose this had to happen, karmically, sooner or later. I have a friend in Japan who is now a Zen abbot and runs a temple, the Daigo-ji Temple just outside Osaka. In the '90s he briefly studied martial arts with me and one of my other friends at our Choy Li Fut studio, and we've seen him on his trips back to the states. He is something of a celebrity these days in Japan, being the second Caucasian to become a Zen abbot in that country, and several TV documentaries have been

Shoulder to the Wheel (2003)

done on his life and work. He just asked us to officially join his temple, and we've agreed to do so, along with an interesting international roster of musicians and writers he's also invited, including a Czech violinist and a Japanese novelist.

I tend to be more Theravada than Zen, but the Dharma is the Dharma, so it's about time, I guess, that I go down on some roster with a specific affiliation, Rinzai Zen in this case.

WHALEN-BRIDGE: *I'd like to return to the Theravada/ Mahayana difference shortly, but first a question on your descriptions of Buddhist communities in* Turning the Wheel. *Is it possible you idealize Buddhist groups in America a little bit? We have had our scandal . . .*

JOHNSON: It's not my intention to idealize the *sangha,* but instead to deliberately give a whack of the bamboo stick to readers who are, in my view, too Eurocentric (or even Afrocentric). We know the *sangha* is a collection of mere human beings (like a Christian monastery), and there one can sometimes find the foolishness of our entire species in microcosm. So in *Wheel* when I talk about Buddhists being the best bosses and employees, or in a recent Harvard lecture say the *sangha* is the "finest" of social groups, I am—well—just poking my finger into the paunch of pompous Westerners; indeed, I want their heads to snap back at those lines, if only for a second, and to wonder, "You mean the West *isn't* the center of the Good, the True, and the Beautiful?"

WHALEN-BRIDGE: *So how do we think about the faults of the teacher? There have been American Buddhist teachers who have created havoc in their communities through sexual and even financial improprieties, as detailed in* Shoes Outside the Door; *and, in phenomenological circles, there is the problem of Heidegger. What to do when the teacher screws up big time?*

JOHNSON: Must the philosopher or Buddhist teacher be perfect? We expect philosophers to always be wise and moral, both in their personal and public lives. But such an expectation is bound to be frustrated by individuals prone to make mistakes.

One could condemn Hume for his racial stupidities, but we simply have to listen to his discussion of the self in *A Treatise of Human Nature,* because there he does not err. The same is true of Heidegger; he stumbled badly in his reading of Hitler, but his major work, *Being and Time,* and essays on art and aesthetics disclose his subject in the best phenomenological fashion. Heck, if we judged all thinkers by their racial mistakes, we'd have nothing to learn from anyone before 1960, including Jefferson, Lincoln, and most likely *every* European thinker before the mid-twentieth century. As for the Buddhists, well, all I can say is that the *sangha,* historically, can be swept up in samsara, overcome by the relative-phenomenal world, but that isn't a judgment on the dharma itself—only on that frail creature called "man."

WHALEN-BRIDGE: *You said a moment ago that you preferred the Theravadin arhat ideal to the Mahayanist bodhisattva ideal because a commitment to actual buddhahood was more available in that approach. Does the American approach throw out the baby of total complete enlightenment when it rejects some of the traditional bathwater*

JOHNSON: Do I talk more about Theravada than Mahayana? Well, the Mahayana suits me fine, and I love the bodhisattva ideal. But, damn, I don't want reincarnation, if there's any truth to that. I want off the Wheel after this go-round. Truth to tell, I'd love to "save all sentient beings," and if that's my *svadharma,* I'll try—but I wistfully envy the arhat who finishes his work in the classroom called life and graduates. I'm all for the Mahayana, like any other good American *upasaka,* but the emphasis on the bodhissatva seems to mute the original "goal" of achieving liberation (oneself) and eliminating suffering caused by thirst and selfish desire. There's a tricky balance to maintain here—realizing egoless peace in one's own life and working to "save all sentient beings." That latter part appeals, I'm sure, to the missionary (Puritan?) strain in the American psyche, that urge which M. L. King knew and expressed so well.

Problem is: he was so at work on "saving sentient beings" he always had to sacrifice the one day a week he wanted for meditation and fasting after his 1959 visit to India. The Theravada tradition (which isn't lacking in compassion) does remind me of the work I have to do on myself at the same time I'm working on and in the relative-phenomenal *saha* world. Ah, it would be so much easier to just check into the monastery!

WHALEN-BRIDGE: *Do you feel, as a practitioner, that we need to encounter actual examples of total enlightenment in the world, or is "enlightenment" more of a luminous archetype? If the answer is yes, which teachers or other exemplary humans stand out, in your experience?*

JOHNSON: The answer for me is, yes. I think it's enormously helpful to all practitioners to have an example of (1) a Buddha in our presence or, lacking that, (2) someone sufficiently advanced on the path of spiritual attainment. He (or she) provides a model as well as a reminder of what the Way is. I'm thinking of how the late Lama Yeshe provided such a model (and fatherly-like loving kindness) for Jan Willis, or my friend Sri Chinmoy (who later this month is going to lift me and others at the University of Washington, a weightlifting feat he does to demonstrate the power of the spirit), or the Dalai Lama, or Thich Nhat Hahn. As always, though, and as the Thai monk reminded me in 1997, the teacher and texts are just tools for our liberation.

WHALEN-BRIDGE: *Thich Nhat Hahn discusses a sutra in* Heart of the Buddha's Teachings *(New York: Broadway Books, 1999) and recommends that one not get angry even if someone is sawing off your limbs one-by-one. That's a mighty high standard. Have you met anyone who could pass this test?*

JOHNSON: Not to my knowledge. Maybe Sri Chinmoy. You know, when I spoke at Elliott Bay Book Store, there was a young man from Europe who did the predictable: he challenged me on the issue of whether the "self" existed. He needed, I could tell, to believe in this. I just, well, deconstructed him. I let him see that if one believed in a "self," the burden of providing empirical evidence for it was on him, and naturally he just couldn't provide such evidence. The look on his face, I noticed, was pained when I categorically denied the existence of an enduring self. Very pained and confused. It was a profound look of fear. Similarly, another young man on the other side of the room kept pressing me to admit that violence was sometimes necessary to solve problems. A retired cop in the audience came to my rescue, explaining to him that he knew from his experience that violence may seem to solve problems in the short term but in the long term it only caused more harm.

I keep coming back to the Buddhist Two Levels of Truth, ultimate and conventional. In the marketplace, we'd be idiots, I think, not to pay attention to what classically since Locke has been called "self-interest." We have to pay our taxes. Avoid con men. Protect the safety of our loved ones—and ourselves. But that doesn't mean we have to be "of the world" in terms of having monkey minds, cravings we can't control, or actually believing in an "I" that is substantive and enduring.

WHALEN-BRIDGE: *A few years ago Donald Lopez recounted in* Tricycle *("The Buddhist and the Buddhologist," Summer 1995) a meeting between the Dalai Lama and his graduate students in which the students more or less suggested that the Buddha was no more than a very good person. The Dalai Lama took exception to their idea of enlightenment. Are the teachers you mention (Sri Chinmoy, Lama Yeshe, Dalai Lama, Thich Nhat Hahn) more than merely exemplary, if I may put it that way? Is a Buddha something like a saint? If so, do we expect such a person to be faultless?*

JOHNSON: I'm troubled by this conclusion that those students thought the Buddha was just "a very good person." My parents and grandmother were "very good people." The triumph of the Buddha is expressed, I believe, very powerfully by Nikunja Vihari Banerjee in his translation of *The Dhammapada* (New Delhi: Munshiram Manoharlal Publishers, 1989). I like this book because he provides a Sanskrit version of the text and transliteration. In his introduction, he says:

In fact, what Buddha found especially objectionable about the Hindu view of life was that it is based on the belief that the soul is a permanent and abiding entity. *It is he who, perhaps, for the first time in the history of human thought, came to realize that there is no certain evidence for the existence of such a thing as the permanent soul. Consequently, he came to hold that the self is a passing idea and not an abiding substance.* (My own emphasis.)

I'd be willing to bet that the above is one reason the Dalai Lama took exception to the students' characterization of the Buddha as merely a "very good person." (Which it is important to be, of course, but good behavior doesn't equal awakening.) As His Holiness once said, if one is a serious Christian, for example, he (or she) will be a "good person," but not enlightened or liberated (as the Dalai Lama put it). From the outside a Buddha will no doubt "look" like a saint to others, but the term is no doubt meaningless to him (or her), and he or she might appear now and then to break "saintly" behavior—for example, the monk in the famous Zen story who carries an old woman across a body of water (to the horror of his companion) when monks are not supposed to touch women (or money).

I think the important point—and difference that we find in Buddhism from other spiritual practices—is that while a Buddha may appear saintly or faultless, the important thing is that he is *awakened* and *liberated.* To be awakened is to have experienced the nonconceptual, impossible to describe (or converse about) intuition of this world after dualism and the fiction of an enduring, separate self have been extinguished (nirvana) and to know—*really* know through experience—that *all* things are void or *shunya* (empty). In my twenty-three years of sitting, I'm convinced this can *only* be achieved, in part or whole, through meditation. For a Buddhist, that is the ultimate truth, compared to the "conventional" truth we employ when moving through the marketplace (much like knowing that the subatomic world is there, that "substance" is an illusion, but nevertheless conducting ourselves in the social world as if the Newtonian universe described completely our physical reality—if one steps out a fifth-floor window, that is, he will go *splat*). The question, I think, is what does a Buddhist do *after* awakening. If he stayed in *samadhi*, he'd probably die within two weeks—he's not eating, not sleeping, he'd just shed the body pretty darned quick. Two weeks is, I've heard, the longest for anyone remaining in *samadhi* and not dying.

If he decides to stay in the world, the marketplace, in order to teach, as Shakyamuni did, or serve in some capacity, he does so—and lives daily—with nonattachment and *metta*. This is what I think most people don't quite understand about *serious* Buddhist laymen: they may appear to be "in the world" like others, but actually they are not "of" it. Their goals are not selfish or self-centered. They try to use samsaric means for nirvanic ends. Theirs is a liberated work (doing, karma) because it is egoless, with no "I," no selfish desire, no clinging involved, and always with the nirvanic knowledge that "All things from the very first have been in a perfect state of tranquility." Certain dualistic terms—*life* and *death,* say—are meaningless to him (or her) and he sees, as Huang Po points out, the unity and the multiplicity *at the same time.* This is why those ever-delightful Zen guys can speak in apparent contradictions: Mumon's poem about Nanchuan's cat captures this paradox nicely; and in his article "Quick! Who Can Save This Cat?" Norman Fischer (*Buddhadharma: The Practitioner's Quarterly,* Spring 2003) comments beautifully that "You and I both know that the cat is already dead. You and I are already dead. All disputes are already settled. All things beyond coming and going, vast and wide, at peace . . . we are always dying and there is no such thing as death."

Soooo . . . the awakened practitioner is not just a "good person." Frankly, he is beyond "good" or "bad," what we conventionally see as "life" and "death," and all the other dualisms. He is without craving, knows how to tame the "monkey mind," and serves daily because what *else* is there to do *after* awakening if one remains in the marketplace?

Especially one like contemporary America. Quite frankly, this was a question I had to face, personally, in 1982 after *Ox* was published, and after I plunged deep into meditation practice while living and working in San Francisco in 1981: How do I remain *in* the world *and* follow the dharma?

WHALEN-BRIDGE: *So there's no getting around it—being a novelist is a form of karmic attachment?*

JOHNSON: Afraid so. My duties as an artist, husband, and father kept me from checking into the monastery, and so I started in 1983 the six year's of work that would result in *Middle Passage*. But after one's work—*svadharma*—is done, even being a novelist is something that one can "let go" as a tool or boat that served its purpose in facilitating our liberation.

WHALEN-BRIDGE: *Thank you very kindly for sharing your thoughts on these matters.* Namaste *and* danyavad.

JOHNSON: *Mahadanyavad*—big thank you!

# WORKS BY CHARLES JOHNSON

LISTED CHRONOLOGICALLY

*Black Humor.* Chicago: Johnson Publishing Company, 1970.
*Half-Past Nation Time.* Westlake Village, CA: Aware Press, 1972.
"Creating the Political Cartoon." *Scholastic Editor/Communications and Graphics,* Feb. 1973: 8–13.
*Faith and the Good Thing.* New York: Viking Press, 1974.
"Essays on Fiction." *Intro 10.* Hendel and Reinke, Publishers, 1979. 10–13.
*Oxherding Tale.* Bloomington, IN: Indiana University Press, 1982.
*The Sorcerer's Apprentice.* New York: Atheneum, 1986.
*Being and Race: Black Writing Since 1970.* Bloomington, IN: Indiana University Press, 1988.
"Where Philosophy and Fiction Meet." *American Visions* 3 (June 1988): 36+.
*Middle Passage.* New York: Atheneum, 1990.
"One Meaning of *Mo' Better Blues.*" *Five for Five: The Films of Spike Lee.* New York: Stewart, Tabori & Chang, 1991. 117–24.

"The Philosopher and the American Novel." *California State Library Foundation Bulletin* 35 (April 1991): 1–16.

"Absence of Black Middle-Class Images Has Global Impact." *National Minority Politics* 4 (Nov. 1993): 7+.

"Java Journey: From Chaos to Serenity." *New York Times* 7 Mar. 1993: 24+.

Introduction. *On Writers and Writing*. By John Gardner. New York: MJF Books, 1994. vii–xxi.

"The Work of the World." *Transforming Vision: Writers on Art*. Ed. Edward Hirsch. Boston: Little, Brown, and Company, 1994. 100–104.

"The Gift of the Osuo." *African American Review* 30.4 (1996): 519–26.

"Green Belt." *African American Review* 30.4 (1996): 559–78.

"John Gardner as Mentor." *African American Review* 30.4 (1996): 619–24.

"The King We Left Behind." *CommonQuest* 1.2 (1996).

*Black Men Speaking*. In collaboration with John McCluskey, Jr. Bloomington, IN: Indiana University Press, 1997.

"Executive Decision." *Outside the Law: Narratives on Justice in America*. Eds. Susan Richards Shreve and Porter Shreve. Boston: Beacon Press, 1997. 93–105.

*Africans in America: America's Journey Through Slavery*. In collaboration with Patricia Smith. San Diego: Harcourt Press, 1998.

*Dreamer*. New York: Scribner, 1998.

*Soulcatcher and Other Stories*. San Diego: Harcourt Press, 1998.

"Fictionalizing King."<http://seattletimes.nwsource.com/mlk/legacy/Johnson_intro.html>

"Creative Adventures: The Fiction Writer's Apprenticeship." *Creating Fiction*. Ed. Julie Checkoway. Cincinnati: Story Press, 1999. 34–42.

"A Soul's Jagged Arc." *The New York Times Magazine* 3 Jan. 1999: 10.

"An Ever-Lifting Song of Black America." *New York Times* 14 Feb. 1999, sec. 2: 1+.

"Accepting the Challenge." *Tricycle: The Buddhist Review* 10.1 (Fall 2000): 63–64.

*King: The Photobiography of Martin Luther King, Jr.* In collaboration with Bob Adelman. New York: Viking Press, 2000.

"Sweet Dreams." *StoryQuarterly* 36 (2000): 111–16.

"Fred Barzyk: PBS' Golden Age Pioneer." *Fred Barzyk: The Search for a Personal Vision in Broadcast Television.* Ed. Curtis L. Carter. Milwaukee: Marquette University, 2001. 39–52.

"Cultural Relativity." *Indiana Review* 24 (Spring 2002): 100–103.

"A Boot Camp for Creative Writers." *Chronicle of Higher Education* 31 Oct. 2003: B7+.

Foreword. *Black Images in the Comics: A Visual History.* By Fredrik Strömberg. Seattle: Fantagraphics Books, 2003. 6–19.

Introduction. *Selected Writings by Ralph Waldo Emerson.* Ed. William H. Gilman. New York: Signet, 2003. vii–xvi.

"Mindfulness and the Beloved Community." *Turning Wheel: The Journal of Socially Engaged Buddhism* (Summer 2003): 37+.

*Turning the Wheel: Essays on Buddhism and Writing.* New York: Scribner, 2003.

"Essie Mae Williams (née Thurmond)." *Wall Street Journal* 23 Dec. 2003: A14.

"Honoring King's Vision." *Seattle Times* 18 Jan. 2004: C1+.

Foreword. *Reading Seattle: The City in Prose.* Ed. Peter Donahue and John Trombold. Seattle: University of Washington Press, 2004. xi–xiii.

"Be Peace Embodied." *Shambhala Sun* (July 2004): 27–33.

# WORKS ABOUT
# CHARLES JOHNSON'S FICTION

LISTED CHRONOLOGICALLY

Kutzinski, Vera. "Johnson Revises Johnson: *Oxherding Tale* and *The Autobiography of An Ex-Colored Man.*" *Pacific Coast Philology* 23.1 (1988): 39–46.

Crouch, Stanley. "Charles Johnson: Free at Last!" *Notes of a Hanging Judge: Essays And Reviews, 1979–1989.* New York: Oxford University Press, 1990. 136–43.

Gleason, William. "The Liberation of Perception: Charles Johnson's *Oxherding Tale.*" *Black American Literature Forum* 25.4 (Winter 1991): 705–28.

Hayward, Jennifer. "Something to Serve: Constructs of the Feminine in Charles Johnson's *Oxherding Tale.*" *Black American Literature Forum* 25.4 (Winter 1991): 689–703.

Little, Jonathan. "Charles Johnson's Revolutionary *Oxherding Tale.*" *Studies in American Fiction* 19 (1991): 141–51.

Rushdy, Ashraf H. A. "The Phenomenology of the Allmuseri: Charles Johnson and the Subject of the Narrative of Slavery." *African American Review* 26 (1992): 373–94.

Benesch, Klaus. "The Education of Mingo." *The African American Short Story, 1970 to 1990.* Ed. Wolfgang Karrer and Barbara Puschmann-Nalenz. Trier: Wissenschaftlicher, 1993. 169–79.

Rushdy, Ashraf H. A. "The Properties of Desire: Forms of Slave Identity in Charles Johnson's *Middle Passage.*" *Arizona Quarterly* 50.2 (1994): 73–108.

Travis, Molly Abel. "*Beloved* and *Middle Passage:* Race, Narrative, and the Critic's Essentialism." *Narrative* 2.3 (1994): 179–200.

Coleman, James W. "Charles Johnson's Quest for Black Freedom in *Oxherding Tale.*" *African American Review* 29.4 (1995): 631–44.

Goudie, S. X. "'Leavin' a Mark on the Wor(l)d': Marksmen and Marked Men in *Middle Passage.*" *African American Review* 29.1 (1995): 109–22.

Scott, Daniel M., III. "Interrogating Identity: Appropriation and Transformation in *Middle Passage.*" *African American Review* 29.4 (1995): 645–55.

Walby, Celestin. "The African Sacrificial Kingship Ritual and Johnson's *Middle Passage.*" *African American Review* 29.4 (1995): 657–69.

Byrd, Rudolph P. "*Oxherding Tale* and *Sidhartha:* Philosophy, Fiction, and the Emergence of a Hidden Tradition." *African American Review* 30.4 (1996): 549–58

Fagel, Brian. "Passages from the Middle: Coloniality and Postcoloniality in Charles Johnson's *Middle Passage.*" *African American Review* 30.4 (1996): 625–34.

Griffiths, Frederick T. "'Sorcery Is Dialectical': Plato and Jean Toomer in Charles Johnson's *The Sorcerer's Apprentice.*" *African American Review* 30.4 (1996): 527–38.

Little, Jonathan. "From the Comic Book to the Comic: Charles Johnson's Variations on Creative Expression." *African American Review* 30.4 (1996): 579–600.

Muther, Elizabeth. "Isadora at Sea: Misogyny as Comic Capital in Charles Johnson's *Middle Passage.*" *African American Review* 30.4 (1996): 649–58.

O'Keefe, Vincent A. "Reading Rigor Mortis: Offstage Violence and Excluded Middles in Johnson's *Middle Passage* and Morrison's *Beloved.*" *African American Review* 30.4 (1996): 635–646

Smith, Virginia Watley. "Sorcery, Double-Consciousness, and War-
ring Souls: An Intertextual Reading of *Middle Passage* and *Captain Blackman*." *African American Review* 30.4 (1996): 659–74.

Storhoff, Gary. "The Artist as Universal Mind: Berkeley's Influence
on Charles Johnson." *African American Review* 30.4 (1996):
539–48.

Brown, Bill. "Global Bodies/Postnationalities: Charles Johnson's
Consumer Culture." *Representations* 58 (Spring 1997): 24–48.

Jablon, Madelyn. "Mimesis of Process: The Thematization of
Art: Charles Johnson, *Middle Passage*." *Black Metafiction: Self-
Consciousness in African American Literature.* Iowa City: Univer-
sity of Iowa Press, 1997. 29–54.

Little, Jonathan. *Charles Johnson's Spiritual Imagination.* Columbia:
University of Missouri Press, 1997.

Thaden, Barbara Z. "Charles Johnson's *Middle Passage* as Historio-
graphic Metafiction." *College English* 59.7 (Nov. 1997): 753–66.

Byrd, Rudolph P., ed. *I Call Myself an Artist: Writings By and About
Charles Johnson.* Bloomington: Indiana University Press, 1999.

Hardack, Richard. "Black Skin, White Tissues: Local Color and
Universal Solvents in the Novels of Charles Johnson." *Callaloo*
22.4 (Fall 1999): 1028–53.

Page, Philip. "'As Within, so It Is Without': The Composite Self in
Charles Johnson's *Oxherding Tale* and *Middle Passage*." *Reclaim-
ing Community in Contemporary African American Fiction.* Jackson: University Press of Mississippi, 1999. 116–56.

Retman, Sonnet. "'Nothing Was Lost in the Masquerade': The Pro-
tean Performance of Genre and Identity in Charles Johnson's
*Oxherding Tale*." *African American Review* 33.3 (Fall 1999):
417–37.

Rushdy, Ashraf H. A. "Revising the Form, Misserving the Order:
Charles Johnson's *Middle Passage*." *Neo-slave Narratives: Studies
in the Social Logic of a Literary Form.* New York: Oxford University Press, 1999. 201–26.

Rushdy, Ashraf H. A. "Serving the Form, Conserving the Order:
Charles Johnson's *Middle Passage*." *Neo-slave Narratives: Studies
in the Social Logic of a Literary Form.* New York: Oxford University Press, 1999. 167–200.

Cox, Timothy J. *Postmodern Tales of Slavery in the Americas: From Alejo Carpentier to Charles Johnson.* New York: Garland Publishing, 2001.

Nash, William R. "'I Was My Father's Father, and He My Child': The Process of Black Fatherhood and Literary Evolution in Charles Johnson's Fiction." *Contemporary Black Men's Fiction and Drama.* Ed. Keith Clark. Urbana: University of Illinois Press, 2001. 108–34.

Selzer, Linda Furgerson. "Charles Johnson's 'Exchange Value': Signifyin(g) on Marx." *The Massachusetts Review* 42.2 (Summer 2001): 253–68.

Nash, William R. *Charles Johnson's Fiction.* Champaign: University of Illinois Press, 2002.

Selzer, Linda. "Master-Slave Dialectics in Charles Johnson's 'The Education of Mingo.'" *African American Review* 37 (2003): 105–14.

Whalen-Bridge, John. "Waking Cain: The Poetics of Integration in Charles Johnson's *Dreamer.*" *Callaloo* 26.2 (2003): 504–521.

# ADDITIONAL INTERVIEWS
# WITH CHARLES JOHNSON

LISTED CHRONOLOGICALLY

McCullough, Ken. "Writers Should Be Able to Write Everything."
 *Coda: Poets & Writers Magazine* 35 (1988): 30–35.
Elsasser, Glen. "Visible Man: As a Book Award Winner, Charles
 Johnson Suddenly Has 'Cash Value.'" *Chicago Tribune* 2 Dec.
 1990, sec. 5: 6.
Newton, Edmund. "Sailing Against a Literary Tide." *Los Angeles
 Times* 20 August 1990. n.p.
Williams, Marjorie. "The Author's Solo Passage." *Washington Post*
 4 Dec. 1990, sec. D: 1+.
Blau, Eleanor. "Charles Johnson's Tale of Slaving, Seafaring and
 Philosophizing." *New York Times* 2 Jan. 1991, sec. C: 9+.
Coffey, Michael. "NBA Winner to Probe Life of Martin Luther
 King for Atheneum." *Publishers Weekly* 12 April 1991: 24–25.
Peterson, V. R. "Charles Johnson." *Essence* April 1991: 36.
Epel, Naomi. "Charles Johnson." *Writers Dreaming*. New York:
 Carol Southern, 1993. 119–32.

Howard, Margaret A. "Interview: Charles Johnson." *Nightlife* 29 Jan. 1993.

Mattmiller, Brian. "Recapturing the Passion." *Southern Illinoisan* 2 Feb. 1993, sec. A: 1+.

Terkel, Studs. *Race: How Blacks and Whites Think and Feel About the American Obsession*. New York: New Press, 1993. 213–18.

Carroll, Rebecca, ed. *Swing Low: Black Men Writing*. New York: Crown, 1995. 113–27.

Barton, David. "Facts of Fiction." *Sacramento Bee* 5 May 1998. <http://www.sacbee.com/static/live/lifestyle/bookclub/archives/johnson2.html>

Rowell, Charles. "An Interview with Charles Johnson." *Callaloo* 20.3 (1998): 531–47.

Crouch, Stanley. "Critic, Not Cynic: Charles Johnson Talks with Stanley Crouch." *I Call Myself an Artist: Writings by and about Charles Johnson*. Ed. Rudolph Byrd. Bloomington: Indiana University Press, 1999. 245–48.

Pautler, Nedra Floyd. "He's Officially *Dr. Johnson*." *University Week* [Seattle, WA] 27 May 1999: 2–3 <http://depts.washington.edu/~uweek/archives/1999.05.MAY_27/_article1.html>

Grady, James. "Fist of Fantasy: Martial Arts & Prose Fiction— A Practictioner's Prejudices." *Journal of Asian Martial Arts* 9.4 (2000): 53–75.

Trucks, Rob. "A Conversation with Charles Johnson." *TriQuarterly* (Winter 2000): 537–60. Reprinted in his book *The Pleasure of Influence: Conversations with American Male Fiction Writers* (2002).

Shoup, Barbara, and Margaret Love Denman. *Novel Ideas: Contemporary Authors Share the Creative Process*. New York: Alpha Books, 2001. 161–68.

De la Paz, Diana. "Author Says 'Mindfulness' Is the Key to Writing, Living." *Tacoma News Tribune* 26 Mar. 2002, sec. Entertainment.

Osen, Diane. "Charles Johnson." *The Book That Changed My Life*. New York: Modern Library, 2002. 32–42.

Malkin, John. "'Buddhism is the Most Radical and Civilized

Choice': A Surprising Conversation about Being Black and Buddhist in America." *Shambhala Sun* (Jan. 2004): 32+.

In addition, one video interview is readily available:
"Remarkable People, Charles Johnson." Ed. / prod. Jean Walkinshaw. *Voices of the West: a Western Writers Collection.* Vol. 4. KCTS Television. PBS, 1996.

# INDEX

A

V ETHEL WILLIS WHITE

BOOK